MAN'S MIND, WHAT IS IT BUT A CONVEX GLASS
WHEREIN ARE GATHERED ALL THE SCATTERED POINTS
PICKED OUT OF THE IMMENSITY OF SKY,
TO REUNITE THERE, BE OUR HEAVEN FOR EARTH,
OUR KNOWN UNKNOWN, OUR GOD REVEALED TO MAN?

   —"The Pope," *The Ring and the Book*

# THE
# CONVEX
# GLASS

*The Mind of
Robert Browning*

By

NORTON B. CROWELL

THE UNIVERSITY OF
NEW MEXICO PRESS

1968

*To*

RUTHMARY,
LAWRENCE,
DRING,
STEVEN,
AND
DONALD

# ACKNOWLEDGMENTS

I wish to acknowledge my gratitude to the American Philosophical Society and to the University of New Mexico for generous grants to further my research on this book. I thank Jack Herring, Director of the Armstrong-Browning Library at Baylor University for aid and kindness which made my task a pleasure. I am particularly grateful to Professors Paul Davis, Joseph Frank, Willis D. Jacobs, Katherine Simons, and Dudley Wynn, and to Dean Hoyt Trowbridge, who read the manuscript and who made valuable suggestions for its improvement. I owe a debt of thanks to The University of New Mexico Press, particularly to Mrs. Winifred Gregory for her helpful counsel.

I alone assume the responsibility for any errors of omission or commission of which time may prove me guilty.

# CONTENTS

How look a brother in the face and say
"Thy right is wrong, eyes hast thou yet art blind,
Thine ears are stuffed and stopped, despite their length:
And, oh, the foolishness thou countest faith!"

—*The Ring and the Book,* XII, 841-844.

# INTRODUCTION

During his lifetime Robert Browning was consistently a controversial figure, and the vitality of his verse was revealed in the rich diversity of the explication and criticism devoted to him. It would be untrue to affirm that since his death he has ceased to be controversial or that explication has waned in like measure with the praise; but the conviction is forced upon one that certain important critical assumptions have become almost sacrosanct and that what might be termed an establishment has arisen in Browning criticism. In my *Triple Soul: Browning's Theory of Knowledge* I attempted to show that one of these critical assumptions—that Browning was a dedicated enemy of the intellect—is demonstrably false. In the present study, I try to focus upon other critical truisms that, in my opinion, are equally mistaken: truisms related to evil, individualism, optimism, truth, and dynamism. My resolution to avoid the topic of Browning's attitude toward the mind has proved difficult—indeed, impossible—to maintain. My labors on this book have shown that Browning's philosophic beliefs are uniquely dovetailed. Every idea is indissolubly linked to every other idea, for one of the central concepts of the poet is the wholeness of man's development. His attitude toward evil, for example, cannot be understood unless one has an accurate understanding of his respect for the triple soul—body, mind, and spirit. Certainly his special kind of optimism and its relation to ethics, which has led to much extravagant speculation since Henry Jones fancied that the poet could not at the same time hold fast to both optimism and ethics, cannot be understood without reference to his markedly intellectual position. Nor can one, in a vacuum, fathom his beliefs on truth, individualism, and dynamism.

In our century it has become a commonplace of Browning criticism to discover that the poet was a woolly thinker, to be deplored as a philosopher, and a "semantic stutterer,"[1] who failed to communicate his beliefs with any marked success. Joseph E. Baker, in his introduc-

1. Stewart Walker Holmes, "Browning: Semantic Stutterer," *Publications of the Modern Language Association*, LX (1945), 231-255.

tion to an edition of Browning's selected verse, notes that as one pursues the study of Browning "seriously," his "philosophy begins to seem so irrational, his learning so pedantic, as to be hardly worthy of the devotion of scholarship."[2] This is far from being an isolated opinion. The long list of critics who have found Browning shallow or incomprehensible may conveniently be seen in Boyd Litzinger's *Time's Revenges: Browning's Reputation as a Thinker, 1889-1962,*[3] a study which I believe to be a fair assessment of his depressing subject. William Clyde DeVane, in his *Browning's Parleyings, the Autobiography of a Mind,* accuses Browning of discounting "the intellect altogether," on the grounds that his childhood faith would crumble if seriously examined, and the poet found no way out of the dilemma except his rejection of mind.[4] Henry Jones finds that "Browning's theory of life, in so far as it is expressed in his philosophical poems, rests on agnosticism; and that such a theory is inconsistent with the moral and religious interests of man."[5]

Any respectable critic will admit that, in the end, Browning's reputation as a poet must rest upon his poetry, not upon his "message," but it must not be forgotten that his thought is an intrinsic part of his poetry, as much as his dramatic characterization and situation, on which his stature as a poet must finally rest. A marked characteristic of contemporary Browning criticism is the easy critical acceptance of any statement hostile to the worth of Browning's thought or of his mind, whereas a contrary position is commonly viewed as a retreat to the shattered battlements of the deplored Browning societies, membership in which amounted to an admission of critical immaturity and pietistic shallowness. It is a mark of scholarship to attack Browning's thought as irrelevant, muddled, and worthless. But the same judgment must be accorded the work of scholars who embrace the opposite position with the same objectivity and care. Critics everywhere utter the some refrain: it is time that Browning's thought cease to occupy our attention, so that we can get on to "valid criticism" of his poetry, which is all that counts, but these same critics

2. *Browning: "Pippa Passes" and Shorter Poems* (New York, 1947), p. xiii.
3. Knoxville, Tennessee, 1964.
4. New Haven, 1927, p. 187.
5. *Browning as a Philosophic and Religious Teacher* (Glasgow, 1902), p. 321.

hail with enthusiasm any critical study of Browning's thought—provided it attempt to show the unworth of what he said. There is no doubt that the London Browning Society spawned much superficial nonsense, much sentimental gush, and much specious religiosity, for which, of course, Browning was not to blame. But the Society also brought forth a small but substantial body of able criticism. Not all the members were little old ladies, their faces working with religious rapture, or dissenting ministers, awash with tea and revelation. George Bernard Shaw, for one, was a charter member, and he is sometimes considered to have been singularly free of such weaknesses.

Roma A. King, Jr., writing in *The Bow and the Lyre,* comments on the effects of the Browning societies, apparently regarding their whole effect as a disaster to both scholarship and to Browning:

> Their dogmatic interest in Browning as a philosopher and teacher discouraged valid literary criticism [*i.e.*, the kind we write today]; their interest in the extrapoetic in his work rendered him suspect for a younger generation, less certain than their seniors concerning the whereabouts of God and the rightness of the world. Early in the twentieth century most young readers turned to newer works such as Ezra Pound's *Personae* and, a little later, to T. S. Eliot's *The Waste Land.* Browning fell into disrepute. Recently, however, serious readers and critics have engaged in an attempt to rescue Browning from the reverent hands of early admirers and to establish his position as a poet. Toward this end impressive work has been done.
>
> Distinguished scholars such as William Clyde DeVane and Joseph Baker have so effectively combatted the misconception of the Browning societies about Browning's "thought," "philosophy," and "optimism" that to pursue the subject further would be useless repetition. Except in a few remote outposts the Browning societies have been routed.[6]

Browning's detractors do not agree on all points in their objections to his philosophy, but on a few they are in substantial agreement:

6. *The Bow and the Lyre, The Art of Robert Browning* (Ann Arbor, Michigan, 1957), pp. 4-5.

almost all find Browning and his "message" to be openly hostile to mind, imperceptive, naïve, indifferent to suffering, and philosophically repellent. Since almost none of his friends came to any such conclusions, it seems apparent that one of two causes may be responsible for the hostile view of critics today: either our standards and mores have changed so drastically as to render Browning's beliefs irrelevant or inadmissible; or Browning's beliefs have been misread. It is my conviction that the latter reason is the true cause. I should be among the first to repudiate Browning as a thinker if I believed that he was a consecrated enemy of the mind, a callously indifferent observer of the teeming evils of life, a man who blandly denied that there is any real evil whatsoever in life, a moralist who believed that man experiences life at its fullest and best when he sins with gusto, and, as John M. Hitner affirms in his doctoral dissertation from the University of Fribourg, a poet who believed only in "the nude and crude."[7]

In my study I examine these and related critical beliefs. The evidence is strong that a large measure of Browning's unpopularity may be traced to his diminished position as a thinker. It is by no means inevitable that a poet's reputation as a poet will suffer fatally because of his philosophy or because of what mistakenly may pass as his philosophy, but Browning has always been regarded as a philosophic poet, a man with a message, and if his message appears to be fatuous or muddy, he is likely to suffer as a poet more than the usual poet might. Baker's invitation to read Browning with as little attention as possible to what the poet is trying unsuccessfully to say is the natural price Browning has paid, ironically, not for his philosophy or for his fancied verbal impotence, but for the monolithic misreadings that mark the establishment. My intent is not to "rescue" Browning either as a poet or as a thinker, but rather to get at the truth, for I am convinced that if he is properly understood, he will take his place as a respectable thinker, if not a great one, and as a poet of lyrical and dramatic power and luminous insight into life and the soul of man.

In my last chapter I have assayed to explore a topic which em-

7. *Browning's Pessimism in "Fifine at the Fair,"* (Colchester, England, 1962), p. 64.

phasizes the life and dynamism of his verse: Browning as a Christian existentialist. No poet of his century or ours has been more dedicated to certain basic concepts of existentialism: that being transcends essence, that life is dynamic evolvement, that each life should be not so much a being as an eternal becoming, that becoming demands the committed life. There is very little in Browning that is negative, and I should be saddened to convey the impression that my attempt to refute certain critical ideas, which I believe to be quite in error and thus destructive of one's understanding of Browning and likely to be injurious to one's assessment of him as a poet, is merely negative in purpose or effect. I shall be gratified if I discover that my critical beliefs carry the conviction that Browning must be reread and re-examined, not so much to discover what errors have been committed but what truth may be found. Browning, in his "Parleying with Francis Furini," finds fault with the evolutionists, not because of their theories and discoveries, but because they looked only behind along the road on which man had come, not forward to the heights yet to scale.

Every poet of lasting value must be re-examined continually. Even if the established critical beliefs are of superb insight, they lose their vitality and their meaning unless they continually reaffirm their truth under impartial inquiry. The truth that seemed so imperishable when new sheds its lustre and becomes an empty husk through thoughtless reiteration and oversimplification. If this fact is true for critical "truths," how much more is careful reinterpretation needed when there was little truth to start with? Browning was a distinguished poet whose close-textured thought has invited errors in explication. Only through renewed explication will his position as a thinker and as a poet be firmly established. Dallas Kenmare, in her sympathetic study, *An End to Darkness,* ably states the problem that is central in Browning criticism: "But the time is already overdue for a completely new approach to, a new attempt at understanding, a poet of such stature. It is essential to begin to realize *what he is saying,* and applying it to the unparalleled difficulties of our own problematical age."[8]

8. *An End to Darkness, A New Approach to Robert Browning and His Work* (London, 1962), p. 7.

with considerable poetic power, this writer seems
to me possessed with a more intense and morbid
self-consciousness than I ever knew in any sane
human being - I should think it a sincere confession
though of a most unloveable state, if the 'Pauline'
were not evidently a mere phantom. All about her
is full of inconsistency - he neither loves her nor
fancies he loves her, yet insists upon talking love
to her - if she existed and loved him, to whom
he treats her most ungenerously and unfeelingly -
In all his aspirings and yearnings and regrets
point to other things, never to her - then he
pays her off towards the end by a piece of
flummery, amounting to the modest request
that she will love him and live with him -
and give herself up to him, without his
loving her, moyennant quoi he will think
her and call her everything that is handsome
and he promises her that she shall find it
mightily pleasant: Then he leaves off by saying
he knows he shall have changed his mind by
tomorrow, & despise 'these intents' which seem so
fair' - but that having been these visions once
no doubt he will again - & is therefore 'in perfect joy'
bad luck to him! as the Irish say.

A cento of most beautiful passages might be
made from this poem - & the psychological history
of himself is powerful and truthful, truth-like certainly
all but the last stage. That he evidently has not yet got
into. The self-seeking & self-worshipping state is
well described - beyond that I should think

the writer had made, as yet, only the next
step; viz. into despising his own state. I even
question whether part even of that self-disdain
is not assumed. He is evidently dissatisfied,
and feels part of the badness of his state, but
he does not write as if it were purged out
of him — if he once could muster a hearty
hatred of his selfishness, it would go — as it
is, he feels only the lack of good, not the positive
evil. He feels not remorse, but only disappointed[?]
a mind in that state can only be regenerated[?]
by some new passion, and I know not what
to wish for him, but that he may meet with
a real Pauline —

Meanwhile he should not attempt to
shew how a person may be recovered from
this morbid state — for he is hardly
convalescent, and "what should we speak
of but that which we know?"

Plate I. Criticism by John Stuart Mill, written at the end of his review copy
of *Pauline*. By courtesy of the Victoria and Albert Museum.

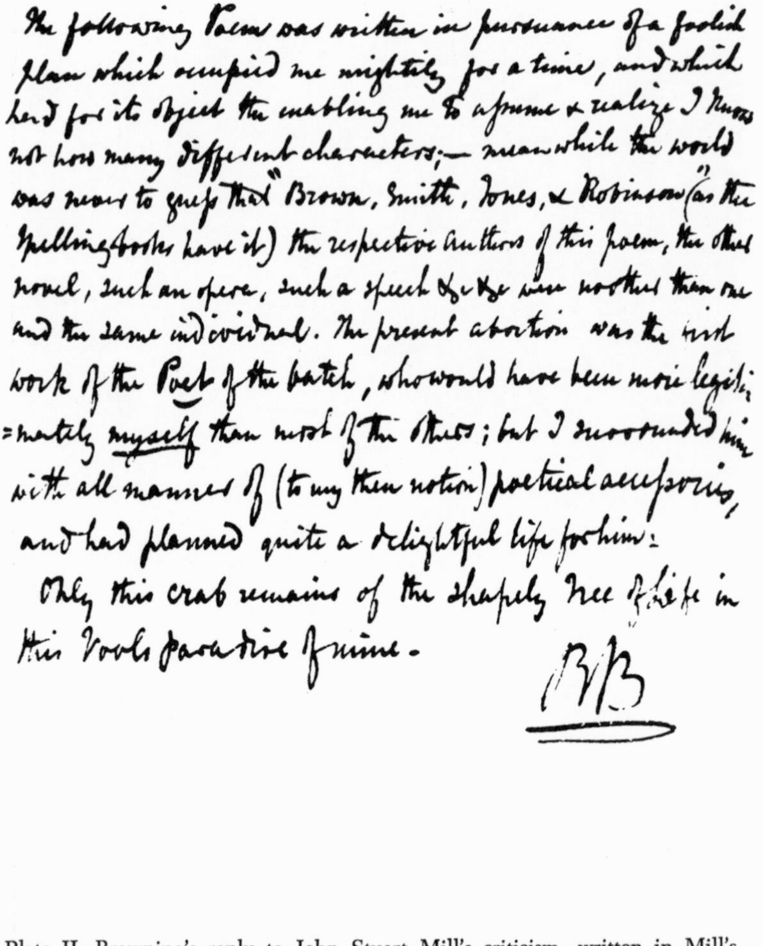

The following Poem was written in pursuance of a foolish plan which occupied me nightily for a time, and which had for its object the enabling me to assume & realize I know not how many different characters;— meanwhile the world was never to guess that "Brown, Smith, Jones, & Robinson" (as the Spelling-books have it) the respective Authors of this poem, the other novel, such an opera, such a speech &c &c were no other than one and the same individual. The present abortion was the first work of the Poet of the batch, who would have been more legiti=mately myself than most of the others; but I surrounded him with all manner of (to my then notion) poetical accessories, and had planned quite a delightful life for him:

Only this crab remains of the shapely Tree of Life in this Fool's paradise of mine.

RB

Plate II. Browning's reply to John Stuart Mill's criticism, written in Mill's review copy, which was returned to Browning by W. J. Fox. By courtesy of the Victoria and Albert Museum.

# PAULINE.

---

PAULINE, mine own, bend o'er me—thy soft breast

Shall pant to mine—bend o'er me—thy sweet eyes,

And loosened hair, and breathing lips, and arms

Drawing me to thee—these build up a screen

To shut me in with thee, and from all fear;

So that I might unlock the sleepless brood

Of fancies from my soul, their lurking place,

Nor doubt that each would pass, ne'er to return

# CHAPTER I

# THE PROBLEM OF EVIL

THE WORLD AND LIFE'S TOO BIG
TO PASS FOR A DREAM. . . .

—"Fra Lippo Lippi"

Among the ironies of literary criticism, one of the most perplexing
is the widespread notion that one is well advised to read Browning,
a poet remarkable for his closely reasoned thought, without regard
to what the poet is saying. Joseph E. Baker, as I noted in my Introduction, is perhaps the best spokesman of this singular position. In
an introduction to a collection of Browning's poetry, he notes that
what the poet spent his life saying is too shallow and tawdry for
contemplation, and one should try to ignore it, like a pebble in the
shoe. Understanding of Browning, it seems, may be had only at the
expense of enjoyment. The truth of the matter is that the standard
misreading of Browning in the most vital of areas has largely destroyed him as a thinker, and has seriously tarnished his fame as a
poet as well.

Among the areas in which Browning's position has been disas-
trously misread is his view of the problem of evil, which informs
almost every poem he wrote. Since Henry Jones's *Browning as a
Philosophical and Religious Teacher* (1891), an inexhaustible source
of error, scholars have embraced, with only an occasional dissenting
voice, the concept that Browning was indifferent to evil, actively
approved of evil, or denied the reality of evil. Hoxie Neale Fairchild,
indeed, discovers an essential identity between Browning and Alex-
ander Pope in their affirmation of the illusory character of evil.[1]

1. "Browning's 'Whatever Is, Is Right,' " *College English,* XII (April, 1951),
pp. 377-382.

Few critics have doubted that the function of evil—real or illusory —in all its guises (doubt, frustration, failure, and crime itself) is very simply, in Browning's philosophy, to test man. But the precise nature of the test and the individual's relation to it have yielded a rich critical mythology. Among the sturdy myths is the theme that W. O. Raymond discovers in "The Statue and the Bust": "It is better . . . to act evilly than to lapse into atrophy of soul."[2] A complementary view is held by Sydney Herbert Mellone, who ingeniously explains Browning's supposed view of evil. He disarmingly admits that in "The Statue and the Bust" Browning's

> . . . doctrine may seem to be immoral; and so far as the morality of a man's actions depends on its consequences to others, it certainly is so. But from Browning's point of view it is not so; for where he says "work," "work out," he is always thinking of the effect of the work *on the worker himself*. Hence he teaches that, when we look deeply enough, we see how strenuousness in evil is better than half-hearted wickedness, which abstains only through weakness from acting out its real nature.[3]

The plain sense of this is that Browning considered the ethics of an act only as it affected for good or ill the doer, without regard to the evil wrought upon others. This is the most entirely libelous view of ethics readily attainable, and Browning has suffered accordingly. Mellone's imperception is equalled by Hjalmar Hjorth Boyesen, who discovers in "A Light Woman," "The Statue and the Bust," "Fra Lippo Lippi," and other poems evidence that Browning's "tendency to glorify the flesh" made "moral obligations sit lightly upon this poet." Concerning "The Statue and the Bust," he notes:

> Those lines, "Let a man contend to the uttermost for his life's set prize be it what it will," might serve for a motto to nearly all that Browning has written. They have a harmless look, and

2. *The Infinite Moment and Other Essays in Robert Browning* (2nd ed.; Toronto, 1965), p. 218.
3. *Leaders of Religious Thought in the Nineteenth Century* (Edinburgh, 1902), p. 268.

might readily be accepted as a maxim of practical wisdom. But this contention to the uttermost implies in Browning a disregard of all rights that clash with your own. It is individualism carried to its extreme limit. Where the sense of duty crops out in Browning, it is frequently as a thing to be brushed aside as unworthy of serious consideration. . . . To be sure he is capable of painting goodness and virtue most beautifully. . . . But how much more gorgeous is the coloring, how much more resplendent the characterization of the guilty lovers, Sebald and Ottima, than of Pippa! It is power Browning admires; power, in whatever shape it may appear. Self-abnegation, abstention, renunciation, are pale negative terms which in no wise attract him, except for the psychological curiosities which they may reveal.[4]

Joseph E. Baker similarly believes that Browning actively counseled man to scorn the pallid virtues and to embrace lusty sin: "The force of Original Sin is not to be resisted but obeyed."[5]

All of these judgments, in my opinion, are wrongheaded. They distort Browning's ethical beliefs, which were of the highest order, and make of him an unprincipled casuist, the twin of his own Mr. Sludge. Never did Browning, from first to last, counsel any individual to elect sin or evil consciously, knowing it to be sin or evil. Never did he counsel acts that bring evil to others, if any better course of action is possible. Unluckily, in life there are occasional dilemmas in which every possible course of action brings some injury or evil, and

4. *Literary and Social Silhouettes* (New York, 1904), pp. 137-138.

5. "Religious Implications in Browning's Poetry," *Philological Quarterly*, XXXVI, No. 4 (October, 1957), 446-448. For a more reasonable view, see Edward Dowden, *Studies in Literature, 1789-1877* (London, 1878), p. 225: "In Mr. Tennyson's poems treating the trials, difficulties and dangers of the heart, the temptation which is commonly represented as the most formidable is the temptation to indulge passion at the expense of duty or in relation to the law of conscience. In Mr. Browning's poems the temptation almost invariably is to sacrifice the passion which ennobles and glorifies life either to prudential motives, or fear of public opinion, or through a supine lethargy or slackness of spirit." Note that Dowden does not say one should indulge an ignoble passion, which might ruin other lives.

man is tested by whether his choice of action yields least evil. From *Pauline* to *Asolando* Browning taught that the game of life is the game of choices, "life being but the terrible choice," as the Pope affirms. The Pope's "terrible choice" in his judgment of Guido is terrible, not because of its effect on his own well-being, but upon Guido's. The Pope clearly states that nothing would be easier or more pleasant for him to do than to free Guido, but he does not, for he has a solemn duty, which personal pleasure must not prevent, although Boyesen says that Browning counseled "a disregard of all rights that clash with your own." And certainly the Pope does not find duty a trifle to be "brushed aside." He is Browning's perfect spokesman, who knows that the test is always one of ethics, as well as of action. He knows that one may not evade the test, but equally important is the rightness of one's decision, which means the rightness of its effect on everyone concerned. Chronic evasion of life's test is a denial of life, virtually a form of suicide, and as such it is among the cardinal sins—perhaps as bad as the worst. But this is not to say that a man must in every instance act without hesitation or sober reflection; it does not mean that a man must act without weighing the consequences well. Nor does it mean that man is ever justified in deliberately seeking out evil and pursuing it lustily merely to avoid atrophy of soul. The test, the "terrible choice," is a test of man's rectitude and principles, and although it is an evil shirking of the demands of life to refuse to make choices, nothing could be further from Browning's ethical idealism than to counsel ardent pursuit of sin. A man may make the wrong choice, but this is the hazard of life. The Pope says that if he sentences Guido to the block through error, in the next life he will face Guido's ghost "nor blench a jot"—because he did all in his power to make the just and right choice.

The Pope perfectly speaks Browning's doctrine of life's test. He wore through "these dismalest of documents"—the mass of lies and distortions in the court record—through a sombre wintry day before he judged, and he makes clear that the task put winter into his soul. He knows that in the mortal state there is no absolute truth, and no man's judgment is infallible. To Guido's ghost, he would say:

> "God who set me to judge thee, meted out
> So much of judging faculty, no more:
> Ask Him if I was slack in use thereof!"[6]

Only because he knows that he did fully exercise his judging faculty, the Pope says

> Therefore I stand on my integrity,
> Nor fear at all: and if I hesitate,
> It is because I need to breathe awhile,
> Rest, as the human right allows, review
> Intent the little seeds of act. . . .[7]

He does not consult his own self-interest in the affair; he does not plunge headlong to a hasty decision; and above all he does not ignore the consequences of his act in the lives of others. In only one sense does the Pope think of "the effect of the work *on the worker himself*": the judgment of God upon his exercise of the judging faculty. And God's judgment is based surely upon the selfless ethical propriety of his verdict, or, more properly, upon the Pope's resolute dedication to that end. It is often a long and taxing process. Ogniben, in *A Soul's Tragedy,* precisely assesses the length of the task:

> A philosopher's life is spent in discovering that, of the half-dozen truths he knew when a child, such an one is a lie, as the world states it in set terms; and then, after a weary lapse of years, and plenty of hard-thinking, it becomes a truth again after all, as he happens to newly consider it and view it in a different relation with the others. . . .[8]

Truth is a slippery business, never static, and the test of life is always shifting, but for all that, a man must judge and risk the error that judging entails. Although Browning never counsels man to sin knowingly, he does clearly throw down the gage to man to run the risk of error in judging. There is a vast difference between say-

6. X, 264-266.    7. X, 275-279.    8. II, 387-394.

ing that Browning holds "it is better . . . to act evilly than to lapse into atrophy of soul" and saying that Browning holds it better to render a reasoned verdict, risk the danger of error, and abide by the consequences than to risk atrophy of soul through refusal to judge. Man is a decision-making being. Life demands that he act, progressing from dark to light as his faculties permit:

> Grant this, then man must pass from old to new,
> From vain to real, from mistake to fact,
> From what once seemed good, to what now proves best.
> How could man have progression otherwise?[9]

To Browning the meaning of life lies in "progression"; this is why, St. John affirms, that truth is made elusive and shifting:

> —this gift of truth
> Once grasped, were this our soul's gain safe, and sure
> To prosper as the body's gain is wont,—
> Why, man's probation would conclude, his earth
> Crumble; for he both reasons and decides,
> Weighs first, then chooses: will he give up fire
> For gold or purple once he knows its worth?
> Could he give Christ up were His worth as plain?[10]

These words of the apostle are very close to the words of Browning's Pope, who has certainly followed the formula well of weighing first and then deciding before rendering his momentous verdict. He knows that man's distinctive attribute is to be mistaken and readily deceived by false and biased testimony, by his own imperfect and dulled senses, by his ignorance, and by every influence that has operated on his life. Man and his judgments are the product of his total context. He is judged by his will to seek out virtue, by his application of his total powers to that end, and by his decisions that are their result—and God judges him in the light of his endowments and limitations and the forces that have operated on him from his

---

9. "A Death in the Desert," ll. 545-548.    10. *Ibid.*, ll. 287-294.

birth. If man makes a decision that proves wrong, he is blameless if he did his best. To make the wrong decision is not so culpable as to elect the wrong reasons for making a decision. In this principle lies the answer to "The Statue and the Bust." Failure to recognize this ethical stricture in Browning has led to most of the attempts to explain away, to justify, or to deny Browning's alleged justification of adultery. It is usually overlooked that both the lady and the Great-Duke Ferdinand are suffering from arrested moral development. The Duke is clearly branded as "an empty sheath of a man"—a hollow husk, a fop who has had little experience in meeting the test of life. As the poem opens he is an abject failure, with no apparent redeeming features except the ability to sit a horse. The lady is little better. She has consented to enter into a loveless marriage to a man of transparently revolting character, but she is either impervious to the evidence or indifferent to it. She has no powers of judging, for she is both immature and irresponsible. When she spies the Duke riding by, she shows her schoolgirl instability by rushing to the window and blushing, while her heart knocks so wildly that the bridesmaids feel it, according to the poet. Until this point, she has been a nullity, a blank, like the Duke:

> She looked at him, as one who awakes:
> The past was a sleep, and her life began.[11]

At the same time, he awakens and the "empty sheath" is filled with a fine blade, and he "grew straightway brave and wise."

Both principals, then, are awakened by love, in a dramatic moment of revelation similar to that in Chaucer's "Knight's Tale," but with a great difference. Palamon and Arcite have not been ciphers, dead to life's demands, but the lady and the Duke have been precisely as if unborn until this awakening. They are immediately subjected to a moral choice worthy of Solomon in all his wisdom. The signs are not auspicious. Both have been caitiff shirkers of responsibility, and in spite of the assurance that the one awakened clear-eyed and the other "straightway grew brave and wise," they are novices in life's

11. Ll. 29-30.

lists. They have no experience in making moral decisions, and they predictably temporize and shilly-shally. Their decision to elope is "brave and wise," but their indecision and procrastination are inexcusable. When the caddish husband, whom Browning pictures as a loveless, heartless brute, incarcerates her, Browning specifically reveals her as a liar. When informed that she must renounce the world and view life only through the eastern window of her room, she assents with her lips and dissents in her heart:

> "Freely I choose too," said the bride—
> "Your window and its world suffice,"
> Replied the tongue, while the heart replied—
>
> "If I spend the night with that devil twice,
> May his window serve as my loop of hell
> Whence a damned soul looks on paradise!"[12]

But her father has come to bless her marriage, and she cannot fly on her wedding night for fear of upsetting him. She reflects that a day's delay is not so long to wait, especially when the Duke is sure to ride past, and "We shall see each other, sure as fate." She turns on her side and sleeps: "So we resolve on a thing and sleep." Her sin here is twofold. To Browning few things are more sinful than relying on fate or chance to bring something about. No Mr. Micawbers are heroes to Browning. Decisive action must follow one's decision. To rely on fate is to refuse the test of life. Sloth and fear paralyze her, not ethical or moral considerations. Neither she nor the Duke has a shred of compunction in violating her marriage vows or in committing adultery. Such matters never occur to them at all, but, it must be said, that Browning elaborately emphasizes the brutish nature of the husband as an apparent justification of their resolution.

The years pass, while irresolution prevents their "leaping over the parapet," irresolution which has nothing to do with moral ambiguities. They rapidly sink back into the sloth that marked their lives before their awakening. She sits by the window, dead to the passing scene and to life, awaiting only the Duke's appearance as he rides by:

12. Ll. 64-69.

> . . . she watched the square like a book
> Holding one picture and only one,
> Which daily to find she undertook:[13]

Love must not be divorced from life, for love is to be lived. Finally "They found love not as it seemed before," for they have killed love by inanition. Then they experience a second awakening, when it is too late. They see with horror that they have wasted their lives as they "dreamed a dream." The lady, in ordering the bust to be made as a warning that life must be lived, ruefully reflects that while in the tomb she can beguile eternity with the reflection:

> " 'What matters it at the end?
> I did no more while my heart was warm
> Than does that image, my pale-faced friend.' "[14]

She learns, too late, one of Browning's great lessons: What is the purpose of beauty or of life

> "Unless we turn, as the soul knows how,
> The earthly gift to an end divine?"[15]

The Duke orders his equestrian statue, not so much as a warning to the slothful, as a monument "That men may admire," while he may "Laugh in my tomb/ At idleness which aspires to strive."

Both know that their evasion of life and its challenge is the greatest of their sins. They are not, to the very end, troubled about their intended adultery, and Browning makes unmistakably clear that their resolution to flee together was right, "Though the end in sight was a vice." It is often forgotten that Browning does consider adultery a vice. It is evil, and not an apparent evil either, in spite of J. Hillis Miller's mistaken belief that to Browning "The only real evil, for man, is inaction."[16] But they commit adultery in their hearts when they resolve to commit it, and they compound their evil tenfold when

13. Ll. 145-147.        14. Ll. 178-180.        15. Ll. 184-185.
16. *The Disappearance of God, Five Nineteenth Century Writers* (Cambridge, Massachusetts, 1963), p. 108.

they fail in their resolution to act. To stay with her unspeakable husband is an evil far greater than to escape to true love, even though it must be adulterous. In this severe test, when two principles collide, there can be no wholly right or virtuous decision: they yearn for fulfillment of their illicit love and remain unrepentant to the end, but it is clear that this resolution involves less sin and evil than allowing the loveless and brutal marriage to perpetuate itself and destroy three lives. Browning's elopement with Elizabeth Barrett supplies an imperfect parallel.

When Henry Jones sees the poem as frankly teaching that "It is better even to seek evil with one's whole mind, than to be lukewarm in goodness," he errs egregiously. This unhappy pair are not seeking evil at all; they are seeking—and they find—the best solution to an intolerable dilemma, adulterous as it is—but they fail to act. Furthermore, they are not being lukewarm in goodness in their refusal to act upon their resolution. No desire for goodness inhibits their act. It logically follows that Jones's dictum puts Guido far ahead of Karshish, Cleon, Andrea, and perhaps even Fra Lippo, to name but a few, if one accepts his thesis that Browning "bids each man let out all the power that is within him and throw himself upon life with the whole energy of his being" without the curb of negative commandments. To say that Browning repudiated all negative commandments, including the Ten, is silly enough on the face of it, and if it were true, it would justify George Santayana's charge[17] that Browning was a vulgar barbarian and confirm Hoxie N. Fairchild's belief[18] that the poet advocated violent, blind, unreasoning activism as the sum of human virtue.

The Pope who judges Guido abundantly answers these charges. His whole soliloquy is a ringing refutation, but perhaps Browning knew that he would not be fully understood, for he sets out to prove that human testimony is false—or appears so:

Some surmise
Perchance, that since man's wit is fallible,

17. *Interpretations of Poetry and Religion* (New York, 1900).
18. "Browning's 'Whatever Is, Is Right,' " *College English, op. cit.,* 377-382.

Mine may fail here? Suppose it so,—what then?
Say,—Guido, I count guilty, there's no babe
So guiltless, for I misconceive the man![19]

He cites the parable of the doctor who while walking through the countryside comes upon a man fallen of an apparent epileptic fit. The evidence prompts the immediate prescription: "Breathe a vein, copiously let blood at once!" Whereupon the patient perishes, and a serpent crawls from his breast. The outraged bystanders accuse the doctor of malpractice, for a cordial would have surely preserved the man whom bleeding slew. But the Pope finds no fault with the doctor, whose prescription was perfectly supported by the symptoms:

So and not otherwise, in after-time,
If some acuter wit, fresh probing, sound
This multifarious mass of words and deeds
Deeper, and reach through guilt to innocence,
I shall face Guido's ghost nor blench a jot.[20]

The Pope does not say that he arrived at his decision under the impetus of the fear that he must do something blindly rather than weigh his judgment with care. The last thing the Pope counsels is the deliberate choice of "acting evilly." He may be rendering the wrong verdict, but, as indicated before, this is the risk that life entails. Man is tested by his resolution to pursue virtue.

I should like to amend Raymond's statement simply but significantly. Instead of saying that Browning believed "It is better . . . to act evilly than to lapse into atrophy of soul," I should prefer to say that he believed "Even though in life man is doomed to make decisions from time to time that are wrong and evil in consequence, it is better to make decisions with all one's heart and soul and mind in an attempt to make the moral choice than it is to lapse into atrophy of soul."

In "Gold Hair" Browning ilustrates the evil of professing to make a choice while repudiating it in deed. A lovely young girl from

19. X, 236-240.        20. X, 259-263.

Pornic, whose hair is a cascade of pure gold, and whose life is famed for its unworldly purity, lies on her deathbed. Her last request, to have her hair undisturbed, astonishes the priest, but her wish is granted. Years later, the paving needing repair, her tomb is opened and thirty pieces of gold are discovered hidden in her hair, revealing her dreadful secret:

> Why I deliver this horrible verse?
>     As the text of a sermon, which now I preach:
> Evil or good may be better or worse
>     In the human heart, but the mixture of each
> Is a marvel and a curse.[21]

Browning's point is not that it would have been equally good to elect evil or good. It is, rather, that to see the good and to profess it, while electing evil—in this instance, miserly greed—is hypocrisy, the most shameful of evils. This theme is similar to that in *Red Cotton Night-Cap Country,* in which Léonce Miranda determines to keep both the fleshly and spiritual delights in nice equipoise, losing nothing of either. He knows it is a sin to keep his mistress in defiance of the church and the moral law, but he cannot give her up. He builds a belvedere, or tower, a symbol of his spiritual aspirations. The turf on which it rests represents the world and the flesh. The symbol of his compromise, a tent, resting on the turf, but elevated slightly toward heaven, represents his desire to have the best of two worlds: good and evil. In an attempt to renounce his mistress symbolically and gain spiritual peace, he plunges her love letters "and coffer and both hands to boot" into the fire and holds them in the purifying flames until all is consumed, even the bones of his hands.

His horrible experience fails of its purpose, for his religious doubts and neurotic guilt increase. What he could do symbolically, he cannot do in reality. He determines to put his doubts to one daring test: he will step off the belvedere and attempt to walk on air. If God suspends the law of gravity, he will know that his way of life is vin-

21.  Ll. 136-140.

dicated. He is predictably killed. The shocked world pronounces him mad, but Browning sees it differently:

> No! sane, I say.
> Such being the conditions of his life,
> Such end of life was not irrational.
> Hold a belief, you only half-believe,
> With all-momentous issues either way,—
> And I advise you imitate this leap,
> Put faith to proof, be cured or killed at once![22]

The point again is that a deliberately uncommitted life is among the worst of evils. If a man elects virtue and occasionally fails through human frailty, there is hope for him. Even the man who elects evil with courage and conviction—bad as he is—has more chance of salvation than the man who professes virtue but embraces evil hypocritically.

Raymond finds support for his thesis—that Browning believed it is better to sin than to be lukewarm in goodness—in the poem "Before," in which two duelers are urged on to their bloody game by a bystander, who says: "Better sin the whole sin, sure that God observes . . . ," and enunciates such enlivening sentiments as are not uncommonly heard at lynchings: "All or nothing, stake it! trusts he God or no?/ Thus far and no farther? farther? be it so!" It is necessary to read the sequel to the poem, entitled "After," to form a reasonably valid judgment of Browning's theme. Did he really mean to say that because atrophy of soul is the result of chronic shirking of life's demands, it is well to fight a duel against a friend with whom one has quarreled? Should one hold "All or nothing" and "Better sin the whole sin" as twin codes of conduct? In "After" the victor does not think so:

> Ha, what avails death to erase
> His offense, my disgrace?
> I would we were boys as of old
> In the field, by the fold:

22.  IV, 351-357.

> His outrage, God's patience, man's scorn
> Were so easily borne!

> I stand here now, he lies in his place:
> Cover the face!

There is no joy here in victory. Nothing could be clearer than the heartbreak and the shame the victor feels. I cannot find the support that Raymond sees in these poems for preferring sin to stagnation. The alternative to sin here is not stagnation, but Christian patience and forgiveness.

Raymond discovers similar evidence in "The Worst of It," "Too Late," and "The Lost Leader." In the first of these poems a man is lamenting the faithlessness of his wife. He wishes that he had been the guilty one, for she was a "swan," snow-white in purity, whereas he has a "speckled hide," smudged in life's struggle, soiled and besmirched by the world. He is not evil or base. He is neither black nor white, but speckled. In his grief he says:

> Far better commit a fault and have done—
> As you, Dear!—forever. . . .

Out of context this appears to link Browning with Oscar Wilde's belief that the only way to get rid of temptation is to yield to it. Care must be exercised in so concluding. Again the poet is saying that it is better to choose the lesser of two evils. If one's life is ravaged by endless temptation, it is better—if there is no other recourse—to yield to it, provided it purge one of the destructive temptation and allow the individual to get on to better things. This proviso is expressly stated:

> . . . and choose the pure,
> And look where the healing waters run,
> And strive and strain to be good again,
> And a place in the other world ensure,
> All glass and gold, with God for its sun.

But far from believing that she sinned in order to be the more free from sin thereafter, he is sure that she is unrepentant: she has not "done" with sinning:

> Most like, you are glad you deceived me—rue
> No whit of the wrong: you endured too long,
> Have done no evil and want no aid,
> Will live the old life out and chance the new.

She is unregenerate. Still sunk in sin, she laments only her delay in sinning. She has achieved no redemption by reason of boldly committing adultery. Her deserted husband—one of Browning's gallery of gallant and forgiving lovers—remarks in genuine pathos:

> Oh, my sweet,
> Think, and be sorry you did this thing!

Although he is eager to place the blame on himself for her faithlessness, he nevertheless knows she has risked her salvation ("Be good! Why want what the angels vaunt?"). She has made a bad bargain to "forfeit heaven for a snapt gold ring." If, by chance, they should meet in heaven, he adds, "I will pass nor turn my face."

As in "Before," I cannot find the evidence in this poem which Raymond discovers in support of his thesis that Browning believed men should prefer "to act evilly . . . than to lapse into atrophy of soul." The alternative to faithlessness in this poem is not atrophy: it is faithfulness. The wife was false to her vows, sinned, and will suffer.

The poem "Too Late" is a highly dramatic, almost hysterical, account of a rejected lover whose beloved Edith, married to a rival poet, is now dead. The lover accepts his rejection with uncommon philosophy, knowing that there may still be hope as long as both live. He holds the firm conviction that their love is ordained of God, and like a stream that is dammed by a great rock thrown by a devil thwarting God, the stream—his Life and love—will find a way around the obstacle, "Since a stone will have rolled from its place," a phrase with a familiar biblical ring. In his grief he fancies that he might have done more to win her, to circumvent the great stone blocking the progress of his love; and he nurtures illusions of how he might have carried her off, Perseus to his Andromeda, in a moment of violence:

> Why, better even have burst like a thief
>    And borne you away to a rock for us two,
> In a moment's horror, bright, bloody and brief:
>    Then changed to myself again—"I slew
> Myself in that moment; a ruffian lies
>    Somewhere: your slave, see, born in his place!"

In this fantasy of violence Raymond finds additional support for his thesis. However, this passage is as dramatic as any passage in Browning and is spoken by a man nearly unhinged by grief. How many young men whose lover has married another have not indulged, however briefly, in fantasies of how different things might have been if only they had been more daring, more violent in their manhood? Even Guido fancies how much different things would have been had he given free rein to his natural violence instead of stagnating in silent acquiescence. It seems strange to advance these wild lines as Browning's sage view of life. The issue in this poem is not a choice between evil and atrophy. It is a choice between doing something and doing nothing. It is clear that he never spoke his love, and she married another, and now is dead:

> I ought to have done more: once my speech,
>    And once your answer, and there, the end,
> And Edith was henceforth out of reach!

Here was no bright evil which would have been better than inaction. As in "The Statue and the Bust" the issue is procrastination, but adultery is not involved. He failed to tell Edith of his love before she married a rival. He finds his heart "marked broad with her mark/ Tekel, found wanting . . . ," but what was found wanting in him was not bold pursuit of evil, but boldness itself.

Raymond, also in "The Jeweled Bow," gives the fullest statement of another disastrous theme which began with Henry Jones and

A. C. Pigou, and which has been very largely unchallenged since: the theme that Browning regarded evil as "stuff for transmuting":

> It is in connection with Browning's belief in evil as "stuff for transmuting" that his ethical standards in "The Statue and the Bust" must be evaluated. Whenever good and evil grapple there is no hesitation whatever in his choice of virtue and his condemnation of the choice of vice. No other poet has been such a militant champion of virtue. . . . Yet, because he does regard evil as "stuff for transmuting" he holds that the shirking of the moral conflict is the worst sin of all.[23]

Raymond is entirely accurate in his assertion that Browning always championed virtue and the moral choice. He is similarly accurate in expressing Browning's views on the evils of shirking the moral conflict, always assuming he means chronic, protracted shirking. Man is never reprehensible, as I have shown, in avoiding temptation in a given instance, or in refusing to make a moral choice until he has weighed the evidence maturely. But the phrase "stuff for transmuting," which is a casuistical phrase in the mouth of the rake Don Juan in *Fifine at the Fair,* must be examined. Don Juan uses the phrase to convince his wife Elvire that his intended adulteries are "stuff for transmuting"—i.e., that evil itself is changed to good in the performance of the act. In effect, as Raymond points out, this means that evil is an illusion. It is ironic that Raymond's statement, which does not at all apply to Browning, does apply to Don Juan. He hopes that his wife will be so entoiled in the web of his casuistry that she will evaluate his ethical standards in the light of his argument that evil is the raw material of good, which it becomes, as base metal supposedly becomes gold, in the alchemist's crucible—or rather the bed. In the history of Browning scholarship nothing is more astounding than the regularity with which he is identified with his characters, even the most revolting of his villains, of whom Don Juan is one. Don Juan, of course, does not believe that evil is an illusion, "stuff for transmuting." He wants to deceive his wife by the sophistry. Evil

23. *The Infinite Moment and Other Essays in Robert Browning,* p. 227.

is real enough, and the more fun for being real, he knows. His argument is that since God planned life as a test, he is furthering the divine plan by wenching, for does not evil—an illusion—become good through transmutation? Surely, he argues, God would not have placed evil on earth if it were truly evil and resisted the transmutation which bold indulgence in it surely brings. To say that evil is "stuff for transmuting" is to say, with Don Juan, that by sinning, sin becomes the shining stuff that he says it really is, upon close examination. Only those who are so weak as to resist temptation see evil as a reality.

Henry Jones expressed much the same view as Raymond, but in different terms. He also held that Browning believed evil to be mere illusion.

> Man confronts evil in order to force it to give up the good, which is all the reality that is in it. He conceives it as his mission to prove that evil is "stuff for transmuting," and that there is nought in the world.[24]

I do not believe that Browning ever denied the reality of evil any more than he denied the reality of any other part of life. Nor did he believe that evil is transmuted or changed to good in its perpetration. Rather he believed—and there is a vast difference between these views—that evil yields fruit of good in that it tests man's strength in resisting it. If man resists successfully, the resulting good is clear; even if he fails in his resistance, good may ultimately result through the lesson learned and the greater insight into character and human frailty and good's opposite. *But evil is real and it is not good.* Nor does it change to good. It only may lead to good or result in good.

Johannes Agricola, like Don Juan, believes he can change all poison to honey and all evil to good because he is, he fancies, absolved from compliance under the Mosaic Law—and Browning loathed him. All men are tested alike, and the test is man's resistance to very real evil. Don Juan employs an ingenious argument to establish the illusory character of evil. He argues that as a man floating

24. *Browning as a Philosophical and Religious Teacher*, p. 102.

in the sea soon learns that if the body sinks into the slimy depths, the face is elevated toward the purity of heaven, so his body, by sinking into promiscuity, elevates the spirit toward God. This is what he means by "stuff for transmuting." Elvire is not deceived. The analogy is patently false. It does not establish that good will grow out of his seduction of Fifine, much less prove that evil is transmuted to good. As I have attempted to show in my *Triple Soul: Browning's Theory of Knowledge,* the casuistical pieces can be understood only if it is recognized that the subtle, convoluted arguments of the speakers are distortions and extensions and misapplications of doctrines that Browning firmly held. These doctrines are made absurd and vicious by these unprincipled casuists, who argue for the sport of the thing, to see how far words can be distorted and misapplied for private advantage:

> By practice with the false, I reach the true? Why, thence
> It follows, that the more I gain self-confidence,
> Get proof I know the trick, can float, sink, rise, at will,
> The better I submit to what I have the skill
> To conquer in my turn, even now, and by and by
> Leave wholly for the land. . . .[25]

Raymond finds that Browning's denial of the reality of evil is a direct result of his "intellectual agnosticism":

> Unfortunately, Browning's representation of this aspect of evil is warped by his intellectual agnosticism. An extreme instance is his argument that although evil is an illusion, it is necessary for man to regard it as real in order to preserve the worth of the moral struggle. This would seem to make man's moral effort dependent on ignorance and delusion, or to hold, as Professor Jones writes, that "the world is a kind of moral gymnasium crowded with phantoms, wherein by exercise man makes moral muscle." As I have stated the confusion of thought engendered by Browning's sceptical theory of knowledge seems to me responsible for much misunderstanding regarding his ethical

25. Ll. 1069-1074.

standards. The poet exposes himself to this because he fails to realize that even from an absolute point of view evil has a relative degree of reality, and is not mere semblance and illusion.[26]

I believe that in this passage may be seen much of the reason for the sixty-year decline in the popularity of Browning, beginning with his death. In my *Triple Soul* I have tried to show how mistaken has been the notion that Browning was an enemy of the mind. The whole of Raymond's statement, quoted above, is found elaborately developed in Jones. It should prove instructive to examine briefly Jones's theory.

Mistaking wholly Browning's belief that on earth knowledge cannot be and must not be absolute—for doubt, ignorance, and uncertainty are among the severest tests of man's fidelity and faith—Jones affirmed that Browning denounced knowledge as nescience simply, renounced the mind as worthless, and recommended uninstructed reliance on intuition, love, and the heart. That this belief is incompatible with almost everything Browning said and wrote did not occur to Jones, but he did find it puzzling that such a keen mind as Browning's would not have recognized the impossible dilemma that such a belief leads to:

> And absolute scepticism is easily shown to be self-contradictory. For a theory of nescience, in condemning all knowledge, condemns itself. If nothing is true, or if nothing is known, then this theory itself is not true, or its truth cannot be known. And if this theory is true, then nothing is true; for this theory, like all others, is the product of a defective intelligence. In whatsoever way the matter is put, there is left no standing ground for the human critic who condemns human thought.[27]

Jones is entirely right in discovering a fatal contradiction here. To condemn the intellect as useless and to counsel pursuit of total ignorance would be shocking enough, but to do so by means of a discredited intellect and on the basis of nescience parading as knowl-

26. *The Infinite Moment and Other Essays in Robert Browning*, p. 230.
27. P. 246.

edge is absurd. Browning's mind was far too subtle to become enmeshed in such a childish contradiction. Of course, Browning never
says what Jones thinks he says. Rather, he declares ceaselessly and
clearly that part of life's test of man is to progress toward truth endlessly, in the sure knowledge only that today's "truth" will yield to
a better "truth" tomorrow and so on during all the days of man's
life. In this spirit, Browning, like Montaigne, continually inveighs
against the folly of "trusting knowledge," by which he means simply
that man must never accept any fact or dogma or belief as final and
absolute, immune from further examination and repudiation if found
wanting. One of the true ironies of literary history is that a man who
held this perfectly intellectual position is widely held to be the chief
of anti-intellectuals. In learning, to Browning, "the prize is in the
process"—a scientific attitude toward the pursuit of knowledge. In two
letters to Dr. F. J. Furnivall, Browning, in reply to a query concerning his meaning in a passage in the "Parleying with Bernard Mandeville," says:

> The meaning of the passages is much as you say—entirely so,
> indeed. "Neither body nor mind is born to attain perfect strength
> or perfect health at its first stage of existence respectively, in
> each case, by the want of and desire for the thing as yet out of
> reach, they get raised towards it, and are educated by the process
> —as would not happen were the body strong all at once—or the
> soul at once perfect in apprehension."[28]

> I should prosaically state the meaning thus: I do not ask a
> full disclosure of Truth, which would be a concession contrary
> to the law of things, which applies equally to the body and the
> soul, that it is only by striving to attain strength (in the one case)
> and truth (in the other) that body and soul do so—the effort
> (common to both) being productive, in each instance, of the
> necessary initiation into all the satisfactions which result from
> partial success; absolute success being only attainable for the

28. *Letters of Robert Browning Collected by Thomas J. Wise,* ed. Thurman L. Hood (New Haven, 1933), p. 301.

body in full manhood—for the soul, in its full apprehension of Truth—which will be, not *here,* at all events.[29]

These two statements perfectly express Browning's respect for intellectual processes and refute Jones, but unluckily Jones has been widely read and the letters, apparently, have not.

Fortunately, the whole matter of Browning's sane and respectful attitude toward the intellect is finally placed beyond reasonable conjecture by the publication of a letter from Browning to Mrs. Thomas FitzGerald on the occasion of her son's mental illness. Repeatedly in his words of comfort and commiseration, he speaks with the greatest emphasis and the strongest conviction that the mind is the *"eyes of the soul,"* the faithful servant of the soul, the guide to man's moral being, without which man is clearly absolved from divine retribution that would follow acts of violence or suicide committed while without the guidance of mind:

I confess I wonder, dear friend, that you could entertain for a moment that doubt which you express—& which Mr. Hussey so strangely declares he cannot solve—as to the liabi[li]ties of any soul deprived by the visitation of God of that reason which is given as a guide to its actions. WHO has said "I will be eyes to the blind"?—and may not the soul want sight much more than the body? What struck me so much in that life of Schopenhauer which you gave me, was that doctrine which he considered his grand discovery—and which I had been persuaded of from my boyhood—and based my whole life upon:—that the soul is above and *behind* the intellect which is merely its servant. I first met with this doctrine's enunciation in a memoir of Robert Hall the Baptist Minister, who was subject to fits of mental alienation, and expected to be eventually deprived altogether of his reasoning faculty. The memoir went on to say that he had a correspondence with some eminent friend on this subject—I believe, Macintosh—who pressed on his consideration that the instru-

29. *Idem.*

ment was not the craftsman, the intelligence—not the soul. The consequences of this doctrine were so momentous to me—so destructive of vanity, on the one hand,—or undue depression at failure, on the other—that I am sure there must be references to and deductions from it throughout the whole of my works. . . . Now, in the case of any one deprived, by no fault of his own, of those *eyes* of the soul—the reasoning powers—could we wrong the justice as well as the goodness of God more offensively than by supposing that He will ignore the consequences of his own act and punish the blind for blindness? In your son's case,—the letters which I read contained positive proof that his religious feeling was very earnest—*that is* the *soul:* and if, like poor L$^d$ Lyttelton who was similarly afflicted, in the absence of his *soul's eyes* he should commit the worst of excesses against himself or others—I should never dare attribute to God what would be injustice in a human being—nay, in a *less* degree,—and think Him capable of punishing what Himself was the agent in producing. That is my opinion, and it is inexplicable to me how people with a belief in the Mercy and Rectitude of God can have any other. Trust in these, dear Friend,—and dismiss all such fancies as derogatory to the All-good and All-wise.

Now let us turn our own servants,—our own intelligence and thoughts,—from the morbid employment about such matters, and make them do legitimate duty by bearing us above what sorrow may be so surmounted.[30]

Of special significance is his forceful pronouncement that this large and humanistic view of intellect everywhere informs his poetry.

In discussing Browning's supposed denial of the reality of evil, which was a direct product of his supposed repudiation of the mind, Jones reveals some doubt about his dubious position:

30. *Learned Lady, Letters from Robert Browning to Mrs. Thomas Fitz-Gerald, 1876-1889,* ed. Edward C. McAleer (Cambridge, Mass., 1966), pp. 34-35.

. . . clear knowledge that evil is illusion and that all other things have their place in an infinite divine order would paralyze all moral effort, as well as stultify itself.[31]

It would indeed. The very real test of life—if evil were but illusion —would become an artificial playacting deceiving no one, or a protracted game of poker played for matches. Edward Berdoe, the prince of Browning idolators, shares what he takes to be Browning's view:

> Browning cautions us against looking upon evil as a real thing. We are to consider it as shade is considered in relation to shine, or as he put it in another way in *Abt Vogler*—
>
> "Evil is null, is naught."[32]

He quotes from *Sordello* ("For mankind springs Salvation by each hindrance interposed") a passage which is the most striking evidence that Browning, far from denying the reality of evil, found evil and good equally real:

> Where the salt marshes, crystals branch
> Blood dries to crimson; Evil's beautified
> In every slope. Thrust Beauty then aside
> And banish Evil! Wherefore? After all,
> Is Evil a result less natural than Good?

Evil is "null" only in the sense that it is good's opposite, and hence it heightens one's sense of what is good—and thence works for good. An adult dismisses as "nothing" a slight injury, but he is never misunderstood to mean it did not happen. It is simply not important, properly looked at, and this is Browning's sense in the passages from both "Abt Vogler" and *Sordello*.

Raymond cites Pippa's famous song by way of proving Browning's denial of evil: "God's in his heaven—/All's right with the world." And he adds what is perhaps the most widely accepted fallacy in

31. P. 255.
32. *Browning and the Christian Faith* (2nd ed.; London, 1897), p. 221.

Browning criticism: ". . . there can be no doubt that they voice the poet's belief."

I very much doubt that they voice the poet's belief, if one accepts Raymond's notion that the lines express a denial of the existence of evil—and this is the standard critical belief. Of all the poets of his day, he saw evil rampant and teeming and knew it for the validity it was. Pippa's words form an ironic contrast with the evil everywhere about her, blighting lives, both literally and figuratively.

What Pippa meant is that the *plan* of life is perfect, for it was made by God to give life a function: to test man's courage and fortitude in the face of evil. Pippa (who is a far more reliable spokesman of Browning's philosophical position than is Don Juan, the rake who is busily engaged in demonstrating that he is a heartless distorter of truth in an evil cause) would have been shocked to hear herself accused of believing that there is no evil in the world or, indeed, that evil is an illusion, which upon close inspection is merely "stuff for transmuting," *i.e.*, really virtue and excellence, not in its results, but actually in itself.[33] All's right with the world because the test of life through suffering and evil is right. The Pope in *The Ring and the Book* paraphrases what Pippa means when he says that the "dread machinery of sin and sorrow" is to stimulate man's moral growth through struggle. It might be noted that Pippa on her one holiday in the dreary year of poverty, long hours of drudgery in the silk mill, and loneliness does not seek comfort in the delusion that her past life has been visited only with good, since there is nothing else in life. She has known little else but evil, and the misery of the past year appears as an earnest of the year to come. She knows that her great day cannot give her the joy that "prosperous ones" expect, "Those who enjoy the higher lot"—perfect evidence that she is pain-

33. Arthur Symons (*An Introduction to the Study of Browning* [London, 1886], pp. 18-19) noted with some alarm the habit of critics of ascribing to Browning the sentiments of his characters: "There is another popular misconception to which also a word in passing may well be devoted. This is the idea that Mr. Browning's personality is apt to get confused with his characters', that his men and women are not separate creations, projected from his brain into an independent existence, but were masks or puppets through whose mouth he spoke."

fully aware of the disparity of fortune—and she is aware that whatever happiness her twelve hours confer, sorrow will close about her
for another full year:

> For, Day, my holiday, if thou ill-usest
> Me, who am only Pippa,—old-year's sorrow
> Cast off last night, will come again to-morrow:
> Whereas, if thou prove gentle, I shall borrow
> Sufficient strength of thee for new-year's sorrow.[34]

To free her holiday from the gloom of the past and dread of the
future, she seeks no comfort in childish denial of evil; rather she
projects herself into the lives of "the four happiest ones in Asolo"—
who are, unknown to her, immersed in evil and unhappiness. Her
little songs, which are by no means as happy as some critics have
found them to be, alter the course of lives at the crossroads, but they
cannot transmute evil into good. Old Lucca remains none the less
murdered after her passing, and the evil of Ottima and Sebald is
still as red as the blood they shed. They have committed a crime as
base and loathsome as any committed by Browning's gallery of rogues
and criminals, and without conscience they are about to make love
while old Lucca's corpse lies as a silent reproach to them, when
Pippa's song brings some measure of good out of evil. Sebald sees
his wickedness, repents and repudiates his guilty love for Ottima,
who now appears hideous in his sight, and stabs himself in atone-
ment. Pippa's song makes him see the horrible *reality* of his sin, not
its illusory character. To say that Browning denied the reality of the
evil in this sordid story is as naïve as to believe that the foul evils of
*The Inn Album* are figments of a disordered fancy. In neither poem
is evil transmuted or explained away somehow, for it is the central
reality. Good may be evil's fruit, but evil remains evil. If Ottima and
Sebald do not sin, then Pippa has no real function in their lives,
since nothing is really changed after her passing, and Sebald's suicide
becomes unmotivated and irrelevant.

John Bury, in discussing *Fifine* and "Bishop Blougram's Apology,"

34. Ll. 30-34.

notes with keen insight that "From God's point of view, doubt and evil are good as means to good; but from man's point of view—as practiser, not theorist—doubt and evil in themselves must be always evil, because imperfect."[35] Life to Browning, Bury knows, is no game or illusion.

William Whitla takes a more moderate position concerning Browning's concept of evil:

> Evil in *The Ring and the Book* (and that poetic world for Browning represents life) is temporal and fleeting. It serves only to illustrate the power and the love of God, because evil is constantly transformed by God into good.[36]

Whitla does not find Browning denying evil, but he does believe, with Raymond and Jones, that evil is "stuff for transmuting"; *i.e.,* it is promptly changed directly into good. Perhaps the danger inherent in adopting this belief may be seen in an anonymous review of Whitla's book:

> No blame to Mr. Whitla, except that his spade was cracked on flint. If the end of the inquiry must lie in this question of belief, then Browning fails. He fails despite interpolated doubts, through over-belief. Mankind, with a new history of concentration camps and their effects on humans, no longer subscribes to that comforting view of evil.[37]

This review strikes at the heart of the problem. As long as Browning is pictured as a fatuous optimist, mystically denying the very existence of evil, and lustily shouting about how all's right with the world because there is no evil at all, his reputation will suffer. This view, which a misreading of Pippa's song ably supports, appears in extended form in Arthur C. Pigou's book, *Robert Browning as a Religious Teacher,* which won the Burney Prize in 1900 at Cambridge University and which has exercised an influence only second to

---

35. "Browning's Philosophy," *Browning Studies* (London, 1895), pp. 28-46.
36. *The Central Truth, The Incarnation in Browning's Poetry* (Toronto, 1963), p. 133.
37. *Times Literary Supplement,* August 30, 1964.

Jones's book, of which it is a summary. In the chapter entitled "The Illusory Character of Evil," Pigou goes to great length to prove his case:

> In the last chapter it has been shown that according to Browning's view all that is commonly designated as evil serves to promote God's ends for man. But this is not sufficient to reconcile its existence with his conception of the nature of God. For if the evil that is present in earthly experience could have been avoided, and the end attained without it, God is not all-loving; whereas, if it was unavoidable, He is not Omnipotent. Hitherto Browning seems to have tacitly inclined towards the second of the two horns of this dilemma. . . .[38]

The reasoning ascribed here to Browning admirably fits Thomas Hardy, Mark Twain, John Stuart Mill, and a host of others, but not Browning. He spent his life defending God's plan (and that is what is *right* about the world) and the function of evil in life, and he makes it clear that God is neither sadistic nor "impotent to tend," as Hardy expressed it. In "A Bean-Stripe: Also Apple-Eating," the question is asked why some people are singled out to see life as largely white, marred by black, whereas many see it as black, relieved occasionally by white:

> " 'Why, if God be just,
> Were sundry fellow-mortals singled out
> To undergo experience for his sake,
> Just that the gift of pain, bestowed on them,
> In him might temper to the due degree
> Joy's else-excessive largess?' Why, indeed!
> Back are we brought thus to the starting-point—
> Man's impotency, God's omnipotence. . . ."[39]

This is the note that Browning sounds throughout his life: God's omnipotence is absolute; man's impotence is real, but not absolute. Man's powers are much limited, but they are never doomed to be

38.  London, 1901, p. 96.    39.  Ll. 209-216.

either static or contemptible. Growth through aspiration and trial and exercise is what life *is*. Man yearns for truth, not semblance. He aspires to knowledge, not nescience, but as man he can only *progress* toward truth:

> "Even so
> I needs must blend the quality of man
> With quality of God, and so assist
> Mere human sight to understand my Life,
> What is, what should be,—understand thereby
> Wherefore I hate the first and love the last,—
> Understand why things so present themselves
> To me, placed here to prove I understand."[40]

Ferishtah's statement makes it unmistakable that man must be convinced of the essential validity of his knowledge, while recognizing always that no human knowledge is absolute. Plainly, he does not intend to say that the false is illusion or that emptiness is solidity, nor that illusion is all or that evil is virtue. Rather it is again the familiar idea that in life there are no absolutes. To man who wearily shouts that he wants "truth at any cost," Ferishtah says:

> "Take one and try conclusions—this, suppose!
> God is all—good, all-wise, all-powerful: truth?
> Take it and rest there. What is man? Not God:
> None of these absolutes therefore,—yet himself,
> A creature with a creature's qualities."[41]

In *La Saisiaz*, without dramatic cover, Browning clearly states his belief in the reality of both good and evil: "the right and the wrong" are "now tangled." Only in the next life will they "lie unraveled." The plain sense here is that two realities are in this life inextricably enmeshed, and the test of life is to separate them as best man can. There is no suggestion that virtue is a real thing, in contrast to evil, which is the illusion Jones, Pigou, Raymond, and others find it to be. Augustus Hopkins Strong discovers that Browning, in denying

40. Ll. 351-358.    41. Ll. 290-294.

the reality of evil is a true pantheist—a strange conclusion in view of Browning's emphatic repudiation of pantheism in *Sordello*:

> Now there are two kinds of optimism: first, Christian optimism, which asserts that *in spite of* moral evil all things are working together for good; and secondly, pantheistic optimism, which asserts that all things *are* good. With every inclination to put the best interpretation upon his works, I am obliged to confess that Browning comes dangerously near to the pantheistic explanation of sin.[42]

He interprets "A Bean-Stripe, Also Apple-Eating"—especially the figure of the chessboard—as proof that Browning so much wanted to find good in everything that he denied evil. He, of course, fails to see that a chessboard, with an equal number of squares of black and of white, may be held by the observer to be predominantly black or white, as he is predisposed to see things. Meanwhile the reality of the white and black squares is unaltered. Predictably, Strong finds the theme of "The Status and the Bust" to be that "vigorous transgression is better than pusillanimous rectitude." Indeed, Strong believes that the message of Browning is "Right is simply might," as evidence of which declaration he cites the fact that "the Pope is a warrior-priest, and Pompilia reaches the height of virtue by becoming energetic":

> Is all moral failure, then, only apparent? Is sin only a phantom? Are right and wrong only illusions to sting men to effort? Is Ottima just as good in her place as Pippa? It certainly seems as if this were at times Browning's doctrine! He says:
>
> > All service ranks the same with God—
> > With God, whose puppets, best and worst,
> > Are we: there is no last nor first.[43]

The assertion that Browning made no distinction between virtuous Pippa and evil Ottima is a natural corollary to the belief that there

42. *The Great Poets and Their Theology* (Philadelphia, 1897), p. 434.
43. *Ibid.*, pp. 434-436.

is, in Browning, a denial of evil—but the assertion serves to illustrate the error of the premise. It is no more absurd, however, than John Meigs Hitner's astonishing theory that Browning found only death and the phallus real:

> The hard core of fact in *Fifine* is the yearning, aspiration, and nostalgia common to all men. Browning's problem as a man is to find an explanation of love which will conform with his philosophy of life. When he decides that the ultimate reality, the sole symbol of truth's permanence, is only the phallic pillar, he reaches the nadir of his pessimism. Browning's problem as a poet is to convey to the reader a clear impression of his mental and emotional disturbance. *Fifine* is a case history of the poet's soul-searching; it is an experiment in introspective psychology, with one-fourth of the poem being given over to a long series of dreams. . . . Infused with paralyzing doubts, the pessimism in *Fifine* develops from the hypothesis that human knowledge is of no use whatever in solving the riddle of man's uncertain doom. The probation theory, so characteristic of Browning, is contemplated briefly in *Fifine,* then discarded. The conclusion reached is that nothing about God can be proved by one's intellect. Only by the intuitive knowledge of the heart can a man find the answer to the meaning of life.[44]

The reader will at once recognize the great indebtedness here to Jones, except for the folly about the phallic pillar. Nowhere in Browning is there the slightest evidence of a phallic fixation, unless one is so perverse as to read it into his wholesome attitude toward sex as a normal part of love and life. Browning defended wholeness all his days and affirmed the virtue of life, of which death is a part, and love, of which sex is a part, but Hitner discovers "In *Fifine phallicism* is the answer to the body's needs, and death is the answer to the soul's"—a dismaying reading, but not surprising as a companion belief to his statement that Browning's "chief interests were the nude and the crude":

44. *Browning's Pessimism in "Fifine at the Fair,"* pp. 40-41.

Everything in his environment points to the conclusion: he sees the symbol of the phallus through the nude form in art, and in architecture through its church spires; he associates the fertility-ritual with that part of science known as creative evolution: he connects the principle of the phallic pillar with dream philos-ophy; he finds sex playing the major role on the stage of life, love, and nature. . . . Behind most of the world's great work and noble deeds stands the phallus. Short of death this is the only reality Browning can hope to know.[45]

These untenable conclusions, wholly out of character with the poet, are the result of Hitner's full identification of Browning with Don Juan, the unprincipled rake, a common blunder in Browning scholar-ship. It must not pass unnoticed that Hitner joins the throng who believe that Browning denied the reality of evil. Pigou, similarly, quotes from "A Bean-Stripe" ("'I know my own appointed patch! the world/ What pleasures me or pains there'") and from *La Saisiaz* ("I myself am what I know not—ignorance which proves no bar/To the knowledge that I am, and, since I am, can recognize/What to me is pain and pleasure: this is sure. . . . )." Pigou neglects to observe that a few lines below, Browning specifically repudiates this sentiment by saying that *if* it were true that earth and evil were "illusions mere" and *if* he could reckon real only his own joys and sorrows, then

> I must say—or choke in silence—"Howsoever came
>     my fate,
> Sorrow did and joy did nowise,—life well weighed,—
>     preponderate."[46]

These two lines are among the most often misunderstood and mis-quoted lines in Browning, and they are, if torn from context—almost unique in their apparent pessimism. It is easy to fail to note that these lines are the main clause coming at the end of fourteen long

45. P. 62.        46. Ll. 333-334.

lines of subordinate subjunctive and "if" clauses. Browning is not at all saying that this is what his life seems to him. He is saying that *if* the dreadful conditions of the subordinate clauses had obtained in his life, then he would have found his life predominantly pain:

> Nay, *were* fancy fact, *were* earth and all it
> holds illusion mere,
> Only a machine for teaching love and hate and
> hope and fear
> To myself, the sole existence, single truth mid
> falsehood,—well!
> *If* the harsh throes of the prelude die not off
> into the swell
> Of that perfect piece they sting me to become
> a-strain for,—*if*
> Roughness of the long rock-clamber lead not to
> the last of cliff,
> First of level country where is sward my
> pilgrim-foot can prize,—
> Plainlier! *if* this life's conception new life
> *fail* to realize,—
> Though earth burst and proved a bubble glassing
> hues of hell, one huge
> Reflex of the devil's doings—God's work by
> no subterfuge—
> (So death's kindly touch informed me as it
> broke the glamour, gave
> Soul and body both release from life's long
> nightmare in the grave)
> Still,—with no more Nature, no more Man as
> riddle to be read,
> Only my own joys and sorrows now to reckon
> real instead,—
> I must say—or choke in silence. . . .[47]

47. Ll. 319-333. The italics are mine.

Henry Charles Duffin, misreading this passage, as most critics have done, condemns Browning for his weakness: "No one doubts that Browning is speaking in his own person in *Prospice,* when he declares his readiness to pay, in the pangs of death, 'glad life's arrears of pain, darkness, and cold.' It is this last handsome admission that makes it hard to forgive that pusillanimous passage in *La Saisiaz* about sorrow preponderating in his own life, which I must regard as a moan out of a temporary depression."[48] It is unfortunate that he did not see that this supposedly pusillanimous passage is in reality as affirmative and courageous as the one he admires from "Prospice." By the use of the subjunctive, implying conditions contrary to fact, Browning is denying that his life has been largely dark with sorrow. But if earth and all it holds (including evil and love) were illusions, and so were man's hopes of purpose in life and ultimate survival, then and only then would he be forced to say that sorrow and not joy marked his life.

J. Hillis Miller singles out this passage as an example of Browning's unfortunate verbal ineptitude. As an introduction to these lines, which he quotes in their entirety, he accuses Browning of the most extreme stylistic bombast, in a critical paragraph not a little remarkable for stylistic bombast:

He has a great many things to say at once, and they all rush out simultaneously—producing a sentence all dashes and parentheses —a sentence which strives to exist all in a moment: all its parts in the same flash of time, not sequentially. A typical sentence in "La Saisiaz" begins with one metaphorical expression of the idea, stops suddenly, begins again with an entirely different metaphor, stops again, tries to pull itself together by adjuring itself to speak "Plainlier!," and then, far from clarifying, collapses into an incoherent coruscation of dashes, parentheses, broken phrases within phrases. Finally the sentence congeals, lamely and with evident difficulty, in a concluding phrase of characteristic

48. *Amphibian, A Reconsideration of Browning* (London, 1956), p. 236.

stuttering staccato, grinding to a halt at last with a single word
full of little dental and labial explosives.[49]

It might be noted that this is not a "typical sentence" from the
poem. Rather it is perhaps the most atypical sentence in the poem in
its length and complexity, but does the sentence really merit such
an immoderate judgment? Is it incoherent? I think not. At most it
can be charged with an overrichness of metaphor and of parentheti-
cal subordination. It is perfectly clear throughout, and it should be
noted that words of one syllable, many of them Anglo-Saxon words,
predominate; and the images are remarkable for their concreteness
and vividness. Out of about one hundred and fifty words (admittedly
an overlong sentence) one word in five (not counting hyphenated
words) is a polysyllable, and, save for *howsoever,* only *preponderate*
has four syllables, a word which Miller seizes upon to illustrate the
blinding and deafening character of Browning's diction. I doubt that
*preponderate* is as rich in explosives as Miller's ". . . far from
clarifying, collapses into an incoherent coruscation of dashes . . ."
or ". . . concluding phrase of characteristic stuttering staccato, grinding. . . ." His phrase "little dental and labial explosives" contains
five such explosives, it might be noted in passing, but in spite of the
linguistic label, the sounds do not deafen the ear or fray the nerves
any more than does *preponderate.*

The Rev. W. Robertson finds evil in *La Saisiaz* very real, but he
finds also that Browning was indifferent to it, or, to put it another
way, did not believe that immortality was necessary to atone for its
harassments in this life. His statement is a tissue of contradictions:

To sum up. It is an error to say, as regards *La Saisiaz,* at least,
that Mr. Browning bases his belief in immortality on the conviction that a second life is needed to atone for the ills of the
present. He does not judge the present world to be a scene of
probation because he believes in immortality; on the contrary,
he believes in immortality because, in his experience, he has

49. *The Disappearance of God,* p. 88

found this present state to be one of probation. It is neither the miseries nor the failures of this present life that oppress him—it is its meaninglessness, and he believes in immortality because in it alone does he find that which confers rationality and intelligibility in life.[50]

This is strange commentary in view of Browning's lifelong explanation of the function of evil. Evil in Browning *does* demand both an explanation and a purpose, and the ultimate purpose is a second life. The chicken-and-the-egg distinction between believing in immortality because he discovers life to be a time of probation, rather than the other way around, is puzzling. If Browning was compelled to believe in immortality because of the meaninglessness of this life—and the meaninglessness of it grows out of the irrational pain and frustration of a life leading to oblivion—surely the probationary period impressed him with its purposeless evils. Meaninglessness in life would be, to Browning, the crowning evil, and a very real one.

A. C. Pigou gave greatest currency to the belief that Browning refuted the existence of evil in *La Saisiaz*:

> Driven to recognize the reality of pain as far as he is concerned, he nevertheless refuses to predicate absolute reality of it. Contrasting the brief minute of this life with the everlasting destiny of man, he holds that the experiences which the soul undergoes in the course of its development may be treated as illusory in contrast to the reality of the soul itself. Pompilia points to the transience of evil in the words
>
> > "I know I wake, but from what?—blank, I say;
> > This is the note of evil, for good lasts."[51]

Pigou here fails to distinguish between *illusory* and *transient*. Pompilia is speaking in the pain occasioned by twenty-two stab wounds, made by a three-bladed Genoese dagger, with tiny hooks along the edges, and she is much aware of the reality of her pain. She is dying,

50. "La Saisiaz," *London Browning Society Papers,* Part XI, No. 51 (London, 1889), p. 16.
51. P. 97.

and she utters what many men before her uttered: now that my
life is ending, what do I know of life? Nothing, men have said, but
they are not denying its reality, but affirming its mystery. Pigou
continues:

> He is therefore driven to regard reality as eternal and timeless
> rather than everlasting. Time is a "mode of man" and not of
> God, so that events in time, though real for man are unreal for
> His absolute vision. It is not enough to say that a thousand years
> in His sight are as a single day. . . . From His standpoint not
> only transient existence but even everlasting existence is divorced
> from reality. Thus pleasure and pain are both ultimately unreal,
> though it is only the latter that Browning cares to prove so.
> Absolute reality cannot be predicated of any event in experience,
> but only of the effect it may leave in the soul, which is eternal
> as well as everlasting. When our end is achieved and the spell
> of illusion is broken by bodily death, God's point of view will
> become ours also.[52]

He cites as evidence from "Reverie" the lines:

> How evil—did mind descry
> Power's object to end pursued—
> Were haply as cloud across
> Good's orb, no orb itself.

It may reasonably be doubted that this quotation means that evil
is an illusion. It does mean the familiar statement that evil is good's
opposite, its obverse, and hence of equal reality. The cloud that
obscures the sun's rays is as real as the rays themselves, although we
think the one to be negative, the other positive. From *Fifine* he
quotes the lines "Evil proves good, wrong right, obscurity explained/
And howling childishness" as evidence of the illusory quality of evil,
neglecting to note that again Don Juan, not Browning, is speaking,
a fact which negates fully the validity of the evidence. If, however, it
were valid, it does not say that evil is unreal; rather it is Don Juan's

52. P. 98.

"stuff-for-transmuting" argument. More interesting is Pigou's quotation from "The Guardian-Angel":

> I think how I should view the earth and skies
> And sea, when once again my brow was bared
> After thy healing, with such different eyes.
> O world, as God has made it! all is beauty:
> And knowing this, is love, and love is duty.
> What further may be sought for or declared?

He concludes that the statement "all is beauty" means that there is no ugliness, no evil, no sin. This is an appalling misreading of the poem. Browning is speculating upon what the world would appear to be *if* the guardian angel, who, in the picture by Guercino at Fano, has his comforting arms about a little child, were to comfort the poet similarly. The poem is a plea for the angel to come with his healing wings and right the teeming evils of the world and to soothe the world-weary nerves:

> If this was ever granted, I would rest
>     My head beneath thine, while thy healing hands
> Close-covered both my eyes beside thy breast,
>     Pressing the brain, which too much thought expands,
> Back to its proper size again, and smoothing
> Distortion down till every nerve had soothing,
>     And all lay quiet, happy and suppressed.
>
> *How soon all worldly wrong would be repaired!*
> I think how I should view the earth. . . .[53]

Of all the poems Browning wrote, this is among the poorest to cite as evidence of his denial of evil. He begs the angel to comfort and sustain his spirit, frayed by the "worldly wrong," which is the hallmark of life.

Little better is Pigou's use of the familiar lines

> This world's no blot for us,
> Nor blank; it means intensely, and means good:

53. The italics are mine.

from "Fra Lippo Lippi," as evidence of the unreality of evil. It is unfortunate that he stops short of the following line ("To find its meaning is my meat and drink"), for it clearly means that the lusty monk regards the riddle of life, its beauty and ugliness, its evil and its good—and their interrelationships—as largely unresolved. It is dismaying to find Fra Lippo Lippi's words quoted for the use Pigou makes of them. He must have forgotten the magnificent autobiography Lippo regales the watch with: an account of sin, starvation, thievery, murder, hypocrisy, and lust—all told by the most buoyant and dynamic spirit in Browning, who finds life a glorious adventure, not because there is no real evil, but because there is. Of all the characters in Browning Lippo would have been most miserable on the planet of Rephan, where there is no evil, no challenge, and hence no growth.

From "Saul" Pigou quotes the lines

> I but open my eyes,—and perfection, no more
>     and no less,
> In the kind I imagined, full-fronts me, and
>     God is seen God
> In the star, in the stone, in the flesh, in
>     the soul and the clod.[54]

David says this immediately after the blinding revelation which comes upon him, when he sees for a moment into the living truth. The revelation, however, is not that evil is not real—Saul stands before him, a catatonic wreck of a man as evidence that evil abounds—but that the plan of life is perfect, that the handiwork of God is everywhere visible. Indeed, the phrase, "In the kind I imagined," is similar in tone to that in "The Guardian Angel." If one must merely imagine that things are perfect, it follows that things are not perfect. David merely sees what the whole poem makes explicit: the perfection of life as a test through evil. Immediately he confirms this judgment by saying that the divine insight he receives is specifically "The submission of Man's *nothing-perfect* to God's All-Complete."

54. Ll. 248-250.

He attains a vision of the perfection that is God's and sees how absurd it is to suppose that God will penalize man, as Caliban is sure he will, for his love and happiness. The sentiment is almost precisely that so often quoted from "Abt Vogler" as proof that evil is mere illusion:

> There shall never be one lost good! What was, shall
>   live as before;
>     The evil is null, is naught, is silence implying
>       sound;
> What was good, shall be good, with, for evil, so
>   much good more;
>     On the earth the broken arcs; in the heaven, a
>       perfect round.

This famous pronouncement that evil is null in no way means that it is illusory any more than a scientist means that there is no such thing as "cold," since there are only varying degrees of heat, or, at absolute zero, no heat at all. For all this, such a scientific definition will only imperfectly prevent frostbite, no matter how resolutely recalled while one is lost in the blizzard. Neither cold nor evil can be explained away by such casuistry. What Browning means by calling evil null and nought is simply that it is to be recognized for what it is: a necessary ingredient, to be little noted, in the scheme of things. In *The Two Poets of Croisic* Browning speaks the clearest warning against regarding life or any part of it as illusory. René Gentilhomme believes that God has spoken directly to him. For a shining moment, he has looked into the Absolute, as did Lazarus in "An Epistle." Browning wants to know

> . . . how a human creature felt
> In after-life, who bore the burden grave
> Of certainly believing God had dealt
> For once directly with him: did not rave
> —A maniac, did not find his reason melt

> —An idiot, but went on, in peace or strife,
> The world's way, lived an ordinary life.[55]

Does he, asks Browning, stand stock-still, like Lazarus, indifferent to
the things of life, now seen as tawdry? Or does he still progress, as
man must, toward truth and perfection? Does he trample life's
"vulgar hindrance"—life's evils and frustrations and obstacles—as a
beast obeys a blind will or instinct to migrate "Where the sun wants
brute-presence to fulfil/Life's purpose in a new far zone" upon the
approach of an ice age? In short, is René now a man or a mere beast,
obeying blindly an instinct, without will or purpose? The next two
stanzas, among the difficult ones in Browning, make clear his belief
that man must be spared such "direct plain truth," for such truth
is inconsonant with man's limited state. The game of life to man is
real; life's walls are solid; its evil and its love are no illusion. But
exposure to absolute truth, again in the manner of Lazarus, destroys
the worth of life and man's values. What hitherto seemed of value
has no worth to eyes that have seen God's truth:

> I think no such direct plain truth consists
>     With actual sense and thought and what they take
> To be the solid walls of life: mere mists—
>     How such would, at that truth's first piercing, break
> Into the nullity they are!—slight lists
>     Wherein the puppet-champions wage, for sake
> Of some mock-mistress, mimic war: laid low
> At trumpet-blast, there's shown the world,
>     one foe![56]

The game of life is not a mimic war; we are not puppet champions;
we do not throw down the gage in defense of a mock-mistress, for
life is real, not sham. Absolute truth on earth, once seen steadily,
would destroy the test of life, remove entirely the purpose of life,
and reduce men to puppets, fighting a purposeless tourney. If any

55.  Ll. 466-472.        56.  Ll. 489-496.

doubt of Browning's intent remains—and this stanza is obscure—the following stanza removes all doubt:

> No, we must play the pageant out, observe
>     The tourney-regulations, and regard
> Success—to meet the blunted spear nor swerve,
>     Failure—to break no bones yet fall on sward;
> Must prove we have—not courage? well then,—nerve!
>     And, at the day's end, boast the crown's award—
> *Be warranted as promising to wield*
> *Weapons, no sham, in a true battle-field.*[57]

Life must be regarded as a true battle, fought on a real battlefield with weapons that draw blood, if man is to be tested. The only sense in which life's struggle may seem unreal is in the light of God's truth, which makes the lists of life seem, from the perspective of heaven, like a child's game far below. In the meanwhile success on earth is to take the spear into the bosom rather than swerve, and failure is to fly the field uninjured. No injury is a sham, and suffering is real.

Pigou finds Pompilia's dying speech rich with the rejection of the reality of evil. Throughout, she makes much of the evil dream that has been her life:

> All since is one blank,
> Over and ended; a terrific dream.
> It is the good of dreams—so soon they go![58]

That Pompilia is not denying the reality of life or the evil in it is seen in her despairing cry that "All human plans and projects come to naught:/My life and what I know of other lives,/Prove that: no plan nor project! God shall care!" Surely this seems like a denial of life as full as could be uttered, but the context makes clear that she is speaking of the terrible disillusionment she experienced at the hands of the cynical Archbishop. If he could prove himself evil, where on earth can there be virtue? She renounces the world in despair:

57.  Ll. 497-504. The italics are mine.      58.  VII, 579-581.

> . . . henceforth I looked to God
> Only, nor cared my desecrated soul
> Should have fair walls, gay windows for the world.
> God's glimmer, that came through the ruin-top,
> Was witness why all lights were quenched inside:
> Henceforth I asked God counsel, not mankind.[59]

Far from proving that she denies evil, it proves that evil is so total on earth that henceforth she will look only to God. The nothingness of this world is an echo of Ecclesiastes on the subject of vanity, which refers to the emptiness of worldly values, not to their non-being. Upon awakening from her fever dream of evil, Pompilia speaks in the certainty of a passage to the world beyond and with the perspective on life that such a passage confers. When Don Celestine counsels her to "remember what is past,/The better to forgive it," she pronounces the advice "vain," for her life has been so filled with grief that "What was fast getting indistinct before,/Vanished outright." In short, her frequent references to her past as an evil dream in no sense mean that it was not real; rather they mean that it was so real that she cannot bear to recall it. If her life with Guido were an illusion, a wild phantasmagoria without substance, wherein would be the point of remembering the dream "The better to forgive it"—since it was unreal, being a dream merely? In Don Celestine's advice, however, she discovers wisdom, for she finds grounds for forgiveness at last. In this way the evil she suffered brought forth good—but the evil remained unchanged for all that and was never "stuff for transmuting," nor was it an illusion. She likens her suffering to an echo, reverberating off the eternal cliffs:

> Echoes die off, scarcely reverberate
> For ever,—why should ill keep echoing ill,
> And never let our ears have done with noise?[60]

Pigou and Jones and some later critics forget that Browning was a Christian—the most Christian poet of his age, in spite of, or because of, his striking individuality. Pompilia, an illiterate child, not in-

59. VII, 848-853.      60. VII, 645-647.

clined to abstruse ratiocination or subtle philosophy, speaks as a primitive Christian might. Evil is transitory (though real) because it partakes of the nature of this life; and it is to be forgiven and forgotten, for man progresses through its offices to good, which is permanent, because it is of heaven, which is eternal. How many casuistical errors in interpretation would be eliminated if it could be kept in mind that Browning spoke of eternal matters in traditional Christian terms! Pompilia knows that in life evil echoes until death intervenes, but in heaven "our ears have done with noise." In this sense only is good more "real" than evil. It is eternal. G. K. Chesterton wisely notes that "Browning's optimism is of that ultimate and unshakeable order that is founded on the absolute sight, and sound, and smell, and handling of things."[61]

Shortly before her death, Pompilia carefully enunciates the value of evil, which vindicates God's plan:

> Therefore, because this man restored my soul,
> All has been right; I have gained my gain, enjoyed
> As well as suffered,—nay, got foretaste too
> Of better life beginning where this ends. . . .[62]

Evil supplied the necessary test; it brought joy out of suffering; and it furnished a foretaste of the delights of heaven. Her forgiveness of Guido is evidence that she is aware of the fourth fruit of evil: the strengthening of bonds of human sympathy, forgiveness, and love. Her extended Christian speech of forgiveness is almost as sublime as that in "Mihrab Shah," in which the outraged citizen finds pity in his heart for the despicable tyrant, who is suffering from stomach ulcers.

Pigou believes that in Browning's philosophy man will embrace God's "point of view" once "the spell of illusion is broken by bodily death." He finds in the "Parleying with Bernard Mandeville" a passage which he believes supports his theory:

61.  P. 182.      62.  VII, 1651-1654.

"Man's fancy makes the fault!
Man, with the narrow mind, must cram inside
His finite God's infinitude. . . ."[63]

This quotation comes near the end of an extended discussion of the rationale which Browning mistakenly ascribes to Mandeville in defense of evil. Mandeville's *Fable of the Bees* is a defense of the thesis that private vices are public benefits and that society flourishes only by reason of flourishing sin and iniquity at all levels. Browning thinks that Mandeville intended to say that evil is a test of man's fortitude in combating it, not adding to it as a stimulus to the economy. In defense of what he in error supposes Mandeville to mean, Browning says:

Sage, once more repeat
Instruction! 'T is a sore to soothe not chafe.
Ah, Fabulist, what luck, could I contrive
To coax from thee another "Grumbling Hive"!
My friend himself wrote fables short and sweet:
Ask him—"Suppose the Gardener of Man's ground
Plants for a purpose, side by side with good,
Evil—(and that he does so—look around!
What does the field show?)—were it understood
That purposely the noxious plant was found
Vexing the virtuous, poison close to food,
If, at first stealing-forth of life in stalk
And leaflet-promise, quick his spud should balk
Evil from budding foliage, bearing fruit?
Such timely treatment of the offending root
Might strike the simple as wise husbandry,
But swift sure extirpation scarce would suit
Shrewder observers. Seed once sown thrives: why
Frustrate its product, miss the quality
Which sower binds himself to count upon?
Had seed fulfilled the destined purpose, gone

63. Ll. 150-152.

> Unhindered up to harvest—what know I
> But proof were gained that every growth of good
> Sprang consequent on evil's neighborhood?"[64]

Browning's recognition of the grim reality of evil is seen ("look around/ What does the field show?"), although Pigou finds an entirely contrary conclusion. It might be recalled that this passage is the one which prompts Joseph E. Baker to conclude that Browning meant to say that in the garden of life the wise man sees not only the futility but the iniquity of trying to pull the weeds of evil which a bountiful Providence put there.[65] If they were unreal evils, as Pigou, Jones, and Raymond suppose, Baker would be right in his assumption, since there would be only a mock battle to fight; but the evils are real. What Browning means is that man should not lament the presence of planned evil or wish its "swift sure extripation"—*i.e.*, its absolute elimination, which, if it were possible, would frustrate God's purpose. There is no danger. Man has no need to moderate his strife with evil lest he win too complete a victory:

> Let the sage
> Concede a use to evil, though there starts
> Full many a burgeon thence, *to disengage*
> *With thumb and finger lest it spoil the yield*
> *Too much of good's main tribute!* But our main
> Tough-tendoned mandrake-monster—purge the field
> Of him for once and all? It follows plain
> Who set him there to grow beholds repealed
> His primal law: his ordinance proves vain:
> And what beseems a king who cannot reign,
> But to drop sceptre valid arm should wield?[66]

If man is counseled to pinch off the buds of evil, the buds are as real as the grain they menace, and at harvest the grain is garnered

64. Ll. 90-113.
65. "Religious Implications in Browning's Poetry," *Philological Quarterly*, *op. cit.*, 446-448.
66. Ll. 121-131. The italics are mine.

safely and "good's foe/ Bundled for burning." But, Browning says, man has great difficulty in fathoming the purpose of the Infinite, and repeatedly asks why God would permit evil to "triumph one sunny minute." At this point appears the quotation Pigou cites to prove that evil is illusion. When Browning says that man "must cram inside/ His finite God's infinitude," he does not mean that the finite is unreal in contrast to the reality of the eternal; what he means is that man cannot comprehend with his finite mind the infinite will. The word "must" does not mean he ought to, but rather that, being man, he falsely thinks he must try to fathom God's purpose. Especially important is his statement that "the divine lies linked/ Fast to the human. . . ." There is no gulf separating the essence of one from the other. The things of this world evolve into the things of the next, with no other hiatus than what man calls death. Man

> . . . discovers—wings in rudiment,
> Such as he boasts, which full-grown, free-distent
> Would lift him skyward, fail of flight while pent
> Within humanity's restricted space.[67]

Only the restrictions of life prevent man's wings in rudiment from carrying him to God. Death is the passport for the flight.

In the poem "Reverie," appearing in the *Asolando* volume, Pigou finds additional evidence of Browning's rejection of the reality of evil:

> I understood
> How evil—did mind descry
> Power's object to end pursued—
>
> Were haply as cloud across
> Good's orb, no orb itself. . . .

This is the same basic image that Browning uses scores of times: that evil is the opposite of good, instead of being a primary quality, as cold is merely the opposite of heat, and shadow the reverse of shine. This is the way Browning, the optimist, likes to look at things,

67. Ll. 163-166.

just as he prefers to consider the chessboard predominantly white, not black, although he grants an equal validity to the contrary view. Bishop Blougram uses a variation of the argument when he says that each man may look upon life as made up of faith darkened by moments of doubt, or of doubt, lightened by moments of faith. One cannot deny the existence of something by the simple tactic of regarding it as the opposite of something else. In "Reverie" Browning clearly regards evil as very real indeed: "Earth's good is with evil blent:/ Good struggles but evil reigns."

Of all the poems in the Browning canon, the one most often cited as supplying proof of the poet's denial of the existence of evil is *La Saisiaz*. This is a poem to be taken seriously, for it is Browning speaking, without a dramatic cover. Furthermore he wrote it in soul-searching and grief over the death of his friend Anne Egerton Smith, with whom he had planned to climb Mount Salève, near Geneva. Her death on the morning of the proposed climb became symbolic of life's mystery and its doubtful purpose and its evil. He was fully aware that the problem of evil in a morally conceived and planned universe admits of no perfect solution, and he was a profound student of the problem, and of the proposed solutions. The many explanations may be, for simplicity's sake, reduced to five:

1. Man may simply refuse to view the problem of evil in teleological terms, substituting necessity in its place. Death, disease, disaster, frustration, and failure may simply be looked upon as natural concomitants, incidental by necessity to life, but not planned by God. They merely happen, without a creator.

2. A compromise between a teleological order and an unplanned necessity may be adopted, in which evil has a necessary function: pain to warn us of disease or impending injury, and adversity to serve as a discipline. Pain, we are told, also is something inescapable in the scheme of things, as an attendant of growth. The problem with this explanation is twofold: there is no assignable reason to suppose that growth must be attended by pain, and if pain is a warning, then it must be a warning of something worse than the pain itself,

which, in turn, must warn of a still greater hazard, and so on. Thus there is no real explanation of evil at all.

3. An exculpation of God may be found in the belief that he himself was in a dilemma: to make life free from evil and thus rob it of any discernible function, since it would by definition overlap with heaven, and to grant man freedom of the will and the right to do evil or good, as a means of conferring on life some means of testing man. According to this view, God has no control over the amount of evil his subjects elect to visit upon the earth, although he wills to have only good, and judges man by his acts. The objection to this theory is that it totally neglects natural evils of which man is innocent, such as earthquakes, hurricanes, and the Black Death. God, by allowing such natural disasters, is tarred by the same brush that blackens his worst villains.

4. A further explanation lies in pantheism or a form of philosophical idealism which identifies all creation with God. According to this theory, there is no satisfactory explanation to the problem of evil as long as God is viewed as something outside the world, a discrete and separate ruler, looking on the world swarming with misery. It will not serve to say that he had to have a reason for his creation of man and his world. He could have declined to create at all and so have obviated the problem. If he were constrained to create in spite of the eons of horror that he must have foreseen, he stands blood-drenched and guilty for permitting unlimited evil, cosmic and human. The test of man would have been equally valid if only much moderated and tempered evil had been made possible. This explanation solves the problem by affirming that God is all creation and all creation is God and the misery I suffer is in reality God's misery since I have no separate existence apart from the Absolute Being. Thus, in extremity, I may be confronted by the assurance that God did not create a sadistic horror of a world, since he *is* creation and suffers every evil in the world; that the groaning of the world is not the fruit of his wrath, neglect, or indifference, since my woe is his. A frequent corollary to this theory, in answer to the question why he elects to suffer, is that, like man, he needs ill, suffering, and woe

as a means of attaining perfect selfhood, an explanation which confers upon him unbounded vanity, or imperception, since by definition he was perfect to start with. Furthermore, if to achieve a state of flawless selfhood more perfect than the absolute perfection with which he began, God discovers the only means to be the endless misery of his helpless creation man, then Caliban's view of God is vindicated. That he shares in the pain of man is irrelevant, since it is well established that masochism almost always accompanies sadism.

5. A final explanation may be found in the simple denial of evil as a fact. This is the explanation that Browning is supposed to have adopted. The great objections to this theory are two: one, life itself becomes unreal, a child's game without substance, and two, it is self-contradictory. To say that the pullulating evils of earth are a figment of the imagination, a mere distortion of a sick mind, a product of imbalance or imperfect perception, does nothing whatever to explain away evil, for evil is an abstraction, a state of mind. Fear of cancer is as great an evil as cancer itself. No greater suffering (evil) can exist than anxiety and fear, which may have no ground whatever in fact. But the anxiety is as much a fact as the thing feared.

*La Saisiaz*, Browning's most direct discussion of evil, contains not one line that supports the idea that evil is illusory. Indeed, the remarkable characteristic of this work is the terrifying sense of the dominant reality of evil in life. The theme of human isolation and desolating loneliness, which is at its strongest in this poem, is reminiscent of Arnold's "The Buried Life" and "To Marguerite—Continued," neither of which suggests that evil is anything other than the reality it is. As he picks up the silent figure of Anne Egerton Smith, he feels the chill of loneliness and terror:

> Did the face, the form I lifted as it lay, reveal the loss
> Not alone of life but soul?[68]

All that remains of her, he is sure, is the memory he has of her, which is, of necessity, a unique memory, differing from all others.

68.  Ll. 173-174.

An atmosphere of desolating loneliness hangs over the poem. Man, he says, forever proposes problems to be solved "By ourselves alone," even though he will never live to see the fruits of his labors, or to discover whether there are fruits at all. He asks whether life be not really "a curse and not a blessing," man's hopes for redress in the next life in reality being an amiable illusion of the coward who cannot face the nothingness of death:

> Why should I want courage here?
> I will ask and have an answer,—with no favor, with no fear,—
> From myself. How much, how little, do I inwardly believe
> True that controverted doctrine?[69]

Perhaps the basis for his belief is nothing more than his love for his wife and his unwillingness to face oblivion without once again seeing her, a reluctance that makes him affirm, with Dante, that he will pass into a better life "Where that lady lives of whom enamored was my soul." He knows that to man there are only two points that are indisputable:

> Question, answer presuppose
> Two points: that the thing itself which questions,
>     answers,—is, it knows;
> As it also knows the thing perceived outside
>     itself,—a force
> Actual ere its own beginning, operative through
>     its course,
> Unaffected by its end,—that this thing likewise
>     needs must be;
> Call this—God, then, call that—soul, and both—
>     the only facts for me.[70]

Man is doomed to know nothing of the cause and the effect behind him or, of course, of the future. Only his experience in the passing moment has a validity which partially warrants the title of reality. But although the fact that "I am" is the starting point of all knowledge to man, "I myself am what I know not." The second of

69. Ll. 207-210.    70. Ll. 217-221.

man's foundations of knowledge is his knowledge of what to him is pain and pleasure: "this is sure, the rest surmise." No man knows for sure whether "my fellows are or are not," nor does he know what to them is pain and pleasure. For each man, then, knowledge stands on the fact of his existence and on his own experience. The rest is conjecture. It must not be forgotten that he specifically says "were earth and all it holds illusion," his life must be considered a dark disappointment of sorrow and pain, in contrast to the joy and purpose he discovers everywhere, since life and all it contains is not illusion.

In the twentieth century the fullest and most critically influential exposition of Browning's supposed belief in the illusory character of evil appears in William Clyde DeVane's *Browning's Parleyings: The Autobiography of a Mind* (1927). His indebtedness to both Henry Jones and to A. C. Pigou is striking. In his chapter on the "Parleying with Bernard Mandeville," DeVane accurately writes upon Browning's purpose in using Mandeville (whom Browning totally misinterprets) as a means of refuting Carlyle and his gloomy pessimism, which he contrasts with what he takes to be the cornerstone of Browning's whole philosophy:

> *God's in his heaven—*
> *All's right with the world!*

DeVane, like most critics, takes this statement literally as a denial of the existence of evil in a world created by absolute love and goodness. I should like to examine the next two or three paragraphs with care, for they contain the critical fallacies which have made Browning appear both intellectually dishonest and philosophically shallow. It is fascinating to see how DeVane becomes enmeshed in the toils of his reasoning. The *fons et origo* of his conclusions are his major premise that Browning rested his whole philosophy on the absurd and untenable belief that there is nothing amiss in the world:

> In his philosophy of optimism, Browning not only asserts that all is right with the world, but insists that things are getting better.[71]

71. Pp. 31-32.

On the face of it, this statement is an amusing contradiction—and no irony is detectable in its context, although one hunts confidently for it under the impetus of a statement that Browning held things to be perfect, but improving rapidly. If one's major premise is wrong, it is certain that grave critical reefs lie ahead.

DeVane discovers that since Browning denied the existence of evil, he straightway set about explaining away the apparent evil which lay everywhere about him, visible to all and crying for redress. There is only one way to deny the clear presence of what one has just denied the existence of: to insist that it is a product of a disordered fancy—an illusion. And this is what DeVane says Browning spent a substantial part of his life doing. It is significant that Browning never actually *says* that evil is illusion, but, according to DeVane, he must have thought so, since there is no alternative way to deny evil. The following statement, which is a close paraphrase of Henry Jones, is so important that it must be quoted at length:

> Whereas Carlyle started with the axiom that evil was essentially real, Browning started with the axiom that God was all-loving and all-powerful. But with the hypothesis that
>
> > God's in his heaven—
> > All's right with the world!
>
> Browning had to meet the problem of evil and its reality. This brought him at once to a philosophical difficulty. For with his optimistic attitude, Browning refused to give up the belief that man, the creation of God, was really great too. Man had a dignity of his own, arising from the power of free will which he exerted in the moral struggle. Browning held with great tenacity to the idea of a universal benevolent order, and at the same time to the idea of man as a morally free person within that order. Yet—and this is the flaw in his argument—If God were all-loving He would wish to destroy evil, and if He were all-powerful He could do so. The idea of such a God is inconsistent with the existence of evil. Yet if man is to have free will, there must be evil for him to discriminate against and to fight against. Browning refused

to degrade either God or man. God was power, wisdom, and love without limit. Man was king in the moral world, and that world in which he was placed to strive was not perfect.

Browning solves the problem of reconciling an all-loving God and the presence of evil in the world by casting doubt upon facts that threaten his hypothesis of universal love. Evil is not really evil; it is only apparent. God has placed it in the world so that man may develop his moral nature. God is thus like a father who while building a house has given his son a few worthless boards to saw in order to make the boy think he is helping. Or, as Jones put it, the world becomes only "a kind of moral gymnasium, crowded with phantoms wherein by exercise man makes moral muscle." It is perilously like playing a trick upon humanity in order to make it progress, for the evil that spurs man on is nothing but illusion.

Browning escapes from *this* difficulty by saying that man ultimately cannot know that the evil is illusory. A certainty of knowledge concerning the existence or non-existence of evil is incompatible with moral life:

A full disclosure? Such would outrage law.[72]

In sum, Browning was dishonest, cynically suppressing any evidence that failed to square with his beliefs. To say that Browning, because he refused to degrade man, degraded his intellect and made him incapable of attaining any knowledge is a contradiction. The final quotation which DeVane supplies is not used by Browning to defend either the illusory character of knowledge or man's supposed doubt of its reality. It is one of many scores of statements in Browning that man must be denied absolute or total knowledge. It says nothing whatever about the reality of evil. Immediately above the words quoted, Browning says:

> Here we alive must needs deal fairly, turn
> To what account Man may Man's portion, learn

72. Pp. 30-31.

Man's proper play with truth in part, before
Entrusted with the whole. I ask no more
Than smiling witness that I do my best
With doubtful doctrine: afterward the rest![73]

DeVane's argument might be summed up as follows:

1. Browning believed that all's right with the world, and, therefore, of necessity, there is nothing wrong that needs righting, but, for all that, things are somehow getting better.

2. Unluckily, to the least vigilant observer, the world is teeming with evils of every description.

3. Man achieves greatness and dignity only through the moral struggle, but he seems doomed to littleness and stagnation of spirit, since there is nothing wrong in a perfect world to struggle against.

4. God is all-loving, all-wise, and all-powerful.

5. But—and this DeVane insists is the flaw in Browning's argument—God, if all-loving, could not permit evil to plague man, and if all-powerful, he would surely have carried out his benevolent resolution. (In point of fact, this seems to be the least flawed idea he ascribes to the poet.)

6. Man must have free will or be degraded, but free will necessarily implies the freedom to make choices between good and evil, a conclusion that plainly puts God in a quandary, since he is wicked if he permits evil and wicked if he does not.

7. It follows that evil is not really evil. It just seems so, since even God cannot make evil and at the same time not make it. (The fact that the illusion of evil, or the imaginary terrors that a fancied evil engenders, is a valid form of evil is here forgotten, a simple reflection that reveals a grave contradiction.)

8. The illusion of evil is essential to man so that his moral nature (which is perfect to begin with, since nothing in the world needs righting) may be improved by the illusion of a struggle (which cannot exist in a world free from stress and strain and onslaught) with the illusion of evil (which in a perfect world would be impossible for

73. "Parleying with Bernard Mandeville," 11. 13-17.

the flawless mind to conceive of, the very conception of evil being an evil).

9. Man is shrewdly kept in ignorance that the evil he fears and fights against (again a three-fold contradiction, for the evil he could not conjure up in a perfect world he would not fear or fight against, both these activities being evils of which he would perforce be ignorant anyway) is an unreal phantom. If he ever saw through the deception, he would catch on to the emptiness of the whole game.

10. Thus man, through therapeutic ignorance and an illimitable capacity for being deceived (a form of evil which cannot be in a world free of evil) is eternally tricked into a useless tilting against illusory windmills, which he must not be permitted to recognize as illusions, as means to improvement of his unimprovable moral nature.

11. Thus it follows that in a world as skillfully disguised as this, things are perfect but improving. Certainly, it seems apparent that there is much room for improvement.

To argue in this fashion is to invite the conclusion that Browning was a credulous fool, incapable of logic, readily imposed upon by the most outrageously contrived syllogism. It is to reduce his philosophy to absurdity and to hold him up to ridicule. And this is exactly what has happened, and it largely explains why Joseph E. Baker can state that the only way to read Browning with enjoyment is to resolutely pay no attention to what the poet is saying—and if this is the measure of Browning's mind, Baker is right. Following Jones and Pigou closely, DeVane portrays one of the nineteenth century's most alert and creative minds as undeveloped and dishonest. With Jones and Pigou, DeVane says that Browning "saw evil as mere stuff for transmuting," like them forgetting that the speaker of these words is Don Juan, whom Browning is in the process of discrediting. Next to Guido—and perhaps Sludge—Don Juan is the least trustworthy and creditable character Browning created. DeVane's statement, again closely paralleling Jones and Pigou, that within the evils of earth "lies the germ of good" is wonderfully wrongheaded. Good does not grow *out of* evil, nor does evil contain the seed of its opposite, as the worm becomes the butterfly. In every instance in Browning, as I have emphasized before, good results—or may result—from the collision of a resolute personality with evil, his struggle against it, and his increased spiritual strength resulting from the encounter. The evil remains evil, whatever good resulted from the collision. And the evil is real. Bernard Mandeville says that "every growth of good" springs "consequent on evil's neighborhood." He does not say that evil is either good or illusory.

DeVane's central belief that Browning denied to man the validity of knowledge and degraded the mind wholly and insisted that a state of ignorance is man's proper state—for he must be kept like a child the better to be imposed upon—is, as I have shown, absolutely false and destructive of Browning as a thinker. Out of this belief grow all the other fallacies which have imperiled the stature of the greatest poet of the Victorian Age. Nowhere does DeVane express this mistaken belief more emphatically than in the *Browning's Parleyings*:

His optimistic philosophy, as we have seen, included an all-loving and all-powerful God, and likewise free will and moral progress for mankind. Under the consequent necessity of admitting or disclaiming the reality of evil, Browning made evil illusion, but insisted that man must not *know* whether it was illusion or not. That is, ignorance became a necessary part of his theory of an all-loving God. Then, too, as he went on showing how good evolves from all things, and how "the last is ever better than the first," he had more and more to deny the evidence which his intellect brought him. Thus Browning preserved his optimism by casting aspersions on the validity of man's knowing faculty; and as he proclaimed with increasing vehemence his faith that God was love,—the faith he had learned as a child from his mother, and had temporarily rejected in his youth—he insisted on the necessity of man's ignorance. His faith is thus ultimately blind, and he is an intellectual agnostic:

> . . . knowledge means
> Ever-renewed assurance by defeat
> That victory is somehow still to reach. . . .[74]

74.  P. 34.

It is instructive to examine this quotation from "A Pillar at Sebzevar." Does it really mean that Browning was an "intellectual agnostic," believing that man must guard his ignorance as a treasure essential to his spiritual health? Ferishtah, the wise dervish, who is Browning in flowing robes, is busily instructing his small band of admiring students in the arcana of learning. DeVane fails to see that Ferishtah's constant warnings that one must doubt knowledge "Even wherein it seems demonstrable" and that knowledge must be regarded as "lacquered ignorance" ("As gain—mistrust it!") means only that one must never regard knowledge as final and complete. The lines which DeVane quotes do not support his contention; they destroy it. To the wise man, newly acquired knowledge is merely a step upward on the endless road leading to full knowledge, which is unattainable on earth, but no "knowledge" must be "trusted" as true. A healthy skepticism of all knowledge is the surest way of preventing error from blocking the road to truth. Today's knowledge will give way to a better knowledge tomorrow; but, far from convincing man that knowledge is nescience, it should vastly encourage him to greater effort. For those who persist in reading "A Pillar at Sebzevar" as a condemnation either of the mind or of man's attempt to attain knowledge, the opening lines should be consulted. It is not Browning and not Ferishtah, but "the foolishest of all the company" who launches the discussion by groaning that knowledge turns nescience because what one learns today yields to a better knowledge tomorrow. "The prize is in the process," Ferishtah says, and this means, not as Raymond assumes that "Browning is denying the efficacy of knowledge," but that man is tested by his tireless pursuit of knowledge in the face of errors that masquerade as knowledge and half-truths that seem whole-truths, a view held by the relentlessly intellectual and scientific Goethe. DeVane forgets that in the "Parleying with Charles Avison" Browning says:

> So works Mind—by stress
> Of faculty, with loose facts, more or less,
> *Builds up our solid knowledge:* all the same,
> Underneath rolls what Mind may hide not tame,
> An element which works beyond our guess,

Soul, the unsounded sea—whose lift of surge,
Spite of all superstructure, lets emerge,
In flower and foam, Feeling from out the deeps
Mind arrogates no mastery upon—
Distinct indisputably.

.   .   .   .   .   .   .   .   .   .   .   .

"So worked Mind: its tribe
Of senses ministrant above, below,
Far, near, or now or haply long ago
Brought to pass knowledge."[75]

The "element which works beyond our guess" is merely the matters
of the Infinite, which Browning warns us against trying to attain in
this world. Providentially the pursuit is futile—but, if man could
attain such forbidden knowledge, the result would be pernicious.
This is the argument of "An Epistle of Karshish," in which Lazarus,
after seeing the white radiance of eternity and attaining absolute
knowledge, is forced to take up again his station in life and wearily
wait in patient boredom until death a second time releases him from
an existence which now is without function or interest.[76]

75. Ll. 156-178. The italics are mine.
76. A. W. Crawford ("Browning's Ideal of Life, an Interpretation of 'An
Epistle of Karshish,'" *Methodist Review*, XCI, No. 2 [March, 1909], 264-269)
misses the point of the poem, not seeing that Lazarus is miserable upon return to earth, not in an "excellent condition," and failing to see that the poem
is not a condemnation of knowledge or science but a warning against the
dangers of seeing into the Absolute while yet on earth: "The poem is an
arraignment of the mere scientific view, that disdains spiritual conditions and
causes, and ignores spiritual phenomena, and by implication is a tremendous
plea for the reality of the spiritual. This is the keynote of Browning's life.
Any interpretation of Browning would seem questionable that involved the
suggestion that one of Christ's miracles was injurious to man's spiritual condition or detracted from his fullness of life. Browning so completely believed
in Christ as the perfect and Divine One that he would not so present any of
his miracles. Moreover, a plain interpretation of the poem seems, rather, to be
that Karshish is incapable of understanding the high spiritual and altogether
excellent condition of Lazarus that resulted from the wonderful miracle
wrought upon him. . . . Lazarus, because of his experience of the eternal,
through the miracle of Christ, is enabled to live the ideal life."

In his discussion of "Francis Furini," DeVane adds one final and devastating blow against the quality of Browning's mind and its fruits. After finding in the poem clear evidence that the poet espouses his "theory of the worthlessness of human intelligence," he cites Jones's often-quoted statement that the heart of Browning's message may be found in his description of the world as "a kind of moral gymnasium, crowded with phantoms, wherein by exercise man makes moral muscle," and adds: "And all this is in preparation for a contest which never happens. This building of moral muscle for no particular end, as I have said, is a characteristic conception of Browning's. . . ."[77] I confess that I do not know whether DeVane means that the contest never happens at all or never happens on this earth alone. I presume he means the former, but whatever the sense, it is a misreading of Browning. Browning so strongly believed in growth through the test of struggles that he could not imagine an after-world in which man did not similarly progress through combat:

> How helpful could we quote
> But one poor instance when he interposed
> Promptly and surely and beyond mistake
> Between oppression and its victim, closed accounts
> With sin for once, and bade us wake
> From our long dream that justice bears no sword,
> Or else forgets whereto its sharpness serves!
> So might we safely mock at what unnerves
> Faith now, be spared the sapping fear's increase
> That haply evil's strife with good shall cease
> Never on earth. Nay, after earth, comes peace
> Born out of life-long battle? Man's lip curves
> With scorn: there, also, what if justice swerves
> From dealing doom, sets free by no swift stroke
> Right fettered here by wrong, but leaves life's yoke—
> Death should loose man from—fresh laid, past
>        release?"[78]

77. *Browning's Parleyings, the Autobiography of a Mind,* p. 189.
78. "Parleying with Bernard Mandeville," 11. 46-61.

"The prize is in the process" of trial and growth. To say that man works out in the gymnasium of life for an athletic event that is not even scheduled fails to see that the working out in the gymnasium *is* the great athletic event, for life from beginning to end—and beyond —is one endless competition. Andrea del Sarto, in a moment of vision, sees the next world as given to competition and growth as much as this world is:

> What would one have?
> In Heaven, perhaps, new chances, one more chance—
> Four great walls in the New Jerusalem
> Meted on each side by the angel's reed,
> For Leonard, Rafael, Agnolo and me
> To cover—the first three without a wife,
> While I have mine! So—still they overcome
> Because there's still Lucrezia,—as I choose.

Andrea, a failure because he aimed for an easily attainable perfection in technique in painting, knows that even in heaven he will fall behind in the competition with his peers. In Browning's heaven one attains through struggle heights only dreamed of in this life.

In his criticism of "Francis Furini" DeVane pursues his theme that Browning denounced the intellect and soberly affirmed that evil is illusion. "Such was his position as he defines it in *Furini*. It is the position of Andromeda on her rock as she awaits the sea beast. A prince charming, Perseus, or God will appear in the nick of time. The outcome of the whole is the same as it was for Browning. God is in his heaven, all-good, all-wise, all-powerful; and evil is only illusion."[79] By way of support for this conclusion, he quotes the lines:

> . . . still wrong must needs seem wrong
> To do right's service, prove men weak or strong,
> Choosers of evil or good.

Let us examine the context of these lines. Furini (or Browning) is discussing the problem of evil and its justification in a morally created and guided world. Browning concludes, predictably, that to

79. P. 192.

achieve his grand design in which "Good strives with evil," God created an earth

> . . . where wage
> War, just for soul's instruction, pain with joy,
> Folly with wisdom, all that works annoy
> With all that quiets and contents. . . .[80]

There is no hint here that the evil is a figment of the mind, a phantasm. It is as real as life and the world, of which it is a prime ingredient:

> Think!
> Could I see plain, be somehow certified
> All was illusion,—evil far and wide
> Was good disguised,—why, out with one huge wipe
> Goes knowledge from me. Type needs antitype:
> As night needs day, as shine needs shade, so good
> Needs evil: how were pity understood
> Unless by pain?[81]

The lines immediately before and after the quotation DeVane chooses to support his belief afford some illumination on Browning's purpose:

> Though wrong were right,
> Could we but know—still wrong must needs seem wrong
> To do right's service, prove men weak or strong,
> Choosers of evil or of good. 'No such
> Illusion possible!'[82]

The verb *were* in the first line is subjunctive, indicating a condition contrary to fact—that wrong is surely not right. He means that even if wrong *were* right (or an illusion, which is much the same thing), man would have to be ignorant of this fact to make the test work. Life is not playacting, and evil is as real as all else in life.

DeVane's corollary to his thesis abundantly reveals the effect it has had on Browning's reputation in our century: ". . . what Browning had to say no longer met the issue. He who had once been a

80. Ll. 463-466.     81. Ll. 479-486.     82. Ll. 504-508.

prophetic voice was now but the voice of a bygone generation."[83] It is not at all surprising to find DeVane pronouncing Browning obsolete. If the charges made against him are correct, he is obsolete, and he cannot speak to the condition of man in our age—or in any other, for that matter. In our century Browning is as pertinent to our lives as Pollyanna—if DeVane, Raymond, Pigou, Jones, and others are right. While denying the reality of the evils that every child can see in battalions and hosts on the plains of life, he denied "any efficacy whatever, or any value, to man's mind and its products," DeVane insists. This is a bleak picture, indeed.

Pigou adds an ingenious and fascinating dimension (much copied and stressed by later critics) to Browning's alleged denial of evil. Since evil is "mere illusion," he says, "and nothing but good is real, there can be no reason why man should follow any one course of conduct rather than another."[84] Why indeed? Man, he adds, might just as well do as he pleases since God's purpose will be achieved anyhow, and try as he may, since there can be no evil, he cannot do evil. The fact that every line Browning wrote gives this the lie direct and is in some way connected with his lifelong belief that man is judged by whether he elects good rather than evil—or strives to follow good—the fact that three-fourths of all Browning wrote concerns towering evil and man's varying degrees of success and failure in facing it—these things in no measure gave Pigou pause in his ruinous conclusion, a conclusion completely at variance with Browning's whole life purpose.

Pigou paraphrases Sordello's argument, which he imperfectly understands, that since "the pain of others serves a divine end, it cannot . . . be our duty to try to relieve it." Sordello means that the *absolute elimination* of evil would rob man of the test of life, of course, and the test *is* to see whether we will try to relieve our brothers of pain and evil. Pigou's belief robs Browning of morality and sense. He finds it impossible "to reason out any clear rule of right" in Browning (which might suggest that Judas and John are of identical worth in God's sight), for Browning's faith "serves to indicate that

83. P. 193.    84. P. 105

the moral law is not only indiscoverable but nonexistent." Under this system, Pigou argues, to attempt to change God's purpose by philanthropic schemes "is at once impious and futile. It is a matter of complete indifference whether we be selfish or self-sacrificing."[85]

If Pigou is right, it might reasonably be expected that Browning would never pass judgment on his villains, and it is true that he rarely does so overtly; but no one can escape the moral direction everywhere visible in Browning. In a letter to Julia Wedgwood, February 22, 1869, in answer to her animadversions against the brutality in *The Ring and the Book*, Browning writes:

> Why, I almost have you at an unfair advantage, in the fact that the whole story is *true*. How do *you* account for the "mere brutal hacking Pompilia to pieces" [Julia Wedgwood's words in the letter of February 21] in a nobleman thirty years long the intimate of Cardinals: is this the case of a drunken operative that kicks his wife to death because she has no money for more gin? But I won't begin and tell my own story over yet another time—I am too glad to get done with it. We differ apparently in our conception of what gross wickedness can be effected by cultivated minds—I belive the *grossest*—all the more, by way of reaction from the enforced habit of self denial which is the condition of men's receiving culture.[86]

It is clear that Pigou dimly discerns the impossibility of his own conclusions, which everywhere in Browning's verse and letters as well is given the lie in the clearest terms. Faced with a dilemma, Pigou discovers a way out. His ingenuity at this point is admirable. Since God created a world to test man's adherence to the good, but falsified the test by neglecting to put anything else but good for him to adhere to, on what basis is man to be judged and rewarded? Man fancies that certain things are evil, whereas in fact they are perfectly good. Man

85. P. 106. Pigou adds: ". . . a Marcus Aurelius or Francis of Assisi is no more acceptable to God than a Borgia or a Catiline"—according to Browning.

86. *Robert Browning and Julia Wedgwood, A Broken Friendship as Revealed in Their Letters*, ed. Richard Curle (London, 1937), p. 177.

is viewed as a child resolutely refusing to step on the cracks in a sidewalk; but God gratefully accepts this childish fancy as a means of creating the illusion of a test, so that men may be judged and given their several rewards, all of which, Pigou neglects to note, supply no means of getting God off the horns of the dilemma, since the rewards must all be perfectly good, that being the only condition to be found in the creation. How then are the illusory rewards and distinctions made? Through the view that Browning allegedly took of time:

> God's "purpose of love" is finally fulfilled in all men, even in those who refuse to make use of the moral gymnasium with which they have been provided, and chosen hate instead of love throughout their earthly lives; but between the good and the bad there is the difference that the course of the former is completed in a shorter time.[87]

Now it is all made clear. God rewards all men equally, for if the truth were known, he has absolutely no interest in the test of life he himself made, for it turned out to fail of its purpose, being a mere delusion, as we have seen. Thus, he gives equal and identical rewards to the just and the unjust alike, since they *are* in fact alike; but those who *think* they did wrong he punishes by denying them their reward for a few millennia, whereas those who *think* they did right (*i.e.,* have in many instances, a numb conscience) are whisked off to their reward without delay. Since evil is only a figment of the imagination and has no objective correlative in God's mind, it seems to follow that a feeling of guilt is the nearest thing on earth to evil (although, of course, not an evil) and those who have the elementary decency implicit in guilt are punished, whereas those who brazen it out and have a casehardened conscience are ushered into the Presence without delay. Pigou seems unaware that this supposed belief of Browning's robs God of his last vestige of rectitude and reduces his judgment to the level of his virtue. He confidently cites as evidence Browning's well-known opposition to the Christian concept

87.  P. 106.

of hell in such poems as *The Ring and the Book,* where the Pope refers to the

> . . . sad obscure sequestered state
> Where God unmakes, but to remake the soul
> He else made first in vain,[88]

and where Pompilia, forgivingly, hopes that even Guido will be saved, although she fails to mention, doubtless because of her wounds, that he is guiltless, as he is since evil is unreal, or that God is as pleased with her twenty-two stab wounds as he is with the birth of her son, since in God's sight all is one:

> But where will God be absent? In His face
> Is light, but in His shadow healing too:
> Let Guido touch the shadow and be healed![89]

Pigou comments:

> Guido, however, and those like him will not reach the end for which they are destined till many ages have gone by, while Pompilia passes at once to the throne of God. The better a man's earthly life is, the sooner will the gates of heaven be opened to receive him.[90]

Since in God's sight a thousand years are as but a day, "many ages" may very well mean a few million years, as time is counted by man, a calculated cruelty which contradicts Pigou's position that God is incapable of creating evil. It is sophistry to suggest that a few eons of time spent in a cheerless limbo outside the heavenly gates is not an evil to the weary petitioner, and it does nothing to say that the evil is only an illusion existing in his mind. In the last analysis all evils exist in the mind. Pigou quotes Don Juan, whose views are rather consistently a caricature of Browning's:

> . . . whatever end we answer by this life,—
> Next time, best chance must be for who, with toil and strife,
> Manages now to live most like what he was meant

88.  X, 2123-2125.     89.  VII, 1703-1705.     90.  P. 107.

Become: since who succeeds so far, 't is evident,
Stands foremost on the file: who fails, has less to hope
From new promotion.[91]

I do not find here the evidence that Pigou discovers to support the
view that God will create an illusion of punishment in the minds of
sinners by keeping them waiting for admittance into heaven. I do
see clear evidence of what Browning said repeatedly, that in the
next world man will grow in direction and degree as his performance
and aspiration in life warrant. In passing, one might note a small
sign of the unreliability of Don Juan's testimony in the idea that one
should "live most like what he was meant/Become. . . ." The
casuistical rake is perverting Browning's belief in self-development
to include the idea that since he is a born lecher, he must fulfill himself wholly in lechery.

Pigou, further, cites from "A Camel-Driver" the words of
Ferishtah:

> "However near I stand in his regard,
> So much the nearer had I stood by steps
> Offered the feet which rashly spurned their help.
> That I call Hell; why further punishment?"

Ferishtah—a fully reliable witness to Browning's word—is recounting
by way of parable how his wise father compiled a book wherein he
wrote words of wisdom to give to his son when he became a man.
Ferishtah, however, at the age of three, threw it into the fire in
ignorance of its value. The lines simply mean that he has since been
aware of his loss, for he knows that however close he was to his
father's wisdom, he would have come even closer if he had not in
ignorance destroyed the valued book. It reveals the sense of loss and
torment of spirit that unwise acts bring upon the doer. A man
creates his own punishment. It has not the slightest connection with
any alleged punishment his father might have inflicted upon him
through postponement of some desired reward. The reason that Pigou
elects these two quotations as evidence, even though they are ir-

91. Ll. 2084-2088.

relevant, is simple: there *are* no relevant ones in the whole of Browning, and something that might seem to serve as evidence must be advanced.

Pigou continues his discussion of punishment by showing that "time is only a mode of man and not of God," and, as a result, "the fulfillment of God's purpose for him is in no way affected by this fact." In short, God's character is admirably preserved, for in delaying reward, he is really not aware that he is doing so, since time is a mode of man which he has not understood. This completes the wreck of God's character: he cannot punish his erring children for two reasons: punishment is an evil, alien to his nature and forbidden to the world; and erring is a thing impossible, since everything is perfect. However, if a man fancies he has done something wrong, he may be punished for his ethical sensitivity, except for the fact that punishment, again, is a thing impossible, and indeed unthinkable in a creation free from evil. God preserves his unblemished character by the ingenious stratagem of simply not being aware of what he is doing by way of punishment. While his guiltless children wait in the chill antechamber for eons of time, he remains of unsmirched character because he has no concept of time or of what they are undergoing. The fact that he keeps only those who are guilty (or fancy they are guilty) waiting and opens wide the doors with admirable promptitude to all others perfectly proves that he has an excellent conception of time, in both celestial and human terms, and, if he maintains that he does not, the truth is not in him or he is capable of illimitable self-deception. This is the God that Browning praised throughout his life, according to Pigou. This is the fantastic web that grew out of the idea that Browning denied the reality of evil.

Henry Jones similarly recognized the moral dilemma that is implicit in this idea: ". . . clear knowledge that evil is an illusion and that all other things have their place in an infinite divine order would paralyze all moral effort, as well as stultify itself."[92] But elsewhere he reaffirms his belief that Browning never really conceived of evil as

92.  P. 255.

illusory, saying that if there were no doubt that evil "is but mere show and semblance," the consequences would be "ruinous to man."[93] And he says elsewhere: ". . . nor, on the other hand, does he limit man's freedom, and stultify ethics by extracting the sting of reality from sin."[94] But later he contradicts his contradiction and henceforth remains constant to the belief that Browning denied evil:

> The apparent existence of evil is the condition of goodness. And yet it must only be apparent. For if evil be regarded as veritably evil, it must remain so for all that man can do; he cannot annihilate any fact nor change its nature, and all effort would, therefore, be futile. And, on the other hand, if evil were known as unreal, then there were no need of moral effort, no quarrel with the present and therefore no aspiration, and no achievement. That which is man's highest and best,—namely, a moral life which is a progress—would thus be impossible, and his existence would be bereft of all meaning and purpose.[95]

Jones frankly confesses that his interpretation of Browning's philosophy leads to nearly insoluble contradictions and dilemmas:

> But now comes the great difficulty. How can the poet combine such earnestness in the moral struggle with so deep a conviction of the ultimate nothingness of evil, and of the complete victory of the good? Again and again we have found him pronounce such victory to be absolutely necessary and inevitable. His belief in God, his trust in His love and might, will brook no limit anywhere. His conviction is that the power of the good subjects evil itself to its authority.[96]

Jones's interpretation destroys Browning's philosophy of the function of life, which becomes not a test but a charade. Since evil is an illusion, no greater moral grandeur is possible in choosing to oppose it than to embrace it, but even more destructive is the conviction that since in the charade of life there are no losers possible, the test is a phantasm and a fraud twice compounded. We are tested, ac-

93. P. 256.    94. P. 116.    95. Pp. 271-272.    96. P. 126.

cording to Jones, to see if we will elect what really is not there in a game in which it matters not a straw whether we select right or wrong, for everybody wins.

He cites "Apparent Failure" by way of proof—the familiar passage in which Browning hopes ("My own hope is, a sun will pierce/The thickest cloud earth ever stretched. . . .") that the three suicides will not be accursed. It is true that here and elsewhere Browning repudiates the concept of hell, but he repeatedly affirms his belief that in heaven there are illimitable degrees of attainment and growth and presumably happiness. The most familiar expression of it occurs in "A Grammarian's Funeral" and in "Andrea del Sarto," where Andrea foresees that the painters who aimed for impossible heights will continue to outstrip him in heaven:

> . . . man's reach should exceed his grasp
> Or what's a heaven for?

Jones—*mirabile dictu*—cites as proof of his allegations Don Juan's words to Elvire:

> As firm is my belief, quick sense perceives the same
> Self-vindicating flash illustrate every man
> And woman of our mass, and prove, throughout the plan,
> No detail but, in place allotted it, was prime
> And perfect.[97]

One is stunned to find Jones advancing this as evidence of God's intent. Don Juan is in the middle of his casuistical argumentation of the great values that will accrue to him and to Elvire from his proposed adultery with Fifine. He has just announced with candid villainy that through knowledge of Fifine's body he will discover her mind and that the inward grace is discovered most directly and attractively through the flesh:

> I thank the smile at last
> Which thins away the tear! Our sky was overcast,
> And something fell; but day clears up: if there chanced rain,

97. Ll. 351-355.

The landscape glistens more. I have not vexed in vain
Elvire: because she knows, now she has stood the test,
How, this and this being good, herself may still be best
O' the beauty in review; because the flesh that claimed
Unduly my regard, she thought, the taste, she blamed
In me, for things extern, was all mistake, she finds,—
Or will find, when I prove that bodies show me minds,
That, through the outward sign, the inward grace allures,
And sparks from heaven transpierce earth's coarsest
    covertures,
All by demonstrating the value of Fifine![98]

To quote Don Juan as an authority on God's plan of salvation is not unlike quoting Belial on grace and original sin.

Since Jones recognizes—as does everyone else—that Browning spent his life in expounding what to him seemed to be the meaning and purpose of life, it occurs to me that Jones might have re-examined his thesis when he discovered that it proved Browning to be a woolly-headed bungler.

John M. Robertson, following Jones, in his *Browning and Tennyson as Teachers,* concurs in the belief that Browning denied evil. After citing the last stanza of "Apparent Failure," he adds:

At the height of his argument he will hold that sin and evil are only apparent flaws in the infinitely perfect whole, visible as perfection to Deity alone at present, but one day also to be so perceived by man. He puts this doctrine, undramatically enough, into one of Pippa's songs:

> . . . God's puppets, best and worst
> Are we; there is no last nor first.[99]

As further evidence, he quotes the lines spoken by the Pope about Guido's presumed salvation: ". . . that sad, obscure, sequestered state? Where God unmakes but to remake the soul/He else made in vain," and comments:

98. Ll. 326-338.    99. London, 1903, p. 114.

This is not the Pope's final philosophy only. It is Robert Browning's. And what a philosophy! Broadly speaking, it leaves off where the real task of philosophy begins. It is only a humanised version of the myths of hell and purgatory: even more naively than they, it negates the very assumption on which it stands, the infinitude of Deity. This conception of Omnipotence as an artificer who chronically makes a misfit, so to speak, what is it but primeval puerility made to look profound?[100]

Here is a perfect instance of the mischief done by this popular belief that Browning denied reality to evil.

In 1867, six years after the death of his wife, Browning wrote to Isa Blagden:

So you go to Lucca. I don't in the least know—or rather in my fancies I change continually as to how I should feel on seeing old sights again. The general impression of the past is as if it had been pain. I would not live it over again, not one day of it. Yet all that seems my real *life*,—and before and after, nothing at all: I look back on all my life, when I look *there*: and life is painful. I always think of this when I read the Odyssey—Homer makes the surviving Greeks, whenever they refer to Troy, just say of it "At Troy, where the Greeks suffered so." Yet all their life was in that ten years at Troy. Lucca, where I suffered so."[101]

This striking, but by no means unique, statement, made to the one person to whom he could speak in candor, perfectly expresses Browning's view of evil and its reality. How well he would have understood Albert Schweitzer's cry: "All life is suffering"—and how fully Pippa would have agreed.

Raymond fully supports Jones, Pigou, and DeVane in the belief that for Browning evil is unreal, a conviction that depends absolutely on man's inability to know anything because of "intellectual agnosticism":

100. P. 115.
101. *Dearest Isa: Robert Browning's Letters to Isabella Blagden,* ed. Edward C. McAleer, p. 267.

Lack of confirmation of its objective reality never makes the poet swerve from the conviction that man should act in accordance with the intuitions and promptings of his conscience which urge him to follow good rather than evil. These are rationally, subjective, confined apparently to each individual's private experience, but they are an absolute for him. A man's ignorance of their ultimate worth the poet regards as a part of his probation on earth. Even though he may not know until the Day of Judgment that they are in accord with divine reality, he must act in obedience to their guidance.[102]

Here again is the old belief, found in its most extended form in Jones's *Browning as a Philosophical and Religious Teacher,* that because Browning had no faith whatsoever in man's intellect as a guide to conduct, he put all his faith in the intuition of the individual. There is no doubt that Browning did place great faith in the emotions and intuition, especially if allied to love; but he denied all absolutes in the mortal state. If there is one guiding principle in understanding either Browning the man or Browning the poet, it is simply that he was a supremely healthy man, in body, mind, and spirit. He was not odd, not freakish, not warped. He was essentially moderate and whole, and he pleaded for moderation and wholeness all his life. John Bury wisely observes: "A main point on which I wish throughout to insist is that Browning realizes the defect and falseness of one-sidedness, and never halts at half-truths: he always gives them their proper place in relation to each other and a higher unity."[103] Few statements as wise have been made about Browning, but, unfortunately, Bury is but little read. Browning scorned dogmatism and absolutes of all kinds, for they stop inquiry. He said that "Love is best," but he never said it is an absolute good or that it is everything. He said the intellect of man is wonderfully subject to error; but, for all that, he never preached the uselessness of intellectual efforts, but ceaselessly affirmed the necessity of pursuing knowledge endlessly, even though for man absolute knowledge ever

102. P. 223.
103. "Browning's Philosophy," *Browning Studies* (London, 1895), p. 41.

recedes in the distance before us. This central belief of the poet is perfectly stated by Henry Charles Duffin:

> Browning is set on justifying the existence of evil. He argues that it is natural and necessary: perfection palls; it is the climb towards perfection *via* the conquest of evil that brings the highest satisfaction (though I do not see why we should strive to attain a condition that is going to bore us when it is achieved).[104]

Duffin is accurate in his belief that the race will not end even in heaven. Illimitably man must evolve, through struggle against ignorance and opposing forces. It seems unlikely that even beyond the screen between this life and the next man will be permitted the luxury—or the stagnation—of dogma. Nor will he be bored. Like John Stuart Mill, Browning believed that no idea should be allowed to petrify into dogma, immune from examination and repudiation if in error. On these grounds Browning repudiates the Roman Catholic Church in *Christmas-Eve:* the intellect is degraded and denied its office, while dogma, which on earth is *always* a compound of truth and error which man must pass beyond, is blindly obeyed. A code of conduct or an ethical principle, Browning knew, may be admirably suited to a given situation or time, but it may equally be catastrophic if applied blindly in all cases. This is the underlying principle of the casuist pieces, where principles are misapplied in an evil cause.

In spite of Browning's lifelong opposition to dogma and to rigidity in application of principle, he is nevertheless accused of the same inelasticity he deplored. He is believed to be guilty of pushing philosophical ideas to extremes, as if he believed a course of conduct appropriate to a given situation were of necessity equally appropriate to all other situations in any way similar, regardless of how irrational and disastrous the results. Thus he is made out to be intellectually shallow and irresponsible. As Raymond says, Browning placed great faith in the individual and his intuitions. But to conclude that Browning never swerved in his belief that man should act in ac-

104. *Amphibian, A Reconsideration of Browning,* p. 232.

cordance with his intuitions and promptings of conscience and that "these are, rationally, subjective, confined apparently to each individual's private experience, but they are an absolute for him" is to make Browning appear to be an uncritical extremist, indeed. Festus warns Paracelsus of his sins of hubris, the pursuit of knowledge to the exclusion of love:

> I know not:
> But know this, you, that 't is no will of mine
> You should abjure the lofty claims you make;
> And this the cause—I can no longer seek
> To overlook the truth, that there would be
> A monstrous spectacle upon the earth,
> Beneath the pleasant sun, among the trees:
> —A being knowing not what love is.[105]

But so great is his awe of the erudition of Paracelsus that he seeks whatever comfort he can find in the illusion that the monomaniacal seeker after knowledge is of a higher order of being, absolved from compliance with the laws of life:

> I dare not judge you.
> The rules of right and wrong thus set aside,
> There's no alternative—I own you one
> Of higher order, under other laws
> Than bind us; therefore, curb not one bold glance![106]

Michal, however, knows that no one is absolved from compliance, for life tests us all equally, and to scorn the limitations of life is to be guilty of hubris:

> Stay with us, Aureole! cast those hopes away,
> And stay with us! An angel warns me, too,
> Man should be humble; you are very proud:
> And God, dethroned, has doleful plagues for such![107]

Paracelsus has spent his entire life in an impossible quest for absolute knowledge, and in this fatal pursuit he divests himself of love and

105. I, 673-679.        106. I, 694-698.        107. I, 700-703.

wholeness. Even love, which to Browning is the most beautiful and wonderful thing in life, can be absolute only as an ideal. Aprile, the poet who seeks for love to the exclusion of knowledge, is guilty of imbalance and a special kind of hubris.

In *Christmas-Eve* Browning offers the most discriminating statement on the nature of love:

> But love is the ever-springing fountain:
> Man may enlarge or narrow his bed
> For the water's play, but the water-head—
> How can he multiply or reduce it?
>     As easy create it, as cause it to cease;
> He may profit by it, or abuse it,
>     But 't is not a thing to bear increase
> As power does: be love less or more
>     In the heart of man, he keeps it shut
>     Or opes it wide, as he pleases, but
> Love's sum remains what it was before.[108]

At first glance this may seem to mean that love *is* an absolute—the only one in life—but the gushing spring of love is not an absolute quantity or quality; it is merely a constant quantity, beyond the power of man to augment or diminish at the source. But he makes clear that once the water has issued from the living rock, man may widen or straighten the bed to keep the waters fast flowing, sparkling, and pure; or he may clog the bed with debris so that the waters of love are stagnant and sour. Thus, one of life's greatest tests is to see whether man will take the great gift of love—which in each heart is not absolute or total, but is "more or less," as Browning notes—and open his heart wide to the growth of love. Love, like everything else in life, is kinetic, growing, becoming, not a stagnant absolute.

If even love is not an absolute, can man rely, as Raymond says Browning taught, upon his individual experience or his intuition as an absolute guide? A guide, yes, but not absolute, for nothing in life

108. Ll. 318-328.

is fully reliable, certainly not man's mind or intuitions. Raymond says very properly that in Browning's verse we learn that man never will be sure of the worth of his experiences and beliefs until eternity permits him to read the record right, so the word *absolute,* as used here, must mean, not that man has total faith in the worth involved, but only in the necessity or advisability of following intuition and individual prompting wherever they lead for want of a better guide: ". . . he must act in obedience to their guidance," Raymond affirms. This is exactly what he must not do. Part of the test of life is to examine eternally the principles, dogmas, intuitions, emotions, and motives behind any act. It is very likely that the intuitions may be reliable guides in life, unless they are corrupted; and when the head and the heart are in direct confrontation (a very rare thing in Browning), the poet unhesitatingly favors the heart if the issue seems to involve equal weight in each pan of the balance. But Browning never said that intuition is an infallible guide which man "must" follow. Blind obedience to intuition as well as to mind is perilous. Man must bring his total resources to the decisions of life.

The point of *Red Cotton Night-Cap Country* is precisely the conflict of head and heart, principles and emotions, and a man's compromise between them. Léonce Miranda, the playboy who has regarded women as objects of seduction, falls madly in love with Clara de Millefleurs, to whom he gives his devotion: "for life, for death, for heaven, for hell, her own." Browning assures us that his love is true, as far as the world which denies absolutes permits truth:

> Truth I say, truth I mean: this love was true,
> And the rest happened by due consequence.
> By which we are to learn that there exists
> A falsish false, for truth's inside the same,
> And truth that's only half true, falsish truth.
> The better for both parties! folk may taunt
> That half your rock-built wall is rubble-heap:
> Answer them, half their flowery turf is stones![109]

109. II, 457-464.

Miranda's mother is opposed to his mistress, and he is uncommonly afflicted with momism. As I have explained earlier, his religion demands that he renounce his mistress, and he is singularly pious. Reason urges that he should let her go and make peace with his mother and with the church, but his emotions are too strong. Thus he attempts to keep the best of two worlds and make an impossible compromise:

> Léonce was found affectionate enough
> To man, to woman, child, bird, beast, alike;
> But all affection, all one fire of heart
> Flaming toward Madame-mother. Had she posed
> The question plainly at the outset "Choose!
> Cut clean in half your all-the-world of love,
> The mother and the mistress: then resolve,
> Take me or take her, throw away the one!"—
> He might have made the choice and marred my tale.
> But, much I apprehend, the problem put
> Was "Keep both halves, yet do no detriment
> To either! Prize each opposite in turn!"[110]

To Browning this kind of uncommitted life, this pusillanimous refusal to take a stand, is entirely mischievous:

> Here's our case.
> Monsieur Léonce Miranda asks of God,
> —May a man, living in illicit tie,
> Continue, by connivance of the Church,
> No matter what amends he please to make
> Short of forthwith relinquishing the sin?
> Physicians, what do you propose for cure?[111]

Browning insists upon a reasoned choice, not a compromise, and certainly not unreflecting adherence to emotion or intuition. When Miranda steps off his belvedere as a means of determining whether God approves of his course of life, Browning applauds his bringing

110.  III, 71-82.    111.  III, 876-882.

to an end his evasive compromise, even though he finds death at the foot of the tower.

The "victor" in the two poems "Before" and "After" acts on impulse, slays his childhood comrade, and lives in remorse. His hot blood proves to be no infallible guide:

> Ha, what avails death to erase
>   His offence, my disgrace?
> I would we were boys as of old
>   In the field, by the fold:
> His outrage, God's patience, man's scorn
>   Were so easily borne!

If man's mind is subject to error, so likewise are his emotions, intuitions, and urges. Pompilia, on her deathbed, tells of a "rough gaunt man in rags, with eyes on fire" whom she saw in the square proclaiming himself Pope:

> " 'I am the Pope, am Sextus, now the Sixth;
> And that Twelfth Innocent, proclaimed to-day,
> Is Lucifer disguised in human flesh!
> The angels met in conclave, crowned me!'—thus
> He gibbered and I listened; but I knew
> All was delusion, ere folk interposed,
> 'Unfasten him, the maniac!' "[112]

Raymond's statement regarding Browning's faith in the "intuitions and promptings of conscience which urge him to follow good rather than evil" reveals a singular fallacy in Browning scholarship. If man could always rely on his intuitions as unfailing guides to conduct, the test of life would be destroyed. In *Easter-Day* Browning says:

> "You must mix some uncertainty
> With faith, if you would have faith be.
> Why, what but faith, do we abhor
> And idolize each other for—
> Faith in our evil or our good,

112.  VII, 1162-1168.

>     Which is or is not understood
>     Aright by those we love or those
>     We hate, thence called our friends or foes?"[113]

Not even man's experience may be relied on as a guide. The moral choice of yesterday, which fitted the exigencies of the moment so well, may not be blindly relied upon to answer the needs of tomorrow. Each test is new and fresh and individual, and life offers no talismans. The Old Man in Hemingway's *The Old Man and the Sea* knows that yesterday's courage has no relevance for today. Each day is unique and its trials are a new challenge. His code of conduct here is very close to Browning's.

113. Ll. 71-78.

# CHAPTER II

# ON THE LIMITS OF INDIVIDUALISM

HERE COMES THE FIRST EXPERIMENTALIST
IN THE NEW ORDER OF THINGS,—HE PLAYS A PRIEST;
DOES HE TAKE INSPIRATION FROM THE CHURCH,
DIRECTLY MAKE HER RULE HIS LAW OF LIFE?
NOT HE: HIS OWN MERE IMPULSE GUIDES THE MAN—

—*The Ring and the Book, X, 1904-1908*

The primary source of the belief that Browning brooked no limits to individualism and affirmed the sacred right of each man to be his own absolute guide in matters of conduct is Henry Jones:

> For a God who, in filling the universe with His presence, encroaches on the freedom and extinguishes the independence of man, precludes the possibility of all that is best for man—namely, moral achievement. Life, deprived of its moral purpose, is worthless to the poet, and so, in consequence, is all that exists in order to maintain that life. Optimism and ethics seem thus to come into immediate collision. The former, finding the presence of God in all things, seems to leave no room for man; and the latter seems to set man to work out his own destiny in solitude, and to give him supreme and absolute authority over his own life; so that any character which he forms, be it good or bad, is entirely the product of his own activity. So far as his life is culpable or praiseworthy, in other words, so far as we pass any moral judgment upon it, we necessarily think of it as the revelation of a self, that is, of an independent will, which cannot divide its responsibility.[1]

1. Pp. 113-114.

In "A Bean-Stripe: Also Apple-Eating," however, Ferishtah sees the matter otherwise:

> "What is man? Not God:
> None of these absolutes therefore,—yet himself,
> A creature with a creature's qualities."[2]

Browning, ironically enough in view of Jones's statement, began his poetic career with three works specifically devoted to the theme of man's obligations (and the poet's in particular) to God, society, and himself, and each includes a warning against the extreme individualism which leads to hubris. The young poet in *Pauline,* who is, of course, Browning, is confessing to Pauline the nature of his sins in an attempt to arrive at an answer to the question which preoccupied Browning as a young man: what are the duty and function of the artist? What are the limits, if any, to his being a law unto himself? The sin of the young poet who pours out his confession to Pauline, it becomes immediately clear, is egocentricity, isolation, and self-indulgence. He has relied too much upon himself; he has "cast away restraint," and his soul has retreated "into the dim orb/ Of self":

> I am made up of an intensest life,
> Of a most clear idea of consciousness
> Of self, distinct from all its qualities,
> From all affections, passions, feelings, powers;
> And thus far it exists, if tracked, in all:
> But linked, in me, to self-supremacy,
> Existing as a centre to all things,
> Most potent to create and rule and call
> Upon all things to minister to it;
> And to a principle of restlessness
> Which would be all, have, see, know, taste, feel, all—
> This is myself; and I should thus have been
> Though gifted lower than the meanest soul.[3]

He soon realizes that this total reliance on self is a sin, ruinous to mind and spirit, and he determines to look within no more:

2.  Ll. 292-294.    3.  Ll. 268-280.

> I'll look within no more.
> I have too trusted my own lawless wants,
> Too trusted my vain self, vague intuition—
> Draining soul's wine alone in the still night,
> And seeing how, as gathering films arose,
> As by an inspiration life seemed bare
> And grinning in its vanity, while ends
> Foul to be dreamed of, smiled at me as fixed
> And fair, while others changed from fair to foul
> As a young witch turns an old hag at night.
> No more of this![4]

*Paracelsus* is similarly a study in individualism, arrogance, and scorn of the paths of traditional learning. Paracelsus seeks one goal in life, to the exclusion of all others: to know. But he has no patience with traditional curricula or courses of inquiry. He learns black magic, lives in the house of a conjuror, and amasses vast knowledge— but finds no love or happiness. He knows that his monomania and his scorn of mankind and his mores have destroyed him. He has become a guide to himself, is guilty of hubris, and must fall from his "proud eminence." Life has its rules and boundaries which man must respect or die. Festus is aware of the sin of Paracelsus:

> I call your sin exceptional;
> It springs from one whose life has passed the bounds
> Prescribed to life.[5]

On his deathbed Paracelsus, seeing the sin of pride that has been his, warns of the dangers of becoming a lawless guide to one's own self:

> For men begin to pass their nature's bound,
> And find new hopes and cares which fast supplant
> Their proper joys and griefs; they grow too great
> For narrow creeds of right and wrong, which fade
> Before the unmeasured thirst for good. . . .[6]

4. Ll. 937-947.    5. III, 861-863.    6. V, 777-781.

Unmindful of his position as a social being, he "gazed on power till" he "grew blind." Central to Browning is the concept that man is tested as an individual, not in groups; but part of the test is his fulfillment of social responsibilities. Man's individualism may be vast, but not absolute. The critical error that has become so entrenched as to amount almost to a dogma is that Browning encourages man to regard truth as absolutely relative and individual, no truth being inherently superior to another so long as an individual seizes upon it as a truth for him. In fact, Browning held that there are two views of truth: God's view and man's. The one is eternal, fixed, imperishable; the other is shifting, relative, impermanent. Man is tested by how closely his view of truth approximates God's. In *Fifine* Don Juan, between lies, utters a belief which squares with Browning's views: "falsehood is change" and "truth is permanence." Man's "truth" by definition is a partial truth, intermixed. It is clear that Browning does not intend to say that *for man* any "truth" that changes is falsehood, for all of man's truths shift and change as he progresses toward absolute truth. As Ogniben, in *A Soul's Tragedy*, remarks: "There is truth in falsehood, falsehood in truth"—a pivotal doctrine in Browning. Man's truth is not false because it changes; it changes because it is false—at least because it is false in part. As the Pope says in his judgment of Guido, man on earth cannot bear the full light of truth, but the partial view spurs him forever onward:

> Clouds obscure—
> But for which obscuration all were bright?
> Too hastily concluded! Sun-suffused,
> A cloud may soothe the eye made blind by blaze,—
> Better the very clarity of heaven:
> The soft streaks are the beautiful and dear.
> What but the weakness in a faith supplies
> The incentive to humanity, no strength
> Absolute, irresistible, comports?[7]

7.  X, 1637-1645.

John Bury, in a paper read before the London Browning Society in 1882, wisely pointed out that to Browning "there are two sides to an individual's Weltanschauung, the individual and the universal." It is tempting to embrace the illusion that Browning's vigorous championing of individualism and the relativity of truth is ample evidence that he denied anything beyond the individual. Similarly his vigorous exaltation of love has appeared to the critics as a condemnation of the intellect. Bury comments:

> From the individual side he [man] considers the universe as his own world; from the universal he looks upon himself as a single unit of that world. Now it is the individual side that comes prominently forward in Browning; but to understand it we must take it in its context; and as the universal side, being less obtrusive, is very likely to escape notice, I shall occupy myself first and principally with it, and afterwards take it in connection with the individual side.[8]

The working assumption underlying Bury's essay is that Browning is a man of sane balance. Bury recognizes that although to the poet love is "the end and purpose of life, knowledge is the means whereby it perfects and fulfills itself," and he quotes as evidence from *The Ring and the Book* the Pope's query:

> Why live
> Except for love—and how love unless they know?[9]

That the individual is not granted a blanket dispensation to formulate his own view of truth, ethics, morality, and God is one of the themes of *Christmas-Eve*, one of the poems most reliably expressing the poet's personal convictions: "Truth remains true, the fault's in the prover. . . ."[10] After bursting out of the close and smelly Zion Chapel, with its unwashed congregation and stupid and dogmatic minister, Browning's persona in a dream journeys to St. Peter's and then to Göttingen, where David Friedrich Strauss (or his twin)

8. "Browning's Philosophy," *Browning Studies*, p. 31.    9. P. 33.
10. L. 229.

lectures aridly on rationalism. Upon his awakening in the Chapel, the persona feels more tolerant towards the poor minister:

> For me,
> I have my own church equally:
> And in this church my faith sprang first![11]

Every man has his own church in his heart "equally" with the sectarian church of his choice. Although Browning was not a regular churchgoer, he did attend from time to time, and he never repudiated the church in favor of his individual private faith, but the evidence is strong that the faith of his heart was infinitely more important to him than any organized religion. As he looks into the glorious firmament, he says:

> Oh, let men keep their ways
> Of seeking thee in a narrow shrine—
> Be this my way![12]

In youth he looked at the skies and probed their immensities and "found God there, his visible power," yet in his heart he felt "an equal evidence" that God's love is greater in nobility than in power. The critical belief that Browning denied to the faculties and to the external world any power of teaching man truth or faith must fall before such affirmation. When he recalls the scriptural promise "Where two or three should meet and pray/He would be in the midst, their friend . . ." he feels that perhaps he has been guilty of the sin of pride in leaving the place of worship. To the berobed figure of God that appears to him, he says in contrition:

> It cannot be
> That thou, indeed, art leaving me—
> Me, that have despised thy friends!
> Did my heart make no amends?[13]

When in his vision he is transported to St. Peter's, he is grievously offended by the anti-intellectualism and dogma of the mass, for he acknowledges that God's greatest guide to truth is the intellect of the

11. Ll. 271-273.        12. Ll. 372-374.        13. Ll. 455-458.

individual man: "The clue God gave me as most fit/To guide my footsteps through life's maze." But even though Rome has placed on man's mind a "gross yoke" of dogma,

> Her teaching is not so obscured
> By errors and perversities,
> That no truth shines athwart the lies. . . .[14]

After visiting the arid, skeletal professor in his loveless lecture hall in Göttingen, Browning awakens from his dream in the little dissenting Chapel and decides that with all its vulgarity, its cheese-and-garlic atmosphere, and its errors, it is superior to the offensively ornate ritual and dogma of St. Peter's and infinitely better than the mephitic atmosphere of the loveless lecture hall:

> I then, in ignorance and weakness,
> Taking God's help, have attained to think
>   My heart does best to receive in meekness
> That mode of worship, as most to his mind,
> Where earthly aids being cast behind,
> His All in All appears serene
> With the thinnest human veil between. . . .[15]

The old Pope, who speaks so very eloquently on the need of evil and doubt to test the individual's moral judgment, and who reaffirms the duty of each man to solve his moral problems through use of his talents in facing the trials of life, yet knows that the lawless individual who puts no bounds to his self-governance is surely failing the test of life:

> But when man walks the garden of this world
> For his own solace, and, unchecked by law,
> Speaks or keeps silence as himself sees fit,
> Without the least incumbency to lie,
> —Why, can he tell you what a rose is like,
> Or how the birds fly, and not slip to false
> Though truth serve better?[16]

14. Ll. 614-616.     15. Ll. 1301-1307.     16. X, 360-366.

The man who elects absolute self-sufficiency of moral judgment very often is deceived—very often, indeed, for self-interest has a way of giving to error the look of truth. Indeed, this is the chief theme of *The Ring and the Book,* as of many other of Browning's most significant works. Man, "Whose appetite if brutish is a truth," is peculiarly subject to self-deception, mistaking base lusts and urges for pure truth, as do Guido, Don Juan, Prince Hohenstiel-Schwangau, Sludge, and Bishop Blougram. To some degree every man is at times a casuist, rationalizing his misdeeds and wishes, arguing with consummate subtlety that fiction is fact.

Raymond makes the point that Browning counseled each individual to repudiate any reliance whatever on cultural codes and to go it alone in all matters moral and ethical. Browning, it is true, was one of the most dedicated individualists of his age. G. K. Chesterton expressed the point with his usual succinctness: "The sense of the absolute sanctity of human difference was the deepest of all his senses."[17] He advocated extraordinary reliance on the individual, in line with his belief that life is a test of each man individually. Every man must stand or fall in the test of life essentially alone. Hence, it follows that the individual is heroically tested in isolation from his fellows. It is tempting to conclude that since there is no sure formula to guide man through life, Browning therefore counseled man to scorn any doctrine not arising from his own experience and intuition in his isolation. Raymond quotes from "A Camel-Driver" the lines—

> "Ask thy lone soul what laws are plain to thee,—
> Thee and no other,—stand or fall by them!—"

as evidence of Browning's repudiation of the mores of his culture. In "A Camel-Driver" Ferishtah discusses the fate of a condemned murderer, sawn asunder between two boards for his misdeeds. Ferishtah approves the justice of the sentence but reproves his companion for believing that God will reserve the hottest part of hell for the partner in the murder who fled to safety in Syria. His companion, amazed, argues that "by parity of reason" God should punish the escaped

17. *Robert Browning* (New York, 1908), p. 187.

villain if Ferishtah approves the execution of the one caught. The wise dervish, however, argues that man must not presume to postulate God's actions by analogy with man's: " 'Man acts as man must: God, as God beseems.' " A camel driver knows no better way to discipline his vicious beast than to thump him across the muzzle. Until such time as man can instruct camels through language, blows must serve. He is asked whether punishment is justified if the malefactor is truly repentant and is resolved to transgress no more. Ferishtah replies that to allow the camel to go unpunished, regardless of his repentance, would encourage insurrection among his brethren. But punishment deferred six months until the offending camel has forgotten his evil deed is both cruel and useless. Thus is man's mind constituted in his search for justice, and he assumes that God will reason similarly, but the only thing man can rationally determine about the mind of God is that it

> ". . . never resembles man's at all
> Teaching or punishing."

His companion immediately concludes that since God's reason is contrary to man's it can be assumed that the felon whom man would punish God would pardon. Ferishtah disabuses him of this easy formula. Man must not "ape omniscience" by trying to peer into God's heart and to reduce His motives to a set of codes analogous to man's, either by way of comparison or contrast. The individual, Ferishtah insists, must find his own answers to the moral problems that life besets him with, and he should abandon the attempt to fathom the mind of the Creator.

Raymond, unluckily, assumes that Browning here is counseling each individual to set up his own code of ethics in a vacuum, absolutely divorced from all others, and perhaps at cross purposes to them. The mad murderer in "Porphyria's Lover" makes his own code of conduct, too, but he is detested of God and man for it. Nowhere does Browning suggest that a man has a right to scorn traditional paths and to make unto himself a light for his feet. Paracelsus dooms himself by spurning traditional paths of knowledge and delving into black magic. In *Christmas-Eve* man is advised to exercise his individualism freely—but within the bounds of life. To do otherwise is hubris. There is a great difference between counseling the individual to rely on himself and on his own code in moments of moral crisis rather than upon formulae set by society, and, on the other hand, instructing him to make up his moral code without regard for its collision with the codes of his culture.[18] Freedom to Browning must always be within set limits. He never advocated the anarchy of absolute individualism. In one of his letters Browning berates a young married couple whose individual code of conduct permitted the public display of such vulgar familiarities as holding hands. They violated an established pattern of conduct and are condemned before the bar of public opinion. Much as he approved of love in all of its meanings, Browning would never excuse such a tasteless display in public merely because the guilty pair might argue that they formed their own set of mores.

The Pope, in judging Guido, says much the same thing as does Ferishtah on the matter of the limits of man's individual ethical standards:

> Thus, bold
> Yet self-mistrusting, should man bear himself,
> Most assured on what now concerns him most—
> The law of his own life, the path he prints,—
> Which law is virtue and not vice, I say,—
> And least inquisitive where search least skills,
> I' the nature we best give the clouds to keep.[19]
>
> Was such a lighting-up of faith, in life,
> Only allowed initiate, set man's step
> In the true way by help of the great glow?
> A way wherein it is ordained he walk,
> Bearing to see the light from heaven still more
> And more encroached on by the light of earth,
> Tentatives earth puts forth to rival heaven,

18. See *Christmas-Eve,* 11. 1018 ff. and *passim.*    19. X, 1747-1753.

Earthly incitements that mankind serve God
For man's sole sake, not God's and therefore man's.[20]

At least some one Pompilia left the world
Will say "I know the right place by foot's feel,
I took it and tread firm there; wherefore change?"
But what a multitude will surely fall
Quite through the crumbling truth, late subjacent,
Sink to the next discoverable base,
Rest upon human nature, settle there
On what is firm, the lust and pride of life![21]

The wise old Pope is surely not preaching anarchy here. He is not saying that each man is a light unto himself and thus has no need for other guidance. If man is a law unto himself, then there is no basis for judging his conduct, and the test of life becomes meaningless. Every act of man *is* judged upon its merits, and there must be some standard of conduct by which God judges man, and the assumption must be that the codes of the church and society, which grow out of God's word, bear a close resemblance to the standards by which God judges our acts. When the Pope says that man should confidently bear himself according to "The law of his own life," he does not mean that such a law must not concern itself with morality, the Golden Rule, the Ten Commandments, and the tenets of the church; rather it means that man must devote his attentions largely to "the path he prints"—*i.e.*, the practical, immediate affairs of life, not the affairs of the next life which man must not pry into until death permits his acquisition of such knowledge. This is what he means in counseling man to be "least inquisitive" about what it were best for the "clouds to keep," the matters of eternity. He makes very clear that the "great glow"—not the full radiance—of God teaches man the "way wherein it is ordained he walk." Within these limits, man has freedom of choice and action, but he must not spurn the "true way of help of the great glow," for to do so is to fail the test. Those pure spirits, like Pompilia, will know the right path "by foot's

20.  X, 1808-1816.        21.  X, 1879-1886.

feel," for it is the straight and narrow path, discernible to all whose hearts are right, and they tread firm through life, content.

Caponsacchi, similarly, walks a path between blind obedience to the church and total moral self-determination. The church says to him:

> "But am not I the Bride, the mystic love
> O' the Lamb, who took thy plighted troth, my priest,
> To fold thy warm heart on my heart of stone
> And freeze thee nor unfasten any more?
> This is a fleshly woman,—let the free
> Bestow their life-blood, thou art pulseless now!"[22]

But the priest, who is a perfect spokesman for Browning's ardent Protestantism, is more St. George than St. Jerome and finds his moral guide less in dogma than in situational ethics. When he and Pompilia met

> The spark of truth was struck from out our souls—
> Made all of me, described in the first glance,
> Seem fair and honest and permissible love
> O' the good and true—as the first glance told me
> There was no duty patent in the world
> Like daring try be good and true myself,
> Leaving the shows of things to the Lord of Show
> And Prince o' the Power of the Air.[23]

He asks why the court could not rise above dogmatic inflexibility and, recognizing that man must be human, proclaim: " 'Here's the exceptional conduct that should claim/ To be exceptionally judged. . . .' " When this trial is history, he vows, "I mean to do my duty and live long," for he is not a rebel. He knows that a priest is yet a man and, in spite of the church's insistence to the contrary, is far from pulseless:

> She and I are mere strangers now: but priests
> Should study passion; how else cure mankind,

22.  VI, 962-967.    23.  VI, 1787-1794.

> Who come for help in passionate extremes?
> I do but play with an imagined life
> Of who, unfettered by a vow, unblessed
> By the higher call,—since you will have it so,—
> Leads it companioned by the woman there.[24]

Others, like Guido, scorn the path of virtue and make their own standards, which are based on "human nature" and "pride of life." Even in the Church, the Pope laments, pseudo-priests make their "mere impulses" serve as their guide. His position is the exact contrary of the view Raymond ascribes to Browning, a view that has largely prevailed since Henry Jones.

In "The Sun" Ferishtah carefully speaks Browning's views of individualism and its relation to social codes. At one time man conceived the sun to be God, for it was "author of all light and life" to him. As man progressed in knowledge, he put away childish things and gained an ever-advancing conception of God. No longer does man regard a beautiful stone as a god because it is pleasant to the eye and, if rolled by the tongue, brings moisture to the parched mouth:

> No,—man once, man forever—man in soul
> As man in body: just as this can use
> Its proper senses only, see and hear,
> Taste, like or loathe according to its law
> And not another creature's,—even so
> Man's soul is moved by what, if it in turn
> Must move, is kindred soul: receiving good
> —Man's way—must make man's due acknowledgment,
> No other. . . .[25]

Man has a large measure of freedom in following his own individual nature, but man's soul is rightly moved by kindred souls, and he makes due acknowledgment of the good that accrues to him from others. No man lives in spiritual isolation.

Raymond quotes the lines from the end of *Sordello*, the passage

24. VI, 2049-2055.    25. Ll. 118-126.

where the aspiring poet is learning the lesson of life and the reason
for his failure:

> . . . I have one appeal—
> I feel, am what I feel, know what I feel;
> So much is truth to me.[26]

Sordello continues in this monologue on the theme of the relativity
of knowledge, taste, and beauty, the apparent absence of any absolutes in life to follow, a condition apparently leaving each man to
make his own code of conduct:

> What Is, then? Since
> One object, viewed diversely, may evince
> Beauty and ugliness—this way attract,
> That way repel,—why gloze upon the fact?
> Why must a single of the sides be right?
> What bids choose this and leave the opposite?
> Where's abstract Right for me?[27]

Browning, in *propria persona,* breaks into the monologue to give one
of his most forceful, if tortuous, judgments on this matter and upon
the plan of life. He recounts Sordello's attempts to be sufficient unto
himself and in pride of life to solve the riddle of existence in isolation—"the very nucleus probe"—which a mortal cannot do with impunity:

> So seemed Sordello's closing-truth evolved
> By his flesh-half's break-up; the sudden swell
> Of his expanding soul showed Ill and Well,
> Sorrow and Joy, Beauty and Ugliness,
> Virtue and Vice, the Larger and the Less,
> All qualities, in fine, recorded here,
> Might be but modes of Time and this one sphere,
> Urgent on these, but not of force to bind
> Eternity, as Time—as Matter—Mind,
> If Mind, Eternity, should choose assert

26.  VI, 439-441.      27.  VI, 441-447.

Their attributes within a Life: thus girt
With circumstance, next change beholds them cinct
Quite otherwise—with Good and Ill distinct. . . .[28]

What Browning means is that Sordello's approaching death makes
sorrow and joy, beauty and ugliness, virtue and vice appear as if
they "Might be but modes of Time"—he does not say they *are* so—*i.e.*,
they might be simply man's view, distorted by an artificial view of
time, and thus without validity in terms of absolute values. Mortal
codes, though of force to bind man, have no force to bind eternity
or to change the values of the Infinite, which are absolutes. Man's
life is "girt/ With Circumstance"—the wedding or the funeral of
Wordsworth's "Immortality Ode"—but in the next life good and ill
will lie distinct, as on earth they lie inextricably mixed. There they
will be no longer relative, shifting, shadowy. Once he understands
this, "all was known":

> What made the secret of his past despair?
> —Most imminent when he seemed most aware
> Of his own self-sufficiency: made mad
> By craving to expand the power he had,
> And not new power to be expanded?—just
> This made it; Soul on Matter being thrust,
> Joy comes when so much Soul is wreaked in Time
> On Matter. . . .[29]

This significant passage is irreconcilable with the belief that Browning taught man to rely wholly and absolutely on his own individual
thinking or intuition. This is exactly what Sordello did, and he suffered and died a failure because of it. His despair was greatest when
he became aware of his own hubristic self-sufficiency—when he
played God and relied solely on himself, his own codes, and standards; scorned mankind; and retreated to Goito to become a recluse,
communicating only with birds and animals. These things he did
because he held that each man may with impunity construct his
own moral code, and he failed. When he burst out of the confine-

28. VI, 466-478.    29. VI, 487-494.

ment of Goito, met the fair Lady Palma, and won the prize in singing at her court of Love, he was totally unprepared for love. When
she placed her scarf around his neck, he could not bear the sensuous
experience of feeling the silk warm from the neck of a beautiful
woman; and he sank into amnesia and stumbled back to the false
safety of Goito. The test of life, he finally learns, is not to seek total
self-sufficiency, but to "Fit to the finite his infinity"—i.e., to adjust
his egoism and his standards to those of God. Man cannot be entirely
self-sufficient. Before he learns this great lesson, he announced in
pride of life, "I feel, am what I feel, know what I feel/ So much is
truth to me," and because of this pride he is humbled in the dust.

No poet was more a middle-of-the-road moderate than Browning,
but ironically since Henry Jones and A. C. Pigou he has regularly
been regarded as one who pushed his individualism to the point of
absurdity. He was a dissenter, he was an enthusiastic individualist,
and he believed fully in the right and duty of each man to meet the
issues of life with all his individual powers and with the principles
and codes that each man must form for himself—within the limits
allotted to man, but not in Goito, not in scorn of human relationships, and not in contempt of love and God's laws. The message of
*Sordello* might well be summed up in John Donne's magnificent
statement against sending to know for whom the bell tolls. Every
man is involved with mankind and his codes and with God, and it
is fatal to scorn such relationships.

From "Francis Furini" Raymond quotes the lines about man's

> ". . . solid standing-place amid
> The wash and welter, whence all doubts are bid
> Back to the ledge they break against in foam,
> Futility: my soul, and my soul's home
> This body,—how each operates on each,
> And how things outside, fact or feigning, teach
> What good is and what evil . . ."[30]

as evidence of Browning's reliance solely on one's own belief, mind,
and existence. Furini, however, adds these words:

30.  Ll. 509-515.

> ". . . blame
> Diffidence nowise if, from this I judge
> My point of vantage, not an inch I budge.
> All—for myself—seems ordered wise and well
> Inside it,—what reigns outside, who can tell?
> Contrariwise, who needs be told 'The space
> Which yields thee knowledge,—do its bounds embrace
> Well-willing and wise-working, each at height?
> Enough: beyond thee lies the infinite—
> Back to thy circumscription!' "[31]

The issue here is not, as Raymond supposes, that Furini is affirming his security within the bounds of his own codes and conclusions and thus defends his isolation from society and its codes. Far from it. Furini is warning of the sin of pride: man must be lowly wise; he must busy himself with the things of his "point of vantage"—his world, as contrasted with the things of the next world—and must not scale the ramparts of heaven, the infinite which lies inscrutably behind the veil. The point of vantage is not each individual's separate little world of individual ethics, but man's world, shared by all. Wise Furini is echoing Browning's many warnings to man to "be mere man and nothing more" and to rest content with the plan of life, which permits and demands continued progress in knowledge and moral growth, but which forbids rending the veil shielding the Absolute from mortal eyes:

> "Only by looking low, ere looking high,
> Comes penetration of the mystery."[32]

If man is counseled to look low—to the ever-widening horizons of things about him—before looking high (to the secrets reserved for the next world), it seems miraculous to discover in this poem evidence that Browning believed man was doomed to follow only "the intuitions and promptings of his conscience," which are "confined apparently to each individual's private experience" and which are for

31. Ll. 516-525.    32. Ll. 546-547.

him supposedly an absolute. Mrs. Percy Lake, writing in *The Ethics of Browning's Poems,* has a clear insight into Browning's sense:

> The intellectual life rather than the sensuous is the subject of his poems. No poet has done more to bring the life of the Mind before us, yet we hear it declared sometimes that he despised Knowledge.
>
> Such a declaration must argue ignorance of the very root-principles of Browning's ideas. No one can read "Paracelsus" without feeling how lofty a view he took of Knowledge, and a little study will show us that he raises it to the heights of the Eternal, and places it as an attribute of God, high above all temporary and fugitive things. It is when any attempt is made to limit its scope, to bind it down to transient concerns, that his impatience is shown: A wrong conception of Knowledge and the uses of Knowledge meet with his well-merited scorn. . . .
>
> If the later poems of Browning seem to extol Love and disparage Knowledge, a very casual glance will show that the reason of it is that he is working out in a general form the thoughts of his early poems "Paracelsus" and "Sordello," that the best in Life is obtained by those who can grasp the true meaning of our limitations and not try and force into this world the developments that are only possible elsewhere.[33]

What a simple and humane doctrine it is! And how it has been misunderstood and distorted by critic and casuist alike.

Of all the casuists in Browning's gallery, Bishop Blougram best illustrates the emptiness of the belief that man, without endangering his soul, may be an absolute guide to himself, and may pursue sin and evil for self-interest, there being no guides to conduct outside one's own soul. It is unfortunate that the plain sense of "Bishop Blougram's Apology" has in our time been so totally distorted that the poem is widely held to mean almost precisely the opposite of what Browning intended. It is not in the least surprising to discover that this has happened, for such a distortion is firmly based on a few

33. London, 1897, pp. 153-155.

adamantine critical assumptions that are almost never questioned. Symptomatic of the extremism that has marked Browning criticism in the twentieth century is the strange affirmation that, in Browning's philosophy if doubt is a form of evil and if evil is a part of life's test—both valid suppositions—then it follows that since man must not shirk the trials and the test of life, the greater the evil he encounters, by accident or design, the greater is the test and the greater is his reward. Today in Browning criticism little is said about the fortitude with which one resists evil, but a very great deal is said about the necessity of dynamically pursuing with one's whole heart something, whether it be good or evil being of no moment. Since one is supposedly self-sufficient to make his own standards and choices, it follows that once the judgment is made, he has an obligation to follow the consequences of his judgment, even after he recognizes that they are evil, with all possible vigor, for (so the argument runs) the vigor of the pursuit is really the mark of man's success, not the thing pursued. Since doubt to Browning is among the greatest of all life's tests, it seems to follow that the greater the doubt one can muster, the healthier his spiritual state.

This is the underlying assumption that informs F. E. L. Priestley's important article, "Browning's Apologetics"[34] and Lord Dunsany's "Browning Is Blougram,"[35] both widely admired and quoted as affording a fresh and luminous insight into Browning. These two articles agree in their assumption that Bishop Blougram is not to be included among Browning's casuists, for the bishop is not a hypocritical scoundrel defending his malign position by whatever means he can find in the bending of truth, but is rather a sympathetic individualist who has made an admirable adjustment of spirit to the demands and limitations of life. Lord Dunsany finds an identity between Browning and the cynical bishop and pronounces the unctuous prelate not an evil but an ideal. These views are not really new and fresh at all. Richard Holt Hutton, in 1906, remarked of Browning that

34. *University of Toronto Quarterly,* XV, No. 2 (January, 1946), 1939-1947.
35. *Nineteenth Century and After,* CXXXIX (April, 1946), 175-177.

His genius has been called dramatic. That is, I think a mistake. His insight into character was very keen, but he never lost himself in the characters he depicted. He translated them all into Browningese forms. Bishop Blougram is Browning as a worldly bishop. The Bishop who orders his tomb at St. Praxed's Church is Browning posing as a sensual superstitious Italian Bishop. Ogniben, the Papal Legate in "A Soul's Tragedy," is Browning posing as ecclesiastical diplomatist.[36]

J. M. Cohen similarly believes that Browning is to be identified with his characters, discovering that "the personality of Don Juan in *Fifine* is no sooner created than it disintegrates, leaving Robert Browning with a mere ventriloquist's dummy to speak his reflective discursions."[37] Indeed, as so many other critics have done, he finds that Browning was incapable of creating any character or trait which he did not discover in himself:

For him, as for Blougram, however, evil and doubt existed only in order to occasion faith. So the temporizing Roman Catholic archbishop, like each one of Browning's men and women, spoke for one aspect of the man himself. For in his great monologues Browning rang the changes on his own constituent moods or personalities, embodying each in turn in a character who should hold the stage and, in defending, expounding and pleading his own case, speak in part also for his creator. . . . All are different, yet all speak for Browning himself. . . .[38]

J. Hillis Miller, in *The Disappearance of God,* is more moderate in his identification of the poet with his characters, but, concerning the opinions of his men and women, he says:

They are not his opinions, not his experiences, not his life, because he has no opinions, no experiences, no life of his own. But in another way, all of these opinions, experiences, and lives *are* his, and W. C. DeVane is right to insist on the self-expressive

36. *Brief Literary Criticisms* (London, 1906), p. 253.
37. *Robert Browning* (London, 1952), p. 140.      38. *Ibid.,* pp. 94-95.

side of Browning's poetry. They are all his because each one represents the fulfillment of one impulse of his spirit. Browning has no separate life of his own because he lives his life in his poetry.[39]

The evidence of Browning's life and poetry makes these conclusions untenable. The theme of "Cleon" is that life is to be lived, not in books or at secondhand, but directly. It is better to love than to write the greatest love odes, great and good as they may be. To ascribe to Browning the urges of all his characters is unkind and naïve, and the critical damage has been extensive to Browning. Miller makes quite clear that in the most literal sense Browning's characters speak for Browning:

> It is only a matter of letting one of his inner impulses flow out, take form, and he can become Sludge, Guido, or Caliban. Since Browning contains all these lives potentially in himself he can imitate them from the inside, marrying his mind and sense to theirs. This correspondence between what he is potentially and what the world is actually, is the basis of Browning's poetry, and of his intuitive method of comprehension.[40]

The effect of this oversimplification is, of course, to destroy Browning as a serious artist. It is to rob him of invention, creativity, and imagination, without which a man is no poet. It is especially disastrous to identify the poet with his casuists and other villains, for the mere act of doing so destroys his moral character and his sincerity as an artist. To say that in creating all of his characters—including the despicable casuists, among whom Guido must be numbered—Browning was but ringing "the changes on his own constituent moods and personalities" or that each villain represents "one impulse of his spirit" is silly. Browning in his casuistical pieces allows a consummate blackguard to defend himself and his life by whatever means he cares to elect, including carefully disguised lies, distortion, untenable analogies, outrageous non sequiturs, and cynical misrepresentations —all forced upon principles of the loftiest and most unimpeachable

39. P. 102.      40. P. 103.

character. Cohen's and Miller's conclusion means that Browning—if as an artist he knew what he was doing—freely identified himself with these bad men, for he had no invention outside his own experience and being. The casuists are the least honest characters he created, and it is important to understand that he did *create* them, not reproduce them from mere introspection, for they are wholly bent on deception at whatever cost. Each is an absolute believer in the right of the individual to be a law to himself, to fulfill himself and his private code of ethics in any way that will leave him vindicated among the gullible. Blougram, like all the other casuists, seeks to prove that his way of life, his private and personal codes of conduct, are in fact identical with God's and follow perfectly God's plan of life for man. He admits not one chink in his moral or spiritual armor. As Alfred Noyes perceptively put it,

> Whatever the vices and lies and doubts and follies of Browning's knaves may be, of one thing they always speak with confidence and composure—their relation to God. . . . Sludge is certain that his lies and conjuring tricks were all in harmony with God. Bishop Blougram is certain that all his compromises were in perfect harmony with God. Prince Hohenstiel-Schwangau is certain that all his political dodges were the true means of fulfilling the harmony of God. Every one of these meagre swindlers, while admitting on the immediate plane a complete failure in all things relative, claims an awful alliance on the ultimate plane with the Absolute—God.[41]

F. E. L. Priestley, however, in his article on "Browning's Apologetics," denies that Blougram is to be included among the casuists for the reason that the bishop is not a blackguard at all, and if he is not a blackguard he cannot be a casuist. This is rather circuitous reasoning, and dubious at best. There is, on the other hand, every reason to believe that Blougram is in fact a casuist, if the testimony of his argumentation is to be trusted, for it is precisely like that of his casuistic brethren: Don Juan, the lecher, who exercises his

41. "In White Cotton Night-cap Country," *The Speaker* (June 13, 1903), pp. 252-253.

ingenuity in defense of his proposed seduction of Fifine; Sludge, the mountebank medium, who defends his impostures and monstrous deceptions; Prince Hohenstiel-Schwangau, who blandly explains away his political charlatanism and vicious opportunism. They all use the same method of argumentation, the same contrived sophistry, the same clever distortion and false analogies. Each bases his defense squarely on Browning's most cherished principles of life and conduct, his reliance on individualism, and the test of man through what seems right to him in a moral crisis. Thus each of the casuists adopts an air of rectitude and reasoned and judicious compromise which seems admirably to fit life's hostility to perfection and to absolutes of all kinds. But each is a hollow fraud, and each is a brother casuist who defends his absolute individualism to the end. If Cohen, Priestley, and Dunsany[42] are right in believing that Blougram is Browning, then it must follow that the casuists are either all admirable men or that Browning was a very bad man indeed. It should prove instructive to examine the "Apology" in some detail as a means of settling this important question, not so much to prove that Blougram is Browning's most subtle casuist, as to refute the critical assumption that has plagued Browning scholarship for nearly a hundred years: namely, that Browning set no limits on individualism, counseled man to follow his own code, and denied the right of society to judge the individual by its standards.

The opening scene of "Bishop Blougram's Apology" casts grave doubts upon the integrity of the bishop's pursuit of truth. He has invited Gigadibs, the thirty-year-old unsuccessful journalist who regards Blougram as a hypocrite, to his sumptuous ecclesiastical quarters for dinner, good wine, and a candid examination of Gigadibs's convictions. Blougram is disarmingly candid in confessing his strategy of putting the journalist at a psychological disadvantage. Instead of meeting in a neutral place, perhaps a restaurant, the bishop uses his station and luxurious circumstances as a means of demonstrating that he has the approval of the world, whereas the penurious journalist has won only its contempt:

42. "Browning Is Blougram," *The Nineteenth Century and After, op. cit.*, pp. 175-177.

> . . . don't you know,
> I promised, if you'd watch a dinner out,
> We'd see truth dawn together?—truth that peeps
> Over the glasses' edge when dinner's done. . . .[43]

He implies that the truth becomes apparent when the dinner is excellent, the surroundings richly appointed, the wine admirable. He intends frankly to buy the good opinion of the journalist and says as much:

> Now's the time:
> Truth's break of day! You do despise me then.
> And if I say, "despise me,"—never fear!
> I know you do not in a certain sense—
> Not in my arm-chair, for example: here,
> I well imagine you respect my place
> (*Status, entourage,* worldly circumstance)
> Quite to its value—very much indeed:
> —Are up to the protesting eyes of you
> In pride at being seated here for once—
> You'll turn it to such capital account!
> When somebody, through years and years to come,
> Hints of the bishop,—names me—that's enough:
> "Blougram? I knew him"—(into it you slide)
> "Dined with him once, a Corpus Christi Day,
> All alone, we two; he's a clever man:
> And after dinner,—why, the wine you know,—
> Oh, there was wine, and good!—what with the wine . . .
> 'Faith, we began upon all sorts of talk!
> He's no bad fellow, Blougram. . . ."[44]

In passing it might be noticed that few passages from the literature of the world might be found to equal this in sheer bad taste, not in villainy, but in bald insensitivity and grotesque egoism. He candidly admits that he is playing a game with rules of his own choosing, and he will force his guest to play his game: "The hand's mine now, and

43. Ll. 15-18.    44. Ll. 20-39.

here you follow suit." It seems self-evident that if a man is really interested in seeing "truth dawn," he is morally bound neither to
stack the deck, nor to place his guest at a disadvantage—and Blougram
does both. To take a half-starved journalist and give him a bountiful
meal and expensive wines is not unlike the "good fat father/ Wiping
his own mouth, 'twas refection-time," bribing Lippo, starving on the
streets at the age of eight, to renounce the world and "swear to never
kiss the girls." Neither boy nor man, while starving, is a worthy opponent, but Blougram is bent upon winning, however much he must
violate the laws of courtesy, etiquette, logic, or simple morality.

In opening his argument Blougram states clearly the differences
that separate them: Gigadibs, in an article, has attacked the bishop's
insincerity and hypocrisy. The bishop founds his argument squarely
upon the testimony of success, as the world counts success. The
journalist is unknown, without position, status, or followers. The
bishop is midway between parishioner and pope. He can never become the pontiff, but he sees the hand of Providence in this limita-
tion, for if he should become pope, he would be at his "tether's
end," with no chance for further progress—a perfect example of sour
grapes. This argument is a distortion of Browning's view that one
must aim for the heights that are beyond his attainment in this
world. The fact that he cannot become pope, if he truly represented
Browning's position, should rather spur his energies and resolution
to be worthy of the office, to be qualified for the post, even though the
goal appears to be impossible of attainment. To say that to attain
the goal would preclude all further achievement is to distort Browning's idea of success. Blougram voices the view of the world, not of
Browning, who believed that the mere achievement of a title would
in no way stop advancement and growth. Indeed, the real test of a
man's development would come after attaining the office, not before.
He was fully aware that the popes, as the Pope in *The Ring and the
Book* observes, ran the gamut from total moral bankruptcy to spiritual excellence, and within the special temptations and opportunities
the office provides, a pope would have illimitable chance for spiritual
growth. Blougram, of course, is not concerned with spiritual growth,
but rather with worldly power. To him the office itself is the goal, not

the opportunity for service and selfless dedication, the new and end-less heights of spiritual attainment to scale. To see the office as an end to growth perfectly illustrates the stunted moral condition of the man. It is clear that his resignation is not at all based on the sober reflection that one is blessed in having unattainable heights to aspire to, which the papal office would deny him. He will eagerly accept any office that will further his worldly position, and if an office is shut to him, he will find the office undesirable. He is the contented man, Browning's picture of failure, the "low man" who "seeks a little thing to do,/ Sees it and does it. . . .":

> So, drawing comfortable breath again,
> You weigh and find, whatever more or less
> I boast of my idea realized
> Is nothing in the balance when opposed
> To your ideal, your grand simple life,
> Of which you will not realize one jot.
> I am much, you are nothing; you would be all,
> I would be merely much: you beat me there.[45]

Blougram's statement is one of contentment in having attained his goal. Unlike the grammarian, he has not aimed for the stars. Like Andrea he has compromised away any idealism he may have had, but unlike Andrea he is not honest enough to admit it. On the other hand, Gigadibs, who fancies that he has set for himself an exalted goal, has in reality no goal at all, for he has confused means with ends. He has made uncompromising idealism an end, whereas it is a means to an end; but in a world which denies all absolutes, it is a false ideal, wholly pernicious to man's growth through action, which it inhibits. Blougram's cynical opportunism is to be preferred to Gigadibs's paralyzing search for absolutes. Blougram defends the value of uncompromising compromise in pursuing the fruits of the world, always disguising his greed behind the mask of morality and practical adjustment to the laws of life. He has abandoned principle, but he is dynamic. He acts, and as long as man acts he is being tested

45. Ll. 78-85.

and given the chance to change and to grow. His philosophical position is preferable to that of Gigadibs, though his ethical one is inferior—but he has a chance to grow. The journalist's error is one of
defective judgment, not of contemptible ethics. His tragedy is that
he cannot act as long as he demands absolute faith as a condition of
accepting Christ, and with no action there can be no test and no
growth.

Blougram knows that the idealistic journalist is in a vulnerable
position, the most vulnerable position in life, for it denies life. The
bishop has looked forward to the unequal argument, for he is perfectly aware that his opponent has adopted an unworkable idealism
that cannot be defended. No man may set such conditions upon
life. In contrast Blougram's position is completely flexible. It is a
foregone conclusion that Blougram will win the debate, no matter
how knavish his principles may be, for the position of Gigadibs is
hopeless. He is like a man who refuses to eat until the world is freed
from all taint of corruption. But it does not follow, as has been assumed, that because the bishop bests the journalist in an unfair
fight, Browning gives his approval to either. Both are on unsound
ground, both are wrong, but only the bishop is contemptible. He is
intelligent and misuses his intelligence to distort the truth. Gigadibs
is not very intelligent, but he is honest up to his lights. He is a perfect opponent for an unscrupulous casuist, and Blougram thoroughly
enjoys his playing at cat-and-mouse with him.

Blougram, like Browning, abhors paralysis of will, whatever may
be the reason:

> No, friend, you do not beat me: hearken why!
> The common problem, yours, mine, every one's,
> Is—not to fancy what were fair in life
> Provided it could be,—but, finding first
> What may be, then find how to make it fair
> Up to our means: a very different thing!
> No abstract intellectual plan of life
> Quite irrespective of life's plainest laws,
> But one, a man, who is man and nothing more,

> May lead within a world which (by your leave)
> Is Rome or London, not Fool's-paradise.
> Embellish Rome, idealize away,
> Make paradise of London if you can,
> You're welcome, nay, you're wise.[46]

It should be emphasized that every syllable of these lines is consistent with Browning's most treasured beliefs. Such an apparent identity between Browning and Blougram betrayed Lord Dunsany and F. E. L. Priestley into concluding that the bishop and the poet were in fact the same. No tribute could be greater to Browning as a writer of casuistical verse than this, for if the critics themselves in the undisturbed quiet of their research are so deceived by the sophistical argumentation, how complete must have been the triumph over Gigadibs? The whole secret of Blougram's deceptive argument is to advance a valid principle, gain his adversary's assent to it, and then supply a non sequitur which skillfully conceals the lie.

To show how impractical Gigadib's uncompromising idealism is, Blougram likens life to an ocean voyage. In the "average cabin of a life" one is sorely limited, indeed cramped, for space. It is all very well to want to take along everything—to have all or nothing—but both Browning and Blougram argue that one must live within the limitations of life. To demand any kind of absolute is to be fatally mistaken. If one refuses to embark on the voyage of life until he has brought along everything that he believes might ideally be of value or delight, one stays on the pier and misses life; if he comes aboard "bare," petulantly refusing to bring anything if denied the privilege of bringing everything, he makes the voyage in lonely bitterness:

> And if, in pique because he overhauls
> Your Jerome, piano, bath, you come on board
> Bare—why, you cut a figure at the first
> While sympathetic landsmen see you off;
> Not afterward, when long ere half seas over,
> You peep up from your utterly naked boards

46. Ll. 86-99.

Into some snug and well-appointed berth,
Like mine for instance (try the cooler jug—
Put back the other, but don't jog the ice!)
And mortified you mutter, "Well and good;
He sits enjoying his sea-furniture;
'Tis stout and proper, and there's store of it:
Though I've the better notion, all agree,
Of fitting rooms up. Hang the carpenter,
Neat ship-shape fixings and contrivances—
I would have brought my Jerome, frame and all!"[47]

It should be noted that from first to last the bishop's only argument is that of tangible reward, physical comfort, and social position; and Browning, to keep the reader aware of the bishop's worldly nature—and it is worthy of another bishop who ordered on his deathbed a vulgarly grandiose tomb—interjects throughout the poem the asides about the wine, the ice, the comforts on every hand.

When Blougram pretends to an elaborate show of fairness in his argumentation, he is in fact being most ingeniously dishonest. He is on valid ground when he says that it is impossible to have a faith absolutely free from doubt. Man is mortal, and nothing mortal is pure: not truth, not doubt, not falsehood, and not faith. But when he says that he will throw overboard his dogmas, along with those of the journalist, as a means of arguing on equal terms, he is not, as he affirms, meeting his opponent "on your own premise." He disarms the journalist by a great show of throwing out his major weapon in argument: the dogmas of the church, built up over two thousand years in the arena of theological combat. But he does not in truth do so. He continues to argue from dogma, using every trick that will deceive and frustrate his opponent:

And now what are we? unbelievers both,
Calm and complete, determinately fixed
To-day, to-morrow, and forever, pray?
You'll guarantee me that? Not so, I think!

47.  Ll. 125-140.

> In no wise! all we've gained is, that belief,
> As unbelief before, shakes us by fits,
> Confounds us like its predecessor. Where's
> The gain? how can we guard our unbelief,
> Make it bear fruit to us?—the problem here.
> Just when we are safest, there's a sunset-touch,
> A fancy from a flower-bell, some one's death,
> A chorus-ending from Euripides,—
> And that's enough for fifty hopes and fears
> As old and new at once as nature's self,
> To rap and knock and enter in our soul,
> Take hands and dance there, a fantastic ring,
> Round the ancient idol, on his base again,—
> The grand Perhaps![48]

Blougram again argues by ingenious casuistry. He knows that in the mortal state man cannot find absolutes. Faith must be shaken by doubt, as doubt by faith, a belief that is a cornerstone in Browning's verse. He intends to present himself as eminently human, with just the proper minimum of doubt to disturb his faith, whereas in truth he is at the opposite pole: he is an unbeliever who argues that since life admits no absolutes, he must have some shred of faith in the warp and the woof of his doubt. He employs a fresh analogy to illustrate the uses of doubt. A road over a mountain may to a traveler walking upon it appear to be hardly a road at all, for it seems to be broken by slides and debris. But to the traveler yet on the plain below, the road is clearly a road and the breaks and debris count for nothing from his point of vantage:

> What if the breaks themselves should prove at last
> The most consummate of contrivances
> To train a man's eye, teach him what is faith?
> And so we stumble at truth's very test!
> All we have gained then by our unbelief
> Is a life of doubt diversified by faith,

48. Ll. 173-190.

For one of faith diversified by doubt:
We called the chess-board white,—we call it black.[49]

Here is a splendid statement of Browning's own view of faith, as seen in "A Death in the Desert" and elsewhere. No one can doubt that Browning shared this view and made it a rock for his whole spiritual belief. It is the use that Blougram makes of it that outrages Browning's belief, for the wily bishop argues that since the individual has free choice in seeing life as black or white or any intermediate shade of gray, it thus follows that it matters not at all how he sees life, how he views faith, or how he lives. This is a corollary that runs exactly counter to Browning, for it makes man's choices all alike in God's sight. Blougram forgets that man is free to make choices for one reason: so that he may be judged by the worth of his choices. Thus, Blougram speaks for all the critics who have held that to Browning there are no limits to individualism, no judgments to be pronounced on man's choices so long as he makes them of his own free will. This view makes a shambles of Browning's philosophy.

Blougram, in the figure of the road through life, is using an argument reminiscent of the outrageous Victorian explanation advanced by certain frightened divines to explain away fossils and the menace they seemed to offer to orthodoxy. God, so they argued, planted fossils in the rocks when he laid down the creation, spurious remains of genera that never existed, all as a means of testing man's fidelity in the face of such upsetting evidence—a fraud on the moral level of the Cardiff giant hoax. Life, in Blougram's view, is filled with apparent objections to belief, as a test; but the emptiness of the bishop is seen in his belief that it really does not matter whether one believes or disbelieves. All is one in the sight of God. The real difference is in what it secures for man's comfort and position on earth:

> "Well," you rejoin, "the end's no worse, at least;
> We've reason for both colors on the board:
> Why not confess then, where I drop the faith
> And you the doubt, that I'm as right as you?"[50]

49. Ll. 205-212.     50. Ll. 213-216.

Blougram replies in greater cynical candor than before. He agrees that "man" has freedom to make any choice he wishes, but a cabin-passenger, "The man made for the special life 'o the world," in reality dares not exercise such theoretical freedom, for in "Turning things topsy-turvy," man forfeits the favor of the world and its fruits as well. The world was not made by man, certainly not by Gigadibs or even Blougram, and the bishop, playing upon Browning's central belief that man must accept the conditions life imposed on him, affirms that he means "to take it as it is." These words might have been spoken by Browning, but not the corollaries that follow. Blougram accuses Gigadibs of finding "One and but one choice suitable to all;/The choice, that you unluckily prefer. . . ," and then blandly issues the stricture that conventional foundations and forms of religion must not be disturbed, much less attacked. Religion permits no tolerance for dissent, but it rewards the believer or the man who professes belief:

> I know the special kind of life I like,
> What suits the most my idiosyncrasy,
> Brings out the best of me and bears me fruit
> In power, peace, pleasantness and length of days.
> I find that positive belief does this
> For me, and unbelief, no whit of this.[51]

He likens his faith to his waking hours, his doubts to his dreams; but man is for life, not sleep. To be consistent, he says, the journalist should keep to his bed of doubt and never rise, and "Abstain from healthy acts that prove you man." The analogy is excellent, but its use is dishonest. Man must accept the challenge of life, leap from bed, and *do*. Blougram has learned the advantage of rising to meet life on its own terms, but he does not rise to *do* but to *get*:

> Well, and the common sense o' the world calls you
> Bed-ridden,—and its good things come to me.
> Its estimation, which is half the fight,

51.  Ll. 234-239.

That's the first-cabin comfort I secure:
The next . . . but you perceive with half an eye![52]

What the journalist must perceive, if he is deceived by the arguments of the bishop, is the glass of excellent wine in his hand, the luxurious surroundings, the sleek ecclesiastical jowls of the bishop, and the bellyful of excellent fare. Blougram would have concurred in Lippo's honest confession of his worldly frailties:

'T was not for nothing—the good bellyful,
The warm serge and the rope that goes all round,
And day-long blessed idleness beside!

Guido voices a similar philosophy, far more cynical and far less honest:

Enough of the hypocrites. But you, Sirs, you—
Who never budged from litter where I lay,
And buried snout i' the draff-box while I fed,
Cried amen to my creed's one article—
"Get pleasure, 'scape pain,—give your preference
To the immediate good, for time is brief,
And death ends good and ill and everything!
What's got is gained, what's gained soon is gained twice,
And,—inasmuch as faith gains most,—feign faith!"[53]

Guido's credo leads him to the block, but Blougram's very similar one leads him to pre-eminence within the bosom of the church. The difference lies largely in their cunning, not in their beliefs.

Since Blougram has so far devoted his argument to discrediting Gigadibs's fatal search for absolute idealism, he proceeds to the kill. If he can make his opponent retreat one inch, he can rout him from the field. If absolute idealism is fatal, it follows—so he argues—that a simple overabundance of idealism is bad, in every degree whatever. One must not, therefore, be overnice in his adherence to principle, especially concerning things important, *i.e.*, vital to one's station and preferment:

52. Ll. 264-267.      53. XI, 761-769.

Next, concede again,
If once we choose belief, on all accounts
We can't be too decisive in our faith,
Conclusive and exclusive in its terms,
To suit the world which gives us the good things.
In every man's career are certain points
Whereon he dares not be indifferent;
The world detects him clearly, if he dare,
As baffled at the game, and losing life.
He may care little or he may care much
For riches, honor, pleasure, work, repose,
Since various theories of life and life's
Success are extant which might easily
Comport with either estimate of these;
And whoso chooses wealth or poverty,
Labor or quiet, is not judged a fool
Because his fellow would choose otherwise:
We let him choose upon his own account
So long as he's consistent with his choice.[54]

Here is the ultimate liberalism in matters of faith and conduct. Man's freedom is tempered only by the likelihood of his suffering the world's displeasure and being denied the good things it offers. But once man has deliberated and made his choice, he must abide by his decision and not change, at least in matters of faith and marriage. Blougram begins to appear less latitudinarian than before, until one sees the monstrous cynicism in his caveat:

But certain points, left wholly to himself,
When once a man has arbitrated on,
We say he must succeed there or go hang.
Thus, *he should wed the woman he loves most
Or needs most, whatsoe'er the love or need—*
For he can't wed twice. *Then, he must avouch,
Or follow,* at the least, sufficiently,

54. Ll. 270-288.

> The form of faith his conscience holds the best,
> Whate'er the process of conviction was. . . .[55]

In a world without absolutes, man, he believes, still must find absolute consistency once his decision is made, even though, Blougram
admits, a man is not to be chided for marrying for personal advantage
or electing a form of faith—or pretending to, since it is all one—solely
for the goods that will accrue to him. Man is free to elect anything he
wishes, however ignoble and greedy his motives, so long as he does
not turn things topsy-turvy and so long as he abides by his choice.
He himself made the choice of the faith he was born in, the "most
potent of all forms/For working on the world"—that is, securing from
the world its comforts and delights. His choice has paid handsome
dividends, for "external forces"

> Exalt me over my fellows in the world
> And make my life an ease and joy and pride;
> It does so,—which for me 's a great point gained,
> Who have a soul and body that exact
> A comfortable care in many ways.[56]

Dunsany and Priestley argue that Browning's well-known love of the
creature comforts is ample evidence of his essential identification with
the worldly bishop, a most dubious conclusion. But no one, I think,
has argued that Browning also sought for ease of soul. Every line he
wrote is in some way related to his great doctrine that the function of
life is to test the soul, not by ease, but by trial and stress and endless
combat. The bishop wants ease of both soul and body, a view of all
others the most abhorrent to Browning, for it evades the dust and heat
of moral combat. Blougram's lust for power and domination, his crass
hypocrisy are everywhere visible in the following lines:

> There 's power in me and will to dominate
> Which I must exercise, they hurt me else:
> In many ways I need mankind's respect,
> Obedience, and the love that 's born of fear:

55. Ll. 289-297. The italics are mine.    56. Ll. 317-321.

> While at the same time, there's a taste I have,
> A toy of soul, a titillating thing,
> Refuses to digest these dainties crude.
> The naked life is gross till clothed upon:
>
> I must take what men offer, with a grace
> As though I would not, could I help it, take!
> An uniform I wear though over-rich—
> Something imposed on me, no choice of mine;
> No fancy-dress worn for pure fancy's sake
> And despicable therefore! now folk kneel
> And kiss my hand—of course the Church's hand.
> Thus I am made, thus life is best for me,
> And thus that I should be I have procured;
> And thus it could not be another way,
> I venture to imagine.[57]

And I venture to imagine that no greater insult could be offered to Browning than to say that since he is Blougram, he therefore was motivated wholly by self-interest, boasted of his pursuit of worldly gain and position, and luxuriated in a life of spiritual and bodily sloth. When Blougram affirms that his mastery of duplicity and deceit have yielded him a life of "ease and joy and pride," one must not forget that for nearly two thousand years in the Christian religion pride was the chief of sins and meant death to the soul. Throughout this astonishing passage Blougram illustrates the Biblical warning that there are paths in life that seem good to a man, but the way leads but to death. He has become a standard unto himself, and his religion is the daughter that greed begot upon pride. Everything is deceit and false seeming. The argument that because Browning was conspicuously anti-ascetic and loved good living, he must surely have approved of Blougram becomes absurd. Browning loathed dishonesty in all its forms, and hypocrisy, coupled with the sin of pride, is the most loathsome of all.

Blougram proceeds to answer an objection before it is made:

57.  Ll. 322-339.

Gigadibs, he says, will doubtless reply that all this reasoning may be very well for men of low tastes and corrupted principles, but if the bishop had "nobler instincts, purer tastes," he would not be content— a conspicuously valid objection, which strikes at the heart of the bishop's cynical position. Unperturbed, Blougram employs a daring strategy: he uses again Browning's sage belief in the necessity of fitting the infinite to the finite, and he distorts the meaning outrageously:

> But, friend,
> We speak of what is; not of what might be,
> And how 't were better if 't were otherwise.
> I am the man you see here plain enough:
> Grant I'm a beast, why, beasts must lead beasts' lives!
> Suppose I own at once to tail and claws;
> The tailless man exceeds me: but being tailed
> I'll lash out lion fashion, and leave apes
> To dock their stump and dress their haunches up.
> My business is not to remake myself,
> But make the absolute best of what God made.[58]

Joseph E. Baker comments upon the last two lines in this quotation: "Browning's own attitude is well summarized in these lines."[59] Indeed this is so, but not in the sense in which Blougram employs them. The poet repeatedly said that man must live as best he can within the limitations imposed upon life and upon him in particular; but the wily bishop has just said that he believes that if God made him greedy and power hungry, then he must fulfill God's plan for him by being greedy and power hungry. The sense in which Browning always uses this sentiment is, of course, opposed to this. If man has base instincts, he is tested by his decision to better himself and free himself from sin—or by his contrary decision. Since Blougram was born a lion, he must behave like a lion and destroy the lives of those who are by natural right his prey. He, then, is the king of beasts because he was born a beast. In this sense only has he

58. Ll. 346-355.
59. *Browning, "Pippa Passes" and Shorter Poems,* footnote, p. 345.

made the best of what God made him. This is the same gross distortion that is used by Prince Hohenstiel-Schwangau, when he justifies his vicious reign by saying that he was much too filial a son of God to attempt to remove any of the evil in the world which God had so carefully put here. Indeed, he went out of his way to add some more as a sign of his submission to the divine will. He has cheerfully and dutifully accepted his own avarice and dishonesty by remaining faithful to God's plan for him by devoting himself to avarice and dishonesty. The Prince admits that he has been singularly uncreative in matters of sin, but he has been fruitful in following all those the world affords. This is precisely what Blougram means. To make the best of the character he was born with is to follow his baseness wherever it will gain him an advantage. It is doubtful that Blougram ever in his life has done an evil deed except for personal gain. The bishop well knows that Christ said that if a man is to be saved he must be born again, which means much the same thing as to remake oneself, but Christ's meaning is not Blougram's.

The bishop proceeds to another deceptive analogy. If there are a million imbeciles who are easily imposed upon, there are perhaps a dozen men of taste, sophistication, and intelligence who know the way of the world, which is the way of the bishop. He says that they

> . . . know me, whether I believe
> In the last winking Virgin, as I vow,
> And am a fool, or disbelieve in her
> And am a knave,—approve in neither case. . . .[60]

These worldly men "See more in a truth than the truth's simple self,/ Confuse themselves." Here is Browning's belief that truth is infinitely complex, relative, and protean; but Blougram uses it to defend his hyprocrisy. No man can be absolutely sure that the winking Virgin is or is not a crude imposture contrived to compel the faith of the credulous. No man can attain absolute truth, and the fraudulent miracle, for which Blougram has nothing but contempt, may possibly be true, at least in part. In life there is no truth untainted by

60. Ll. 376-379.

error, and no error unrelieved by truth. Thus, he argues, since all is relative, what does it matter what one believes? All that matters is that one profess to believe something, and the wise man professes only what will work to his advantage. Only a fool is honest to his own hurt. Mr. Sludge, the medium, justifies his fraudulent seances by blandly affirming that since no deception can be absolute, his spurious contacts with the spirit world must have a grain of truth to leaven the lump of the lie. Once Blougram has established that absolute belief is impossible, he has the means, by conscienceless extension of the principle, of routing Gigadibs completely: "we can't believe, you know," he crows, "We're still at that admission, recollect!"

He admits that he has no desire to become a Shakespeare: "I prefer remaining my poor self. . . ." He rejects what he believes Gigadibs will urge, a philosophical principle dear to the heart of Browning:

> "But try," you urge, "the trying shall suffice;
> The aim, if reached or not, makes great the life. . . ."[61]

But the bishop has no desire to aim for the heights; he is content with his low and base aims and desires. He has what he wants. Shakespeare, he believes, if alive and in the prelate's shoes, doubtless would not write plays at all, but would "sit at home/ And get himself in dreams the Vatican," together with all tangible wealth pertaining to the office:

> Greek busts, Venetian paintings, Roman walls,
> And English books, none equal to his own,
> Which I read, bound in gold (he never did).
> —Terni's fall, Naples' bay, and Gothard's top—
> Eh, friend? I could not fancy one of these;
> But, as I pour this claret, there they are:
> I've gained them—crossed St. Gothard last July
> With ten mules to the carriage and a bed
> Slung inside; is my hap the worse for that?
> We want the same things, Shakespeare and myself,
> And what I want, I have. . . .[62]

61.  Ll. 490-491.      62.  Ll. 530-540.

In this blatant casuistry the bishop assumes that every man is, like him, a hypocrite who will lie and deceive for profit. Shakespeare, if he had the chance, would elect to be surrounded by beautiful books, bound in vellum, rather than write them, a dreary drudgery forced upon him in the fight against adversity. But he would have preferred to be sitting as the bishop is, a cool glass of claret in his hand, and the evidence of the world's esteem all about him. In the end all men want the same thing, he says, and what they want is success on the world's terms.

Blougram presses home the attack by insisting that Gigadibs is not merely impractical in his uncompromising idealism, but is destructive of God's test of man through doubt:

> Once own the use of faith, I'll find you faith.
> We're back on Christian ground. You call for faith:
> I show you doubt, to prove that faith exists.
> The more of doubt, the stronger faith, I say,
> If faith o'ercomes doubt. How I know it does?
> By life and man's free will, God gave for that![63]

This is a far cry from Browning's position. He never said that if doubt is a test, one should therefore find himself in a superior state of grace when he is as skeptical as mortal limitations permit. Blougram confesses that he has "Head-doubts, heart-doubts, doubts at my fingers' ends/ Doubts in the trivial work of very day,/ Doubts at the very basis of my soul. . . ." but his doubts, far from casting doubt on his sincerity, confer upon him, he believes, a special sanctity:

All's doubt in me; where's break of faith in this?

His point is not Browning's, that one should greet the doubts and frustrations of life with a shout of joy because of the renewed opportunity of gaining strength through trial. He explains away the very need to have faith at all. His faith is not strengthened by trial. It is sufficient, if you do not believe in Christianity, merely to wish that it were true:

63. Ll. 600-605.

> It may be false, but will you wish it true?
> Has it your vote to be so if it can?
>
> .   .   .   .   .   .   .   .   .   .   .   .   .   .   .   .   .   .
>
> If you desire faith—then you've faith enough. . . .

This is exactly the same as saying that if you are dishonest, you may continue unsullied by sin to embezzle, so long as you wish you could quit. He makes a particular point of acknowledging his debt to "man's free will" in arriving at his great truth. He believes that as long as a man freely elects a belief—or unbelief—his freedom as an individual removes all distinctions that may exist in vulgar minds regarding good and evil.

He proceeds to another of Browning's favorite premises: just as one must be denied the full sight of God and God's word—for the white light blinds mortal eyes—so "Naked belief in God the Omnipotent/ Omniscient, Omnipresent, sears too much/ The sense of conscious creatures to be borne." From this valid premise, he devises his usual form of non sequitur. If we are denied the vision of the white light of eternity, the creation is meant not to reveal God, but "to hide him all it can/ And that's what all the blessed evil's for." This is the equivalent of saying that since the full rays of the sun can blind, man is well advised to put out his eyes. The belief that all the evil is merely to hide God is merely an extension of Browning's belief that evil is a test of fidelity, of faith that does not die in spite of doubt and uncertainty.

Blougram is on solid ground when he says that "when the fight begins within himself,/ A man's worth something." The battle is to be prolonged through life. And through battle "the soul wakes/ And grows." But to the bishop, struggle is quite a different thing from what Browning meant. The bishop means not struggle, but surrender: "Who am I, the worm, to argue with my Pope?" There is no struggle, because one must give assent to things which fail to command his belief or respect. Today, he says, we have become callously indifferent to the Virgin's winks, which used to be a very live issue in matters of faith, but today "Men have outgrown the shame of being fools." If profit lies in paying lip service, pay it by all means, for since nothing is wholly right and nothing wholly wrong, nothing really matters except one's position in life. "Up with the Immaculate Conception, then," he says. Even this fiction we do not gag at, he affirms, shame being dead within us. When he says

> The sum of all is—yes, my doubt is great,
> My faith's still greater, then my faith 's enough,[64]

one is disarmed, and Priestley's and Lord Dunsany's case seems much strengthened. This appears to be the very spirit of Browning. But, as always, the bishop shows that his meaning is dishonest and time serving. He would rather die, he says, than show his fear that the "Naples liquefaction may be false." He "knows" it is, he makes clear, but he has learned, not the value of faith, but of expediency. If this palpable fraud is denied, then "To such a process I see no end"—i.e., once avow one's denial of the least part of belief, and everything goes, for nothing is more or less believable than this obvious deception. There must be total assent or none at all. The bishop has come full circle in his argument against the journalist for his insistence on absolute faith or none. The bishop is now demanding the same thing, except that he is not talking about real faith of the heart but mere assent by the mouth. In this unworthy aim he too demands absolutes, and his position has all the weakness of the journalist's, with hypocrisy as well. He freely admits that the journalist's position is as sound as his own, but there is always the ultimate issue of gain. Everything hinges on that, and his way pays off and the journalist's does not. Individualism and the right of each man to arrive at truth in his own fashion, which he urged earlier, are now forgotten:

> Clearing off one excrescence to see two,
> There's ever a next in size, now grown as big,
> That meets the knife: I cut and cut again!
> First cut the Liquefaction, what comes last
> But Fichte's clever cut at God himself?
> Experimentalize on sacred things!

64. Ll. 724-725.

I trust nor hand nor eye nor heart nor brain
To stop betimes: they all get drunk alike.
The first step, I am master not to take.

. . . . . . . . . . . . . . . .

Your taste's worth mine; but my taste proves more wise
When we consider that the steadfast hold
On the extreme end of the chain of faith
Gives all the advantage, makes the difference
With the rough purblind mass we seek to rule:
We are their lords, or they are free of us,
Just as we tighten or relax our hold.
So, other matters equal, we'll revert
To the first problem—which, if solved my way
And thrown into the balance, turns the scale—
How we may lead a comfortable life,
How suit our luggage to the cabin's size.[65]

Absolute conformity to all matters of dogma and faith is of the first importance in imposing on the gullible, for the greater power and glory of the church. The argument here has nothing to do with bringing the masses to faith, but much with bringing them to heel. This is really what counts to the bishop: power, place, and wealth—and whatever brings them about is right; and in the meanwhile the bishop is enabled to live a comfortable life:

Of course you are remarking all this time
How narrowly and grossly I view life,
Respect the creature-comforts, care to rule
The masses, and regard complacently
"The cabin," in our old phrase. Well, I do.
I act for, talk for, live for this world now,
As this world prizes action, life and talk:
No prejudice to what next world may prove,
Whose new laws and requirements, my best pledge
To observe then, is that I observe these now,

65. Ll. 740-763.

> Shall do hereafter what I do meanwhile.
> Let us concede (gratuitously though)
> Next life relieves the soul of body, yields
> Pure spiritual enjoyment: well, my friend,
> Why lose this life i' the meantime, since its use
> May be to make the next life more intense?[66]

Among the most frequently expressed ideas in Browning is the familiar concept that in the next life man will continue to strive for the heights he sought in life, to make for the great goals that proved too high. Thus, this life's aspirations determine the quality of man's life in the next world. Browning unfailingly interpreted this as an illimitable opportunity for growth and glorious attainment of worthy goals, but Blougram employs the belief to justify his worldly life. When Browning said that this life should be lived intensely, he did not mean that one should seek sensuality and domination. Man is judged by the quality of the goals he seeks, but Blougram is a complete utilitarian and denies that aspirations differ in quality. When individualism serves his purpose, he is a passionate partisan in its favor, but when it does not, he denounces it in righteous indignation.

Blougram next uses Browning's belief that man must comport himself within the limitations of life, living as mere man must in his struggle toward perfection. In the bishop's version, however, this comes out somewhat altered: to accept the laws of life becomes the justification for accepting the way of the world, its grossness, its luxury, its Mammon worship:

> I'm at ease now, friend; worldly in this world,
> I take and like its way of life; I think
> My brothers, who administer the means,
> Live better for my comfort—that's good too;
> And God, if he pronounce upon such life,
> Approves my service, which is better still.

66. Ll. 764-779.

> If he keep silence,—why, for you or me
> Or that brute beast pulled-up in to-day's "Times,"
> What odds is 't, save to ourselves, what life we lead?[67]

Blougram is not the first man to affirm that God is pleased with his devotion to the things of the flesh, but he is one of the most consumately clever in his casuistical affirmation. He is a master of verbal deception. When all is said, unless God specifically thunders a denunciation from the heavens, "What odds is 't, save to ourselves, what life we lead?" We are now back again to the belief in individual choice, which constitutes a denial of values, "Since there's no higher law that counterchecks." This is precisely the view of individual liberty that is widely held to be Browning's own view.

Since "Men are not angels, neither are they brutes," Blougram is imperfect in his view of truth. Blougram pays lip service to the ideal that man is tested by his pursuit of truth, but, in reality, man, he says, is not expected to work very hard at it:

> There needs no crucial effort to find truth
> If here or there or anywhere about. . . .[68]

The implicit premise here is that if God fashions man between angel and brute, man, being free, may cite his kinship with the brute as a justification for a half-hearted search for truth. Since there can be no absolutes, it matters not whether man elects to take his place near the brutes in the grand scale, since man's will is free. And if truth is not so very important—and it must not be so for absolute truth is carefully denied us—it follows that to lie in a good cause (for place, power, and position) is eminently justifiable. In matters that he finds unbelievable, he admits that he swears "to each detail the most minute," even if he sees nothing at all. The word *truth* is slippery, and the bishop makes it more so by a semantic shift, asking the journalist "In truth's name, don't you want my bishopric/ My daily bread, my influence, and my state?" This is *truth* to the bishop.

67. Ll. 797-805.    68. Ll. 858-859.

The great test of truth is how it pays off. If it does not pay at all, it is an untruth.

Gigadibs, paralyzed by his impractical desire for absolute truth and faith, may plead a theoretical superiority over the bishop, but "in truth's name" he knows that he is pursuing a will-o'-the-wisp. He may fancy that it pleases him to "graze through life without one lie":

> But do you, in truth's name?
> If so, you beat—which means you are not I—
> Who needs must make earth mine and feed my fill
> Not simply unbutted at, unbickered with,
> But motioned to the velvet of the sward. . . .[69]

Near the end of the monologue, the bishop makes it unmistakably clear that he knows his words have been a shocking confession of moral bankruptcy. He is under no illusion that what he has said justifies his worldly grossness, nor indeed has he tried to justify his sanctity or spirit. He has frankly argued that hypocrisy pays excellent dividends, and his contempt for the position and influence of the journalist is seen in the bald candor of his confession:

> But you—the highest honor in your life,
> The thing you'll crown yourself with, all your days,
> Is—dining here and drinking this last glass
> I pour you out in sign of amity
> Before we part forever. Of your power
> And social influence, worldly worth in short,
> Judge what's my estimation by the fact,
> I do not condescend to enjoin, beseech,
> Hint secrecy on one of all these words!
> You're shrewd and know that should you publish one
> The world would brand the lie—my enemies first,
> Who'd sneer—"the bishop's an arch-hypocrite
> And knave perhaps, but not so frank a fool."
> Whereas I should not dare for both my ears

69. Ll. 891-895.

> Breathe one such syllable, smile one such smile,
> Before the chaplain who reflects myself—
> My shade's so much more potent than your flesh.[70]

If Browning identifies himself with Blougram and if he finds in Blougram's argument justification for his way of life, why does the bishop admit that if the journalist were a person of any social standing whatever, whose words might win the credence of the world, he, Blougram, would never have dreamed of making such a confession of moral weakness and hypocrisy? If the bishop in truth believes that his argument vindicates his way of life, it seems unlikely that he would make such an elaborate show of not enjoining the journalist to secrecy. Instead, he does not do so, for he knows that if Gigadibs should tell the world, the story would be too monstrous for credence. His enemies, he knows, already have found him out and know that he is too dishonest, shrewd, and self-seeking to expose himself to anyone as a moral pauper. His extraordinary rudeness to his guest, whom he dismisses with a sneer of contempt, is an index to the bishop's heart, which may help one to understand the conclusion. Browning, in his own person, says that the bishop believed only half of what he spoke and used argument as whim dictated, saying true things but calling them by wrong names. This is an excellent picture of the heartless casuist, who exhausts his invention to confuse, to deceive, and to frustrate. A prince among individualists, he thoroughly discredits individualism, that is, untempered by moral sense and love.

If any doubts remain concerning the character of Blougram and the nature of his monologue, it is useful to contrast it with the wise humanity of the old Pope, who speaks so very eloquently on the need of evil and doubt as a test of man's moral judgment, and who reaffirms the duty of each man to solve his moral problems in the arena of life. He is the perfect spokesman of Browning's philosophy of individualism, for he knows that each man is tested *alone,* and he is tested not against a rigid scale of conduct, but against his own capacities and his use of them in specific situations. Man must solve his

70.  Ll. 916-932.

own problems, the Pope knows, but he is tireless in warning of the perils awaiting the lawless individual who puts no bounds to his self-reliance. Man has a right to seek for a code of moral conduct, but he is ultimately judged on the code he finds. Freedom in Browning is never license. Even though a man has no desire to speak falsely, he must forever slip into the penumbra that on earth darkens truth. The man who elects total self-sufficiency of moral judgment often is deceived. Man, "Whose appetite if brutish is a truth," is peculiarly subject to self-deception, mistaking base lusts and urges for pure truth, as did Guido—and I fancy that the Pope would have found the shoe to fit Blougram perfectly. The test ever is to seek good, to strive for excellence, whatever the temptation or the trial:

> Was the trial sore?
> Temptation sharp? Thank God a second time!
> Why comes temptation but for man to meet
> And master and make crouch beneath his foot,
> And so be pedestaled in triumph? Pray
> "Lead us into no such temptations, Lord!"
> Yea, but, O Thou whose servants are the bold,
> Lead such temptations by the head and hair,
> Reluctant dragons, up to who dares fight,
> That so he may do battle and have praise![71]

There is an apparent paradox in the Pope's statement which cannot lightly be explained away. It is justifiable for man to pray for immunity to temptation, as the Lord's prayer directs, the Pope says. But the bold, those eager for the battle with Satan and confident of their power to conquer, should welcome temptation and eagerly close with it in combat. But Browning never counsels man to seek out temptation, to expose himself to evil; the Pope implores God to lead the dragon to the bold warrior. The very avoidance of evil is a triumph over it. The belief that Browning in his exuberance advocated indulgence in sin as a means of fulfilling God's plan is simply not to be found in Browning. It may be all very well for the

71. X, 1178-1187.

man certain of victory over temptation to seek out the dragon for combat, but what of those who are not St. George? It is precisely these men for whom the test has the most validity, for the issue is in doubt. But in reality life is not this simple and clear-cut. There is never a battle in which the issue is not to some degree doubtful, nor is there a temptation which must inevitably be sought out and overcome, for if not met at all, it is then no temptation. If a man wins a thousand contests with evil, he may fail the thousand and first trial; and if a man has lost an equal number of battles, he may win in the next encounter. Life is never predictable. No one can foretell the issue of a battle, not the bystanders and not the principals. The unbeaten gladiator may flee from the arena tomorrow, and David may slay Goliath. Each day brings a new test and a clean slate, and the triumph of yesterday is forgotten today:

> White shall not neutralize the black, nor good
> Compensate bad in man, absolve him so:
> Life's business being just the terrible choice.[72]

The terrible choice is made doubly terrible because no choice can be absolutely perfect—of course, there is the small comfort that no choice can be wholly wrong; unluckily, in the test of life this comfort is at best academic: man's acts are tested by absolutes. The Pope finds Caponsacchi a splendid "warrior priest," whose performance under stress he vastly approves, but with reservations:

> Nay, Caponsacchi, much I find amiss,
> Blameworthy, punishable in this freak
> Of thine, this youth prolonged, though age was ripe,
> This masquerade in sober day, with change
> Of motley too,—now hypocrite's disguise,
> Now fool's-costume. . . .[73]

The Pope is not dismayed by the fusion of good and evil, for he well knows that the long succession of the popes themselves has been a chronicle of hate, greed, and violence. What matters the garb of

72. X, 1231-1233.    73. X, 1123-1128.

Caponsacchi when he heard "the first moan of the martyr-maid/ At the uncaging of the beasts," so long as he ripped it off the better to fight the good fight and "leaped over post and pale/ Right into the midcirque, free fighting-place"? The curtain and counterpane and coverlet which Fra Lippo ripped to form a ladder similarly went in a worthy cause, although his methods may be subject to censure. Life to Browning is of never-ending fascination, for it is never predictable and nothing that happens is exactly like anything that went before. The Pope, while finding fault with Caponsacchi, nevertheless asks where were "the men-at-arms with cross on coat" whose duty it was to leap into the arena to do battle for Pompilia against the lions of oppression. They were "Aloof, bewraying their attire," and they are the true sinners. In other arenas and at other times they may have fought valiantly, but in this crisis they were found wanting, and the least likely of heroes emerged, the dandyish priest "In mask and motley, pledged to dance not fight." Nowhere is there the suggestion that the priest would have the praise of God or of the Pope if he had courted temptation, picked a fight, or turned loose the lions on hapless Pompilia for the glory of saving her in the nick of time. God alone must bring the temptations to us, for he makes the test of life, not man.

The Pope does not fail to see that as all the principals in the sordid drama are tested and in the reckoning won or lost before God, so he himself is being tested. The issues before him are of life and death, and he is old, judged by some as being "of wellnigh decayed intelligence," and the evidence is a rotten fabric of contradiction, bias, and perjury. He is limited in intelligence, insight, and strength, just as all men are, and the sanctity of his position cannot be depended upon to give him either guidance or immunity from error. He is at times nearly overwhelmed by the evils of life and the endless war against them, and he knows that it is the worst form of perversity to think that a man should deliberately seek out temptation in order to cover himself with glory in the encounter. God supplies the test:

> I can believe this dread machinery
> Of sin and sorrow, would confound me else,

> Devised,—all pain, at most expenditure
> Of pain by Who devised pain,—to evolve,
> By new machinery in counterpart,
> The moral qualities of man. . . .[74]

The law of life is that man boldly pursue truth, with due regard to every aid that is available to him. Never must his heart sink under the burden of the test, nor must he in pride lead himself into temptation, under the illusion that he cannot fall into error. That man's freedom is always to be within prescribed limits—or rather that man is tested according to whether or not he remains within these limits—the Pope makes clear. In the early Christian days man was granted the thrill of dawn, the clear light of faith, which "set man's step/ In the true way," and, the old Pope adds: "A way wherein it is ordained he walk. . . ."

As the earth puts forth more blandishments, comforts, and temptations, the test of life becomes more severe, for the light of earth obscures the light of heaven, and greater powers of discrimination are demanded. The early martyrs and saints could hardly misconceive the light, but modern man is blinded by the plenitude of radiance:

> Till at last, who distinguishes the sun
> From a mere Druid fire on a far mount?
> More praise to him who with his subtle prism
> Shall decompose both beams and name the true.
> In such sense, who is last proves first indeed;
> For how could saints and martyrs fail see truth
> Streak the night's blackness? Who is faithful now?
> Who untwists heaven's white from the yellow flare
> O' the world's gross torch, without night's foil that helped
> Produce the Christian act so possible
> When in the way stood Nero's cross and stake,—
> So hard now when the world smiles "Right and wise!"[75]

This warning against worldliness—which might be taken as a direct indictment of Blougram—is less pressing upon the conscience of the

74. X, 1370-1375.     75. X, 1817-1828.

Pope than is a far graver danger yet: the danger of unquestioning assurance, undisturbed faith, serene unquestioning acquiescence; for the Pope, speaking outrageous heresy, affirms Browning's militantly anti-Catholic belief that the greatest of God's tests of man is faith through doubt. Man must doubt; he must question the most fundamental matters of theology and morals, for his spiritual health depends upon it. Man today, the Pope says sadly, has become smug and complacent, and he regards moral conduct and belief as the best of all investments, sure to pay off a thousandfold. The real test is whether a man will elect the right belief and the right course of conduct because it is right, without the crass expectation of a certain reward. If man knows that a shilling's worth of self-denial infallibly brings a thousand pounds' worth of eternal reward, wherein is he tested? No whit. No more than Lazarus was tested after his return from the grave with the vision of the Absolute burned upon his brain. Man must have doubt to be tested. He must not bet on a sure thing:

> Is it not this ignoble confidence,
> Cowardly hardihood, that dulls and damps,
> Makes the old heroism impossible?[76]

But the Pope has a heartening vision—entirely unpapal—of a brighter future when doubt and therefore the test will be reinstated and man will shed

> This torpor of assurance from our creed,
> Re-introduce the doubt discarded, bring
> That formidable danger back, we drove
> Long ago to the distance and the dark?
> No wild beast now prowls round the infant camp:
> We have built wall and sleep in city safe:
> But if some earthquake try the towers that laugh
> To think they once saw lions rule outside,
> And man stand out again, pale, resolute,
> Prepared to die,—which means, alive at last?[77]

76. X, 1842-1844.        77. X, 1848-1857.

The Molinists will introduce helpful heresy to challenge faith and will seek to substitute in man's mind man's God for God's God—the ultimate heresy. Many will meet the challenge successfully and rise to greater heights of faith, but others, failing the test, will sink to the old depths, and will, like Bishop Blougram,

> Rest upon human nature, settle there
> On what is firm, the lust and pride of life![78]

The Pope is Browning's greatest spokesman for the poet's conception of individualism. He knows that each individual is called upon to meet the challenge alone, as an individual, but the Pope never says that each man is sovereign in matters of faith and morals. Man is not necessarily rewarded because of the individualism of his beliefs, or indeed their eccentricity. He gives full approval to those who say "I know the right place by foot's feel,/ I took it and tread firm there: wherefore change?" That the Pope does not by any means indicate that one's sovereign guide to life is private impulse he states directly:

> Here comes the first experimentalist
> In the new order of things,—he plays a priest;
> Does he take inspiration from the Church,
> Directly make her rule his law of life?
> Not he: his own mere impulse guides the man—
> Happily sometimes, since ourselves allow
> He has danced, in gayety of heart, i' the main
> The right step through the maze we bade him foot.
> But if his heart had prompted him break loose
> And mar the measure? Why, we must submit,
> And thank the chance that brought him safe so far.
> Will he repeat the prodigy? Perhaps.
> Can he teach others how to quit themselves,
> Show why this step was right while that were wrong?
> How should he? "Ask your hearts as I ask mine,
> And get discreetly through the morrice too;

78. X, 1885-1887.

> If your hearts misdirect you,—quit the stage,
> And make amends,—be there amends to make!"[79]

Such a man of obedience to impulse will counsel others to follow his example, just as the wicked Abate argues, defending his choice in life of "the lowest of life's appetites" as equal to any other choice, since in reality all choices are of identical value, each individual making his own life choice. There is indeed no disputing about tastes, he argues. In weary disgust, the Pope laments:

> At last we have the instinct of the world
> Ruling its household without tutelage. . . .[80]

It seems impossible to reconcile these lines—spoken with rejection by the Pope—with Pigou's statement that in life, according to Browning, "We know by direct perception what our duty is" and that the poet's "optimistic faith seems to indicate that the moral law is not only indiscoverable but nonexistent." All men need know is that God's purpose is beneficent and marches steadily onwards towards its glorious goal regardless of what we do, collectively or individually: "It is a matter of complete indifference whether we be selfish or self-sacrificing, for a Marcus Aurelius or a Francis of Assisi is no more acceptable to God than a Borgia or a Catiline. . . ."[81]

Two conclusions are forced upon one when he reads words of such fatuity: one is that the author failed to exercise ordinary diligence in reading evidence; and the second is that the vitality of Browning's poetry must be truly remarkable to have withstood the march toward oblivion to which such judgments seem to consign it. Pigou in effect says that (1) each man (according to Browning) is absolutely a free agent in forming his own moral codes in life; (2) but this fact is of little significance or reality because there is no such thing as a moral code in the first place; (3) the plan of life, which has no function, is a blind clockwork, click-clacking its way to a foregone and unchangeable goal; and (4) the most towering villainy and the most consummate goodness are alike in God's eye and equally acceptable in his

79. X, 1904-1921.    80. X, 1986-1987.    81. Pp. 105-106.

sight—as unflattering a view of God's character as imperfect man can devise. This view of Browning has brought forth much bitter fruit in the Browning scholarship in our century. It is unique, not in its substance, but in its affirmation of as libelous an untruth as a poet ever withstood. These fictions have become commonplace in the criticism of the poet, and the result has been unhappy. Browning was a poet with a moral message, an ethical view of life, which underlies every line he ever wrote, directly or indirectly; and to say that in spite of the apparent evidence, he in reality had no faith in the superiority of the good life over the bad, or of the desirability of good rather than evil, or of the moral acumen of God, is the equivalent of discovering in the *Summa* of St. Thomas Aquinas clear support of the Black Mass. The whole range of criticism supplies few twins of these beliefs.

William F. Revell, a contemporary of Henry Jones, voiced one of the earlist assumptions that Browning denied any hierarchy of values in life, especially in the matter of truth, which by definition embraces ethics and moral values:

> All talk of truth strictly so called, is irrelevant; nothing is left but myriads of differing human experiences which we may disregard but no established truth. One system of truth is just as good as another; all systems are in fact only summaries of differing or contradictory human experiences, which have an equal validity. If grass is green to you, it is green; if red, it is red; if blue, it is blue. . . .
>
> And one surmise is as good as another. At least to choose between them would imply some standard of judging between them; and according to Browning there is none.
>
> No words can be used which state with greater plainness and emphasis than these which we have quoted, how complete is the disqualification which attaches to the human intellect as a faculty for the attainment of knowledge and truth. . . .[82]

82. *Browning's Criticism of Life* (London, 1892), p. 61.

The quotations to which he refers are those from "A Pillar at Seb-zevar," used by Jones and by most later critics as well who seek to establish the alleged anti-intellectualism of Browning. As I have ex-plained at some length, and with specific attention to these quota-tions, in my *Triple Soul: Browning's Theory of Knowledge*, not one line in "A Pillar at Sebzevar" is in opposition to the intellect or to the value of man's pursuit of truth. The issue throughout is that to-day's knowledge is tomorrow's fallacy, simply because man must progress towards perfect truth through endless steps of partial truth. The injunction of Ferishtah to "Wholly distrust thy knowledge" means only that man must be eternally vigilant to discover the error lurking in man's apparent "truth"—for only through such intellectual and scholarly determination to arrive at the best "truth" permitted us can man progress.

# CHAPTER III

# BROWNING'S OPTIMISM

NOTHING HAS BEEN WHICH SHALL NOT BETTERED BE
HEREAFTER. . . .

—"Parleying with Gerard de Lairesse"

The long-entrenched belief of Jones, Pigou, DeVane, and Raymond—a view which, as I have indicated, has dominated Browning criticism in this century—that the poet denied the existence of
evil by showing it to be only "stuff for transmuting"—was the
fountainhead of the almost uncontested truism that Browning was
an optimist who assumed the duty of explaining away every evil of
life. Jones discovers a corollary to his axiom that Browning denied
the existence of evil: he was motivated, Jones affirms, from first to
last in his career, not so much to write poetry as to prove "with the
persistence and impressive candour of a scientific investigator" that
his view of· evil fits every circumstance and fact in life:

> He stakes the value of his view of life on its power to meet *all*
> facts; one fact, ultimately irreconcilable with his hypothesis,
> will, he knows, destroy it.[1]

As evidence, he quotes the passage from "A Bean-Stripe":

> "All the same,
> Of absolute and irretrievable
> And all-subduing black,—black's soul of black
> Beyond white's power to disintensify,—
> Of that I saw no sample: such may wreck

1. P. 100.

My life and ruin my philosophy
To-morrow, doubtless. . . ."[2]

And Jones adds that "to justify God, he had to justify *all* His ways to man; that if the good rules at all, it rules absolutely; and that a single exception would confute his optimism."[3]

I choose to ignore Jones's statement that Browning, who, according to Jones, despised the intellect and science, applied himself in the manner of a scientific investigator, but I do wish to call attention to one of his beliefs that does great violence to one of Browning's first premises: in life nothing by definition can be absolute ("None of these absolutes therefore," exclaims Ferishtah): not evil, not good, not truth, not falsehood. The theme of *The Ring and the Book* is to establish this thesis: everything is imperfect in this world—all except God and the plan of life he made, which challenges man to oppose evil. As I have explained before, the quotation which Jones uses means simply that in life the affairs of men are like a checker-board—half the squares black, half white—and a man may elect to determine which is the primary shade and which its obverse. There is no "absolute and irretrievable black," but on the other hand there is no white in a like condition. It does not at all mean, as Jones thinks, that if Browning could discover a single instance of absolute, unrelieved *real* evil, his whole philosophy must fall, but that if he could find a single instance of evil which fell outside God's plan of working good *through* evil—i.e., if he could find an instance of evil that God did not plan, but which happened in spite of God and thus served no purpose—then his philosophy must fall. There is an unbridgeable gulf between these two positions. The one denies the reality of evil; the other accepts it as real and finds its function in life.

Jones's next quotation in support of his thesis is even less germane and proves nothing to the point. He quotes from *Christmas-Eve:*

So, gazing up, in my youth, at love
As seen through power, ever above

2.  Ll. 199-205.      3.  P. 101.

All modes which make it manifest,
My soul brought all to a single test—
That he, the Eternal First and Last,
Who, in his power, had so surpassed
All man conceives of what is might,—
Whose wisdom, too, showed infinite,
—Would prove as infinitely good;
Would never, (my soul understood,)
With power to work all love desires,
Bestow e'en less than man requires. . . .

. . . . . . . . . . . .

No: love which, on earth, amid all the shows of it,
  Has ever been seen the sole good of life in it,
  The love, ever growing there, spite of the strife in it,
Shall arise, made perfect, from death's repose of it.
And I shall behold thee, face to face,
O God, and in thy light retrace
How in all I loved here, still wast thou![4]

This says very fittingly that his faith is founded on the belief that God made the scheme of things without blunder or miscalculation and that he provided for man's needs, the greatest of which is love, and next is strength and judgment to meet the issues of life with all diligence. It says nothing whatever about Browning's compelling need to prove that *all* evil—every instance of it—must upon examination be proved nonexistent. In fact, the line, "The love, ever growing there, spite of the strife in it," perfectly expresses Browning's faith in the necessity of strife and evil in life—and it must be real, as I have tried to establish above. Jones insists that a single instance of "real" evil "would confute his optimism."[5]

Fortified somehow by this quotation, Jones affirms that "this knight of the Holy Spirit goes forth over all the world seeking out wrongs"—to prove them not wrongs but illusory wrongs, good masked by false appearance. "I believe further," he maintains, "that it was in order to justify this conviction that he set on his quest. . . .

4. L1. 329-365.    5. P. 102.

He conceives it as his mission to prove that evil is 'stuff for transmuting,' and that there is nought in this world."[6] Thus he seeks out
evil in its own haunts and creates such a monster—second in villainy only to Iago, Jones believes,—as Guido, only to prove it again
"stuff for transmuting." Having all but exhausted overt evil, moral
depravity in its physical manifestations, Browning courageously
launched out into a new realm of evil: subtle, ratiocinative argumentation in defense of evil: "Having, in *The Ring and the Book*, chal-
lenged evil at its worst as it manifests itself practically in concrete
characters and external action, and having wrung from it the victory
of the good, in *Fifine* and in his other later poems he meets it again
in the region of dialectic."[7] He now ventures into a realm never before investigated by the poet, so Jones believes, in which his struggle
is with something far more insidious even than Guido, "the subtle
powers of darkness grown vocal and argumentative." Since Don
Juan, a heartless villain, is arguing casuistically to prove how great
will be the virtue of seducing Fifine, Jones exercises the most incredible ingenuity in explaining Browning's theme in a manner that
will not do violence to Jones's contention that the poet spent his life
in denying the existence of evil. His explanation is exactly what his
initial fallacy forces upon him: Fifine is not evil and adultery with
her is really virtue all the while, although to uncultivated observers,
adultery may appear to involve some evil. In short, Jones finds for
the plaintiff, Don Juan, who we discover is right all along. Jones
quotes the lines:

> That, through the outward sign, the inward grace
>    allures,
> And sparks from heaven transpierce earth's
>    coarsest covertures,
> All by demonstrating the value of Fifine.[8]

This is Don Juan speaking, be it recalled, not Browning, but Jones,
forgetting this, concludes: "Within his scheme of the universal good,

6. P. 102. For a balanced view, see Philip Drew, "Henry Jones on Browning's Optimism," *Victorian Poetry*, II (1964), 29-41.
7. P. 107.        8. P. 107.

he seeks to find a place even for the gypsy creature. . . ." The quotation, although it signally fails to establish Browning's defense of Fifine or Don Juan or adultery, perfectly establishes Don Juan's opinion of the value of Fifine—in bed.

One of the greatest misfortunes to beset Browning, as I emphasized earlier, has been the persistent and wrong-headed identification of the poet with the creatures he creates. He is everywhere considered to be Don Juan and Bishop Blougram and others, and, appalling as this error is, it persists. This practice is almost time-honored, lamentable as it is. Philip H. Wickstead perhaps best expresses the catastrophic lengths to which such an indefensible practice can be carried:

> Whether he [Browning] has any definite theory of conduct may well be doubted, for a theory of conduct could hardly be dissociated from a theory of society, and of that there is scarcely a trace to be found in Browning; but he evidently recognizes principles of a personal conduct, not differing greatly from those of other high-minded men amongst his contemporaries. His system of religion, however, his theory of life, and his principles of conduct, are far from allowing full scope to his vast energy of sympathy and exuberance of thought. He can sympathise, sometimes subtly, sometimes passionately, with systems of religion as remote from his own as those of Caliban and Johannes Agricola. He can adopt with complete *abandon* a theory of life as unlike his own as that of Count Guido Franceschini or the soliloquising brother in the "Spanish Cloister."[9]

This is one of the most extraordinary pieces of criticism extant. Wickstead assumes that Browning must approve and embrace all the beliefs and acts of all his characters, not excluding Guido. Thus it follows that he cannot have "any definite theory of conduct," and if one accepts Wickstead's premise, it is certain that he does not indeed. Wickstead has by no means exhausted his critical talents:

9. "Robert Browning," *Contemporary Review*, LXXXIII (January, 1903), 86.

Once more, then, how does he get room for all his sympathies without violating his systematic scheme?

He finds the escape he needs by dramatic self-identification with all manner of "Men and Women." This enables him to be as irresponsible as he chooses. He may fling himself without reserve into the position of Caliban, and may freely indulge under some assumed character in speculation which he would have to check, qualify and balance at every turn, if he were treating them with reference to his general scheme. . . .

Thus Browning may expatiate to his heart's content, without being responsible for anything which he does not choose to mark with his sign manual.[10] Wickstead goes beyond a mere identification of Browning with all his villains and their villainy, through which he experiences a vicarious joy. Browning, it seems, paid little more than lip service to virtue and secretly loved vice, especially if pursued with manly dedication:

There is often moral exaltation but there is seldom ethical enthusiasm, or even a sound moral indignation in Browning's work. Caponsacchi's denunciation of Guido has more of virulence than of proper indignation in it; and it is convincing only dramatically. Browning sympathizes too much with vice and evil passion of every kind, is too thoroughly convinced that it is human, is, in a word, too much interested in it, to experience any moral repulsion. Pity and tenderness he has in abundance, and precious indeed are these; but they are not everything, and sometimes this absence of repugnance becomes painful to us. Connected with the want of ethical earnestness is the absence of everything approaching to social enthusiasm. There is no resentment of social wrong, no vision of the kingdom of heaven on earth, to be found in Browning's poetry.[11]

The perversity of this judgment leaves one speechless. Browning's presentation of evil characters is successful *only dramatically,* in-

10. P. 87.      11. P. 96.

deed! Wickstead represents Victorian criticism at its worst, with its "we-are-not-amused" abhorrence of life, which is illustrated by his repudiation of *The Inn Album* because it simply is un-British: " . . . the vulgarities of "The Inn Album" are unrelieved by any accompanying sense of expanding sympathy or intelligence. That such a man should have seduced such a woman and imposed himself as a hero on the "Boy" is wholly incredible, when we are asked to accept the story as a piece of contemporary English life."[12]

Henry Jones, with similar logic, argues that since the cornerstone of Browning's life and works is that

> *God's in his heaven,—*
> *All's right with the world!*

then somehow the evil of a whore must be denied and the erotic adventures of an unprincipled rake must be freed from the untenable charge of evil. He insists that the purpose of *Fifine* is not to present "an exhibition of the argumentative subtlety of a mind whose strength has been lawless, and which spends itself in intellectual gymnastics," but it is "to try those fundamental principles on which the moral life of man is based; *i.e.,* 'all's right with the world.'" The reason for this emphasis, of course, is that, according to Jones, optimism must fall if one evil is found to be real. Wickstead found Browning's picture of evil altogether so real that Browning must have been vicious to draw it with such fidelity to fact; but Jones finds that Browning presented no evil at all, but merely its facsimile. Henry Charles Duffin, who believes Pippa's song to be a fair account of Browning's optimism, is aware of the implications of his belief: "Browning's thinking about evil is initiated by the assumption that whatever is is right." Duffin's failure to understand that to Browning things are "right" only because they are wrong and because they challenge us to right them is seen in his statement: ". . . if it is right to alleviate that form of evil called pain, why was it said [by Browning] to be wrong to try to eradicate evil itself?"[13] The answer is simple, as I have explained earlier: "to eradicate" evil, as Browning uses

12.  P. 88.      13.  P. 233.

the word, is to remove it entirely, root and branch, leaving a world free of evil for all time, and, thus, a world robbed of its capacity to test man. Duffin, like Jones, warmly defends Pippa's song as speaking Browning's philosophy of optimism and finds fault with the critics who attribute the song only to Pippa, who clearly must speak Browning's sentiments, just as everyone else does, including Ottima and Sebald and the despicable Bluphocks. Charles Dickens is rarely charged with embracing the sentiments of Fagin, and Henry Fielding is not often thought to pursue as an ideal the Greatness of Jonathan Wild; but Browning is regularly charged by grave critics with shameless approval of the basest lies and misdeeds of Prince Hohenstiel-Schwangau, whom he despised, and of Don Juan, whom he loathed. Duffin, however, says:

> Browning's personal happiness and his religious conviction that all is for the best constitute the joint basis of the optimism for which he was long loved and is now, in an age of passing shallow cynicism, disliked. Optimism is a philosophy, a considered judgment on life, often, though not necessarily, associated with happiness, which is mainly a matter of temperament. In the well-known lines from *Fra Lippo,* the middle sentence, 'the world's no blot nor blank . . . it means good'—are the judgments of optimism. Optimism looks at life, weighs it impartially up, and concludes that it is good, that is, with a reasonable preponderance of good, or with the good mattering more than the bad. When the pessimist says he has dug deeper and found the source of tears the optimist delves one yard below his mines and blows him to the moon. Optimism is a philosophy: pessimism is an angry reaction to life; but both are tenable and respectable. It is cynicism that is a disease and a sin. . . .

. . . It was with Pippa's briefest song that he first infuriated the unco-guid.

> *God's in his heaven—*
> *All's right with the world!*

They were driven to explain that this was the ignorant little mill-hand's idea, not the poet's, as they had fobbed Keats's epigram off on the urn. But Browning, like Keats, spoke from the heart. . . . It is a simple deduction from intelligent observation of the natural phenomena enumerated that the world is God's creation, whence all must—ultimately—be right with the world, and all would, on a fine spring morning that was a whole holiday, be entirely right here and now not only to a little mill-hand but to any adult as sane and fit as Browning, and willing to sink logic in intuitive apprehension.[14]

Duffin's tribute to Browning as sane and fit is entirely perceptive, but his conviction that Browning embraced the whole of Pippa's song in its literal sense is based on the same fallacy that mars the judgments of Jones, Pigou, DeVane, Raymond, Baker, and others: the belief that a philosophy of optimism cannot stand in the presence of one clear instance of *real* evil in the world. Duffin forgets that Pippa's song is not a mature philosophical credo, but is rather a simple, joyous outburst of a pitiably overworked and underprivileged waif on the glorious morning of her one holiday in the year. Her acute awareness of the universal malignity of evil is really the burden of the whole drama, not her denial of evil. She knows how short and transitory is her one day of freedom from the mill, with its sorrow and its cruelty and its hopelessness—making it a microcosm of the world's evil. Thus, she will play a mad game for the twelve hours of holiday: she will pretend that she is not Pippa, who has known such sorrow, and she will in fancy live other lives in other happier habitations. At the end of her day of magic, which she hoped she could protract forever in the ineffable bliss of escaping from her own world of misery, she returns to her dreary chamber in weariness and depression:

> The summer of life so easy to spend,
> And care for to-morrow so soon put away!

14.  Pp. 238-239.

> But winter hastens at summer's end,
> And fire-fly, hedge-shrew, lob-worm, pray,
> How fare they?[15]

After summer comes winter, and after holiday comes twelve months of suffering, and she knows that the firefly and shrew and worm must suffer and die. "How fare they?" This is the ancient query of all those of gentle heart, those abused by the world, those perplexed by the irrationality of evil and suffering, and it is the implied question in Browning, the gentle-hearted observer of human misery. Pippa knows of the illicit love of Ottima and Sebald, and she knows it is evil, not an illusion of evil, for evil has been her familiar since her birth:

> For, Day, my holiday, if thou ill-usest
> Me, who am only Pippa,—old-year's sorrow,
> Cast off last night, will come again to-morrow:
> Whereas, if thou prove gentle, I shall borrow
> Sufficient strength of thee for new-year's sorrow.[16]

It is not only her personal sorrow that depresses her; she is fully aware of the canker in the bud of life and love, life's crown:

> Lovers grow cold, men learn to hate their wives,
> And only parents' love can last our lives.[17]

If Pippa's famous song is so universally held to represent Browning's view of life, one wonders by what sophistry her song outside Luigi's tower is not equally held to illustrate his measureless pessimism:

> *Among the rocks his city was:*
> *Before his palace, in the sun,*
> *He sat to see his people pass,*
> *And judge them every one*
> *From its threshold of smooth stone.*
> *They haled him many a valley-thief*

15. IV, 247-251.    16. Introduction, 11. 30-34.
17. Introduction, 11. 163-164.

*Caught in the sheep-pens, robber-chief*
*Swarthy and shameless, beggar-cheat,*
*Spy-prowler, or rough pirate found*
*On the sea-sand left aground;*
*And sometimes clung about his feet,*
*With bleeding lip and burning cheek,*
*A woman, bitterest wrong to speak*
*Of one with sullen thickset brows:*
*And sometimes from the prison-house*
*The angry priests a pale wretch brought,*
*Who through some chink had pushed and pressed*
*On knees and elbows, belly and breast,*
*Worm-like into the temple,—caught*
*He was by the very god,*
*Who ever in the darkness strode*
*Backward and forward, keeping watch*
*O'er his brazen bowls, such rogues to catch!*
*These, all and every one,*
*The king judged, sitting in the sun.*[18]

It seems apparent that no one should be held responsible for the utterances couched in the songs he sings, in the tub or out; and if Pippa is to be absolved, surely Browning must be. No one has discovered in this ditty concerning the assizes—wherein the king judges robbers, murderers, pirates, sheep-stealers, confidence men, rapists, and church-breakers—evidence that Browning's view of life is Hardy's or Housman's, and one wonders why not.

*Fifine,* from the beginning, has fulfilled the misgivings that Browning felt about the probable reception of the poem. In a letter to Furnivall, he expressed his doubts that, human nature being what it is, people would believe that the purpose of the poem "was to show merely how a Don Juan might justify himself, partly by truth, somewhat by sophistry." J. M. Cohen, as if to enforce the cogency of Browning's doubts, finds the critics of the twentieth century guilty of failing to make a closer identification of Don Juan and

18.  III, 179-203.

Browning. Mrs. Sutherland Orr summarizes a typical reaction to the poem in her review of Mr. Mortimer's "Note on Browning," in the *Scottish Art Review,* December, 1889, in which the author finds *Fifine* a twin of "The Statue and the Bust," which "prescribes action at any price, even that of defying the restrictions of moral law." Or, to put it more directly, Browning "in the person of Don Juan, defends a husband's claims to relieve the fixity of conjugal affection by varied adventure in the world of contemporary loves."

The fact that every shred of evidence from Browning's life is a denial of this interpretation has done nothing to deter the critics from Mortimer on. Swinburne, W. O. Raymond notes, found *Fifine* to be Browning's "true province," and, I have no doubt, he assumed it was written in the boudoir of the lipless Faustine or Dolores. Browning's disavowal of Don Juan's position, made to Furnivall in the clearest terms, superfluous as it was, did not silence those who fancied they had discovered the leering satyr under the robes of the priest. Mrs. Sutherland Orr, a close acquaintance of the poet, encouraged the identification of the poet with Don Juan by remarking mysteriously that the poem was marked by "some leaven of bitterness" and by the judgment that he wrote it as a plea for understanding of the man who seeks relief from conjugal boredom:

> The author put forth a plea for self-indulgence with a much slighter attempt at dramatic disguise than his special pleadings generally assume; and while allowing circumstances to expose the sophistry of the position, and punish its attendant act, he does not sufficiently condemn it. But, in identifying himself for the moment with the conception of a Don Juan, he has infused into it a tenderness and a poetry with which the true type had very little in common, and which retard its dramatic development. Those who know Mr. Browning, or who thoroughly know his work, may censure, regret, fail to understand *Fifine at the Fair;* they will never in any important sense misconstrue it.[19]

19. Mrs. Sutherland Orr, *Life and Letters of Robert Browning,* revised by Frederick G. Kenyon (Boston, 1908), p. 283.

Since Mrs. Orr wrote these words the critics have apparently been wholly bent on misconstruing *Fifine,* chiefly through attempts to perfect the identification of Browning and Don Juan. Perhaps it is corrective to read in Mary Gladstone's *Her Diaries and Letters* that "somewhere about 1885, sitting next him [Browning] at dinner, he talked to me about La Saisiaz, and later, dining with the Bensons at Lambeth, he talked again about his poems, and told me about Mrs. Sutherland Orr (Leighton's sister) and what an astonishing interpretation of him was her handbook."[20] Browning's wry comment should serve to lay to rest the sturdy fiction that since Browning read the handbook in manuscript, it must be understood to be fully authorized and oracular. Indeed, Mrs. Orr's works constitute a tribute to the breadth of his mind, his tolerance of subjective judgment, and his forbearance in rectifying critical eccentricity.

William O. Raymond sagely repudiates the absurdity of identifying Don Juan and his creator "in any literal sense," but he does find in *Fifine* "the reflection . . . of a mood which has its inception in the poet's personal history," *i.e.,* in the familiar and painful episode of his proposal to Lady Louisa Ashburton:

> Amidst a maze of intermingled truth and sophistry, the cardinal motif of *Fifine,* as it revolves about Elvire and the gypsy, is the subtle lure that lawlessness has in linking itself with the desire for change, with the impulse that represents, in a left-handed way, freedom of the spirit as attained through an outburst into a realm of fresh thought and emotion.[21]

As evidence, he quotes the lines

> Frenetic to be free! And, do you know, there beats
> Something within my breast, as sensitive?—repeats
> The fever of the flag? My heart makes just the same
> Passionate stretch, fires up for lawlessness,
>       lays claim
> To share the life they lead. . . .[22]

20. Lucy Masterman, ed. (New York, 1930), p. 454.
21. *The Infinite Moment and Other Essays in Robert Browning,* p. 113.
22. VI, 43-47.

If this were Browning speaking, as he does in *Sordello,* the evidence would be weighty, indeed, that he is allowing Don Juan to speak for him, and the whole character of the poem would be altered from what it is, a brilliant experiment in case making, to a really shocking confession of moral insecurity. If Browning broke off the painful relationship with Lady Ashburton sometime in the fall of 1871, after she had refused his offer of marriage as a convenience to Pen, his composition of *Fifine,* begun in December of the same year, must, as Raymond says, bear some of the marks of this traumatic experience, but whether it reveals his unconscious desire to castigate himself for his faithlessness to his dead wife may be questioned. It must not be forgotten that *Fifine* is the last of a series of casuistical works, each concerned with what a scoundrel might say in his own defense. "Bishop Blougram's Apology," which appeared in *Men and Women* (1855), is a study of a brilliant, oily hypocrite; "Mr. Sludge, 'The Medium,'" which appeared in *Dramatis Personae* (1864), is a study of a cynically fraudulent medium; Guido, in *The Ring and the Book* (1868-1869), is a study of a malignant casuistical murderer; *Prince Hohenstiel-Schwangau,* which appeared in December, 1871, the month in which Browning began work on *Fifine,* is a study of an unprincipled political tyrant, Napoleon III, after his flight to England. Each of these casuists is a moral derelict, without a shred of real integrity or honor which he will not sacrifice in the cause of self-interest. The evil of Don Juan is so repellent in its Belial-like unctuousness that one has no difficulty in determining his moral stature. Both the reader and Elvire see through his shoddy casuistry immediately. Generations familiar with Bishop Blougram, who is far cleverer and more intelligent than Don Juan, may be confused by his sinuous arguments, but the patent dishonesty and irrationality of Don Juan is everywhere seen. Certainly Elvire is not deluded for one moment. It is preposterous to suppose that she could be deceived into suspending her judgment of her lecherous husband or be persuaded that his lustful acts are "stuff for transmuting." This being the case, it seems in the highest degree absurd to suppose that Browning would hold himself up to ridicule as a lecher. Perhaps the most telling argument against the thesis that Browning identified himself with Don Juan is the nature of his proposal to Lady Louisa. It was couched in terms the least consonant with the traditional character of Don Juan that one can conceive: far from being a romantic, dashing, impetuous affair of love and the flesh, the terms of his proposed marriage had all the detachment of a writ of *habeas corpus* or a codicil to a will. He offered to marry her, not for love, but for the benefits that would accrue to his son. Why, then, is he widely considered to have pilloried himself in the character of Don Juan as a particularly devious adulterer, a man lost to honor and shame? We know that by the time of the composition of *Fifine* he was experiencing a furious distaste for Lady Louisa and referred to her in the most insulting terms. On April 4, 1872, he wrote to Edith Marion Story, daughter of the American sculptor, William Wetmore Story, about his unhappy proposal of marriage and the resulting quarrel with Lady Ashburton:

> I suppose that Lady A. did not suppress what she considered the capital point of her quarrel with me when she foamed out into the couple of letters she bespattered me with,—yet the worst she charged me with was,—having said that my heart was buried in Florence, and the attractiveness of a marriage with her lay in its advantage to Pen—two simple facts,—as I told her,—which I had never left her in ignorance about, for a moment, though that I ever paraded this in a gross form to anybody is simply false. . . .[23]

Although these words seem lacking in the true note of sexual passion and abandon and appear markedly deficient in casuistry, Raymond discovers that

> As a matter of fact, Don Juan is but a stalking-horse for the reflections of the poet on the inconstancies of sex, leading up to consideration of the Bohemian instincts of life in general, the

23. *Letters of Robert Browning, Collected by Thomas J. Wise,* ed. Thurman L. Hood, p. 155.

relation of reality to illusion and of truth to falsehood. The dramatic element in *Fifine* is a shadow rather than a substance.[24]

That this view did not originate with Raymond may be seen in a review of *Fifine*, which appeared in 1872:

> This poem has been even more unfortunate than the other poems of Robert Browning. Others have not been understood: this has been most woefully misunderstood. Some critics of high authority and unusually clear insight have pronounced it, in effect, to contain Browning's views of the higher realities. How absurd and unfortunate such a statement is appears from the fact that it is really Don Juan's defense of his own fickleness and wide-ranging affections.[25]

The words of this anonymous reviewer, perceptive as they are, have done nothing to disabuse the critics of their cherished belief that in Don Juan the hitherto well-hidden rot in Browning's soul is finally seen.

Both Raymond and Jones hold that *Fifine* illustrates Browning's strenuous dedication to optimism, because, supposedly, Don Juan speaks the truth about sexual adventurism and establishes against all comers that it is—like all other illusions of evil—"stuff for transmuting." The truth of the matter is, of course, that nothing whatever can be adduced from *Fifine* about Browning's optimism or pessimism, for he was writing a dramatic account of a liar's defense of his wretched life, not revealing the author's lust. Arthur W. Symons warned of the pitfalls awaiting those who embrace the biographical fallacy:

> I think that at the root of much mistake lies an erroneous conception of the basal principle of Browning's art. Browning is a dramatic poet, and as such he gives utterance dramatically, to all manner of opinions; his own opinions, for the time, being held in abeyance or merged in those of the imaginary typical

24. *The Infinite Moment and Other Essays in Robert Browning*, p. 120.
25. *Old and New*, VI, No. 5 (November, 1872), 609.

personality to which he acts as mouthpiece. We must guard against estimating him by any such purely dramatic passages. To do so were to insult the poet's art as well as to misjudge his religious belief. Browning himself warns us against it, when he says that his poetry is 'always dramatic in principle, and so many utterances of so many imaginary persons, not mine.' In fact, we can get at his real opinions and beliefs by taking as our standard the poems (such as *Christmas-Eve* and *Easter-Day, Epilogue to Dramatis Personae, La Saisiaz*, etc.) which are written manifestly *in propria persona*, and applying that standard to the impersonal dramatic process. The mistake lies in reversing the process.[26]

It is not my intent to discuss in detail the theme of *Fifine* and the underlying principle that Browning uses, for I have done so in my *Triple Soul*. It is enough to say here that the false identification of Don Juan and Browning stems from the fact that the poet permits his casuists free reign in using every argument, including the poet's own most cherished principles, which they push to extremes and distort for purposes of deception. One of the most difficult tests in life, Browning knew, is to detect the misapplication of principle in a bad cause. Certainly Browning, who wrote "House" and "Shop" to discredit self-revelation of the artist, would have been horrified to find himself believed to be the original of Don Juan, who uses every trick and deceit of which only a sick mind is master. Raymond, however, disagrees. He believes that "The arguments of this prince of casuists are not those of an unbridled libertine seeking to condone his debauchery, but those of a man of sensibility, endowed with great gifts of thought and poetic feeling."[27] I do not suppose that Elvire would necessarily agree. Elsewhere Raymond, curiously enough, refers to Don Juan as "the arch-voluptuary Don Juan."

If, however, as Raymond and Jones both say, Browning meant quite literally that "All's right with the world," and all evil is mere

26. "Robert Browning as a Religious Poet," *The Wesleyan-Methodist Magazine*, VI (December, 1882), 943-947.
27. *Ibid.*, p. 120.

illusion, it seems strange that *Fifine,* assuming that it really represents Browning's preoccupation with illicit sex, reveals Browning's "dark mood," as Raymond labels it. Why should his mood be dark if he held, with Don Juan, that evil is "stuff for transmuting," the phrase he uses to impose on Elvire's credulity? Indeed, if Browning's optimism was so total as to deny all evil whatever, where would be the evil in his proposal to Lady Louisa, or in Don Juan's lustful casuistry, or in Browning's alleged enthusiasm for adultery? The question reveals the untenable position that Jones's and Raymond's premises place one in. Browning was an optimist, but an optimist does not deny the very existence of all evil and place the hand over the eyes before the pain of life simply to force all things to conform to the "All's-right-with-the-world" principle. Jones is more extreme than Raymond in his insistence that Browning's philosophy could not tolerate any evil whatsoever. Raymond, indeed, finds *Fifine* one of the few notable instances where Browning's optimism failed him.

If Raymond finds traces of a dark mood in *Fifine,* John Meigs Hitner, in *Browning's Pessimism in "Fifine at the Fair,"* considers Browning, as revealed in the character of Don Juan, to be as pessimistic as Schopenhauer and as deistic as Voltaire. Hitner finds *Fifine* to represent not only Browning's lascivious longings but those of all other men. In a similar vein, he dismisses Browning's entire literary output after 1872 as "an old man's vanity." Hitner makes no distinction between Don Juan and Browning, and he attributes the sentiments and moods of the one to the other. He finds that Browning early in the poem "becomes personally involved"—whatever that means—and "he grows more intense and pessimistic":

> Yet there is sound sense in some of Juan's perambulatory sophisms, and beneath the surface foam and froth of casuistry there flows a dark undercurrent of pessimism. Such a versified philosophy is a sharp branching off from the mainstream of Browning's usual optimism. The poem is conceived in a spirit of defeatism and is dedicated to a sense of failure and frustration.[28]

28. P. 3.

Hitner finds evidence not only of a dark mood in *Fifine*, resulting from the Lady Ashburton affair, but the full-blown phallic fixation, already mentioned. In the poem Browning refers to the Druid's stone as a symbol of a mystery hidden in the mists of antiquity which yields its secrets as well to guesswork as to science. Hitner discovers the stone to be a phallic symbol:

Only the imperishable Druid monument of long ago, with its enduring message of phallicism, can tell man about truth. The phallic stone makes no false promises in dream and therefore is the ultimate reality.[29]

Hitner gives no evidence from the poem or elsewhere in support of this electrifying assertion, apparently assuming that everyone knows that a Druid monument is always a phallic symbol, that a phallic symbol can, of course, tell man about truth, and that if it makes no false promises in dreams, it therefore must be the ultimate reality. If the Ancient Mariner's ship, as Arthur Wormhoudt[30] assures us, supplies us evidence of the homosexual character of the poem, since the vessel is equipped with both a hold and a mast, Hitner's discovery should not unduly dismay one—but it does. At least he does not find the evils of Don Juan's desires to be "stuff for transmuting." Hitner discovers abundant evidence of Browning's pessimism in the "pedestrian" Alexandrine meter, which keeps the poem "down to earth," to match his mood, an explanation which seems to suggest that the classical Greeks must have been victims of a settled depression. Perhaps the most notable characteristic of Hitner's criticism is that little or no evidence is supplied to support the most alarming of judgments, like the following:

He is appalled and desolated that death, disease, and disaster are realities and seem to dominate life. He has lost his youthful vigour and his former animal excitability has cooled down. Gone

29. P. 9.
30. *The Demon-Lover: A Psychoanalytical Approach to Literature,* New York, 1949.

is his healthy toughness; he has become soft. The pride of life and the glory of the world have shrunk to the vanishing point in his eye, and the poet-philosopher has shrivelled to the melancholy metaphysician. Having no invisible means of support, he is impoverished spiritually. His naturalistic look at life ends inevitably in desolation. His sadness lies at the heart of any purely agnostic scheme of philosophy. . . .[31]

Hitner is on more solid ground in his belief that "The Householder" is singularly dour: "There is no escape except through death," he affirms, but he also believes that "In *Fifine phallicism* is the answer to the body's needs, and death is the answer to the soul's."[32] He objects to the final line as being "glib and inconsistent" with the "mood of frustrated emotion": "I end with—Love is all, and Death is nought! quoth She." I suspect that his real objection to this line is that it does violence to his tortuously wrought thesis. If the Householder is Don Juan, as the context makes clear, one must assume that after Elvire's disappearance Don Juan suffered remorse, which may or may not have led to his reform. In any event he seems to have learned Browning's great lesson, that love is the meaning of life—not lust, not adultery, not phallicism—and the final line is perfectly relevant and certainly not flippant. From one point of view "The Householder" seems pessimistic and grim, for it reveals the dreary days of loss he experienced after the death of his wife—and one cannot help comparing his plight with Browning's lonely days in London after 1861—and it takes heroic imagination to fancy that Browning would agree that the pain of these days was an illusion. But, properly looked at, this conclusion may be considered one of the most genuinely optimistic poems in his canon. The true theme is not the defeatist commentary on the futility of life that Hitner believes it to be, but rather it is a joyous epiphany of growth and fulfillment, for it embraces the vision of the enduring power of love. It is fully Christian and is no more a pagan hymn to the phallic pillar than is The Sermon on the Mount. In his vision Don Juan dies and joins his beloved wife and finds that pursuit of phallicism

31. Pp. 57-58.    32. P. 56.

and adultery is a kind of spiritual death, not the answer to man's needs. Love renders death nought, for death is the gateway to the greater life and endless love.

Hitner's failure to understand that the last line, to which he objects, is really the point of the poem is forgotten when one reads his judgment on Browning's style in *Fifine:*

> His use of poetically beautiful words is more or less accidental; if the metre or the rhyme suggests a certain word, it is used; otherwise not. Most poets have certain favourite words which they guard with their poetic lives, but to Browning one word appears as good as another.[33]

And Browning said that this earth could provide no example of absolute error!

Frances Theresa Russell in 1927 was among the first of the critics to prophesy that Browning was soon to be subjected to psychoanalytic criticism, which usually entails wholesale discovery of neurosis, unhappiness, and pessimism. Since the high tide of Browning-the-missionary criticism, she says, criticism has strewn the cultural beach with enough material to last the Freudians for all time: "So great a change has recently occurred . . . that the time seems ripe for the *Zeitgeist* to manifest itself in a Cynic's Calendar for Browning."[34] She herself takes a few initial steps in this direction by proposing the thesis not only that Browning was a pessimist, but that "In quality, the pessimism is the more sincere and spontaneous, the optimism labored and rationalized":

> From the youthful melancholy of *Pauline* to the aged sadness of the *Epilogue* to *Ferishtah's Fancies,* the poet pours forth a fairly steady stream of testimony to the unlivableness of life. His indictments are both specific and general, and are filed against both camps in the cosmic battle—the visible pygmy, Humanity, and the hidden giant, Fate.[35]

33. P. 22.
34. *One Word More on Robert Browning* (Palo Alto, 1927), p. 132.
35. P. 49.

She discovers in *Paracelsus* the theme that she believes Browning intended to illustrate: "Life is a poor cheat, a stupid bungle, a wretched failure, and he for one protests against it and hurls it back in scorn. With equal scorn he hurls back also the sustaining solace of immortality. Why should this world be only a makeshift, a mere foil to some fine life to come?"[36] Proof of her belief may possibly be found in the extraordinary ingenuity that Browning exercised his whole life long to conceal any evidence that might support it. She lifts from context the familiar cry of Paracelsus, who, in pursuing knowledge at the expense of love, finds that life is a lonely wasteland and that "mind is nothing but disease/ And natural health is ignorance," affirming that this is a fair statement of Browning's pessimism, a notable example of the biographical fallacy, compounded with misinterpretation of Paracelsus' vision of his sin in seeking absolute knowledge at the expense of love. She also finds in the poem the depressing theme that "We may be God's creatures . . . but it is certain that He takes no pride in us. . . . Blind and endless is the struggle with evil, futile the frenzy to instruct those who lack the capacity to understand." And in Paracelsus' eloquence "over the fallacy of a beneficent Providence," she finds Browning's own beliefs, for "Paracelsus is but a transparent mask for the youth of Camberwell. . . ."[37] Browning wrote the poems in an astringently pessimistic mood, typical, of course, of all his moods, properly understood: "Not more bitter is Thomas Hardy over the treatment of his Tess by the President of the Immortals than is this medieval rebel over a world of Durbeyfields." It should be recalled, however, that in the poem, Festus and Michal, the married pair who represent perfect balance of complementary qualities, are serene and happy, for they represent the life of wholeness and sanity and love. Paracelsus and Aprile, the poet, represent hubristic imbalance, and they pay the price exacted of such reckless pride.

*Pippa Passes,* she notes, carries the unanswerable indictment of pessimism, for she calls attention to a parade of adultery, murder, ingratitude, cruelty, lust, and malignity. So likewise does *The Ring*

36. *Idem.*      37. P. 49.

*and the Book,* she adds, and the *Epilogue* includes the fullest indictment of all: "Is not that final *Epilogue* the last word? Years before the poet had said: 'I shall know, being old.' Now that he is old, what does he know? Quite literally, he does not know what he is talking about. His subject is himself and his career in the next life. As to the first, the portrait drawn is so subtly specious, mistaking as it does disposition for character and accomplishment, that it is invalidated as a trustworthy report. The second is a concluding instance of his habit of accepting hope for certainty."[38]

One wonders how she could have failed to see that her charges admirably support the view that Browning was indeed an optimist. The charge that he did not know what he was talking about may be charitably dismissed as irrelevant and without any real meaning. To say that facing death his theme is himself and his survival is to prove his optimism, not his pessimism, for is his picture of himself not one which leads him assuredly to believe that he will survive and "strive and thrive" forever? Whether his estimate of himself and his next life is valid is of no consequence at the moment; the fact that he confidently affirmed his unshakable belief in his worth and his certain survival is. To form the habit of "accepting hope for certainty" may not measurably heighten one's stature as a philosopher or thinker, but it does not support the charge of pessimism. I should say that Miss Russell's position is that any man who faces the reality of life is a pessimist. Browning loved to scent out life, its evil and its good, and thus is in the direct line of Chaucer, Shakespeare, and Fielding—and their keen-eyed awareness of evil has not made them appear to be pessimists. Can anyone read *The Canterbury Tales,* with their immortal gallery of scoundrels, rogues, and petty villains, and call Chaucer a pessimist? No work ever written is so full of the *joie de vivre,* light-hearted delight in the simple fact of existence as this grand and heartening chronicle. But on this pilgrimage—which is life in small—are a depraved and rascally miller, a foul and lustful and hypocritical monk; a fraudulent merchant; a fornicating friar; a piratical and murderous shipman; a lecherous wife; a truly aban-

38. Pp. 51-52.

doned pardoner, and others chiefly notable for human frailty, among a minority distinguished by luminous virtue. Can anyone who has read the *Tales* deny that with all the villainy (which surely excels even that in *Pippa Passes*) the pilgrimage remains perhaps the single most inspiriting, enlivening, and heartening account written on the life of man? No one ever put down these tales without feeling the better for them and the more alive to the fascination of the gift of life. As Browning said of the "Old Yellow Book," "the thing's restorative":

> The Book! I turn its medicinable leaves
> In London now till, as in Florence erst,
> A spirit laughs and leaps through every limb,
> And lights my eye, and lifts me by the hair,
> Letting me have my will again with these
> —How title I the dead alive once more?[39]

Is this the true ring of weary pessimism, dispirited *Weltschmerz*? It is rather the lusty, hearty sound of the happy, healthy man who has a thirst hydroptic for life.

Frances Russell believes that the optimistic poems and passages "have been allowed by default" and that Browning "will now have to start living them down," a puzzling judgment in view of her arraignment of him for being steeped in pessimism. The reason his optimism offends modern readers, she says, is that his *"aes triplex* of happy environment, buoyant disposition, and naïve theology" jars upon ears attuned to the several varieties of wasteland, from Dreiser through Henry Miller. "Since life for you never was reduced to its lowest terms," she charges, "you naturally are not qualified to grapple with ultimates." This is one of the judgments of memorable imperception on Browning. It seems that Browning is so pessimistic and dark in outlook that modern readers are offended by his optimism. His preoccupation with such sordid affairs as appear in the "Old Yellow Book," which so jaundiced his outlook on life that a spirit of laughter leapt through every limb, lightened his eye, and lifted his hair in sheer joy, clearly tars him with the brush of pessimism, but at the

39. *The Ring and the Book,* I, 766-771.

same time his fortunate life insulated him from life's evils and made him a naïve optimist. His theology, she affirms, is ninety-five per cent Christianity, five per cent pure Browning.

Far closer to the truth about Browning's attitude toward life is William Lyon Phelps's essay "Browning, Schopenhauer, and Music":

> Schopenhauer was the greatest pessimist, and Browning the greatest optimist, of the nineteenth century, yet they both believed that behind all the phenomena of existence—originating, controlling, supporting, and driving all things that appear to the senses—was the supreme force, the ultimate reality, which both called Will. To Schopenhauer this Immanent Will (as in Thomas Hardy's *Dynasts*) was Unconscious, totally unlike anything called Providence. To Robert Browning (as to Lotze) the Immanent Will was not only intelligent, but it was Conscious Love.[40]

Henry Jones devotes two chapters in his *Browning As a Philosophical and Religious Teacher* to a searching study of Browning's optimism. The second chapter, entitled "Optimism and Ethics," is one of the most formative and seminal critical discussions on Browning written in the last century or in this. It seems apparent that this chapter must have been a decisive part in prompting William Clyde DeVane, in *The Victorian Poets: A Guide to Research,* to pronounce Jones's book as still authoritative. Certainly there is no doubt that Jones's words directly influenced Pigou, DeVane, Raymond, Joseph E. Baker, Richard Altick, and others, directly or indirectly. I should like to examine Jones's thesis with care, for few scholars have probed the nature and the implications of Browning's optimism and the clash between his optimism and his ethics, which Jones finds in Browning to be a head-on collision:

> But now comes the great difficulty. How can the poet combine such earnestness in the moral struggle with so deep a conviction of the ultimate nothingness of evil, and of the complete victory of the good? Again and again we have found him pronounce

40. *North American Review,* CCVI (October, 1917), 623.

such victory to be absolutely necessary and inevitable. His belief in God, his trust in His love and might, will brook no limit anywhere. His conviction is that the power of the good subjects itself to its authority.[41]

Jones's point is most important. Why, indeed, should Browning regard the struggle against evil to be of such transcendent importance, when evil is ultimately nothing—so that the struggle is a make-believe —and the triumph of good is complete and inevitable regardless of how the fight is conducted, or whether it is conducted at all? Where is the victory over a phantom enemy when the only possibility is victory? This is the dilemma forced upon us, Jones discovers, for every devout spirit "adheres to Pippa's doctrine that 'God's in his heaven—/ All's right with the world!'" The pious man, he says, cannot tolerate the concept that a loving God can be guilty of one brutal, stupid, or ignoble act. This is the unassailable position of religion:

But what of its moral consequences? Religion, when thoroughly consistent, is the triumphant reconciliation of all contradictions. It is optimism, the justification of things as the process of evolving the good; and its peace and joy are just the outcome of the conviction, won by faith, that the ideal is actual, and that every detail of life is, in its own place, illumined with divine goodness. But morality is the condemnation of things as they are, by reference to a conception of a good which ought to be. The absolute identification of the actual and ideal extinguishes morality, either in something lower or something higher. But the moral ideal, when reached, turns at once into a stepping-stone, a dead self; and the good formulates itself anew as an ideal in the future. So that morality is the sphere of discrepancy, and the moral life a progressive realization of a good that can never be complete. It would thus seem to be irreconcilably different from religion, which must, in some way or other, find the good to be present, actual, absolute, without shadow of change, or hint of limit or imperfection.[42]

41. P. 126.    42. Pp. 128-129.

Here then, according to Jones, is Browning's dilemma. Religion demands that he believe that this is—here and now—the best of all possible worlds; and morality demands that he condemn the world from root to branch as a sinkhole of evil, injustice, suffering, grotesque inequity, and boundless pathos that cry out for redress. To Jones this is the central fact in Browning, the formative dilemma underlying all his works, and the fundamental cause of his supposed hostility to mind and his moral bumbling.

It is in the highest degree strange that Jones does not recognize the fallacy in his reasoning. Browning, he well knows, repudiated scores of times the concept of absolutes in this life. The law of life is imperfection, and it would never have occurred to Browning to find any contradiction whatever between religion and morality. It would have outraged his whole philosophy to hear religion defined as a belief that this world is the equivalent of heaven, a compound of total good, free of the least tincture of evil:

> I ask no more
> Than smiling witness that I do my best
> With doubtful doctrine: afterward the rest!
> So, silent face me while I think and speak!
> A full disclosure? Such would outrage law.
> Law deals the same with soul and body: seek
> Full truth my soul may, when some babe, I saw
> A new-born weakling, starts up strong—not weak—
> Man every whit, absolved from earning awe,
> Pride, rapture, if the soul attains to wreak
> Its will on flesh, at last can thrust, lift, draw,
> As mind bids muscle—mind which long has striven,
> Painfully urging body's impotence
> To effort whereby—once law's barrier riven,
> Life's rule abolished—body might dispense
> With infancy's probation, straight be given
> —Not by foiled darings, fond attempts back-driven,
> Fine faults of growth, brave sins which saint

when shriven—
To stand full-statured in magnificence.[43]

It is significant that not once in anything that Browning wrote is there the slightest support for Jones's belief that he must have found religion and morality in conflict. It is a contrived dilemma, based upon carefully limited definitions. One moment's reflection on the myriads of religious people who have not once felt constrained because of their religion to suppose that the world must therefore be free of all evil, pain, and suffering will explode Jones's artificial dilemma. Although Jones supposes that *all* religious people must believe that in the most literal sense "All's right with the world," the slightest acquaintance with the world and its religions disproves him. True, one of the most enduring problems to beset philosophy is the swarming evil in a world made by a loving and all-powerful God; but history does not support Jones's case that all men who ask the question must at that moment be men of irreligion. There *is* such a thing as faith, and mystery has often heightened piety, not abolished it. The very cornerstone of Browning's thinking is that the world must teem with imperfection, but Jones ascribes to him doubts which never menaced Browning's religious faith. Browning makes the apparent conflict the heart of his faith in the moral order of the universe. His view, in short, is precisely the opposite of what Jones believes it to be, one of the strangest ironies in literary criticism. It would not be worth the effort to demolish the folly of Jones's belief if it were not for the fact that he has been accepted as a towering and oracular figure in Browning scholarship, a man to be quoted in reverential tones.

Jones, then, finds this dilemma to grow out of the poet's supposedly absolute refusal to compromise. In fact, Browning, he believes, holds both positions at once in delicate equipoise. He simultaneously "holds both the absoluteness of God's presence in history, and the complete independence of the moral consciousness." He will not degrade God or reduce the stature of man by absolving him under the moral law of the duty to redress grievances and right injustices wherever they

43. II, 16-34. "Parleying with Bernard De Mandeville."

may be found. Jones believes that Browning held absolute faith in both positions and absolutely refused any compromise whatever.

Before proceeding in this fascinating argument, I should like to examine the premises so far outlined. The fundamental error Jones makes is in misunderstanding Browning's dramatic purpose in writing Pippa's song. Browning would have been appalled to learn of the incalculable mischief this short poem has spawned. He never dreamed that anyone would ascribe to him—the author of a drama—these words of a simple child, nor did he think that his whole philosophy would be equated with them, with all the destructive charges that have followed. Pippa merely means that on her one glorious day of freedom the world looks glorious indeed, in spite of the blackness in men's hearts and lives, which somehow has a vital role in the scheme of things, which alone is perfect. Let us for a moment suppose that Jones is right and Browning did mean that there is no evil, and that the thousand evils of which he wrote are mere illusions, his religion demanding that he absolve God of all cruelty or mismanagement. Jones holds that Browning could not for a moment attribute the smallest evil to God, but the least attentive reader must discover everywhere in Browning that on earth doubt is a condition of spiritual health, as absolutes are a mark of spiritual death. In "Rabbi Ben Ezra" he said

> Rather I prize the doubt
> Low kinds exist without,
> Finished and finite clods, untroubled by a spark.

This passage clearly means that Browning valued doubt—the supreme test of man's faith in spite of grave uncertainties—which low kinds, finished clods, untroubled by the pricking of doubt, do not have. These "low kinds" are precisely those who hold absolute beliefs about religion, morality, and God, and who refuse to compromise or alter their views, simply because they fancy they have the absolute truth— a condition that Jones imagines Browning to be in. Browning was no clod. St. John, in "A Death in the Desert," warns his followers of the

dangers of seizing any "truth" as absolute, for to do so is to bring
death to the soul:

> "—this gift of truth
> Once grasped, were this our soul's gain safe, and sure
> To prosper as the body's gain is wont,—
> Why, man's probation would conclude, his earth
> Crumble; for he both reasons and decides,
> Weighs first, then chooses. . . ."[44]

And what he chooses must never be held inviolate, immune from
further examination, for growth to Browning is everything:

> "I say that man was made to grow, not stop;
> That help, he needed once, and needs no more,
> Having grown but an inch by, is withdrawn:
> For he hath new needs, and new helps to these.
> This imports solely, man should mount on each
> New height in view; the help whereby he mounts,
> The ladder-rung his foot has left, may fall,
> Since all things suffer change save God the Truth.
> Man apprehends Him newly at each stage
> Whereat earth's ladder drops, its service done;
> And nothing shall prove twice what once was proved."[45]

All in life is change and struggle and pain: "When pain ends, gain
ends too," says St. John.

That Browning never dreamed of saying that there is no pain and
evil in the world may be seen most strikingly in "Gerard de Lairesse":

> What were life
> Did soul stand still therein, forego her strife
> Through the ambiguous Present to the goal
> Of some all-reconciling Future? Soul,
> Nothing has been which shall not bettered be
> Hereafter. . . .[46]

44. L1. 287-292.     45. L1. 424-434.     46. XIII, 367-372.

Paracelsus, his mind radiant with the light of eternity which he faces, sees his folly of attempting to attain absolute knowledge, at the expense of love, which, if attained, would destroy the function of life. His words, which give the retort direct to Frances Russell's notion that he recognizes life to be "a poor cheat, a stupid bungle, a wretched failure," is a joyous recognition of life's plan and heartfelt penance for his hubris:

> You may be sure I was not all exempt
> From human trouble; just so much of doubt
> As bade me plant a surer foot upon
> The sun-road, kept my eye unruined 'mid
> The fierce and flashing splendor. . . .[47]

If Browning built his optimistic faith on the foundation stone of growth through struggle against doubt and evil, and from first to last not only denied that man can attain absolute certainty, but that such an attainment would be tantamount to spiritual suicide, how can Jones argue that Browning attained absolute certitude in his denial of evil in life, an adamantine certitude that was immune from compromise or change? It cannot be said that Browning's prohibition against absolutes applies to everything else but matters spiritual and theological, for these are precisely the matters that he singles out when he cautions man against the folly of embracing what he thinks to be absolutes. In "The Sun" Ferishtah heartily approves of man's eternally shifting concepts of God, for change is the condition of life, without which there is only stagnation. In Ferishtah's words—as everywhere else—can be seen Browning's indignant opposition to the mental and spiritual paralysis which he found in the dogmas of Catholicism, which destroy the test of life through choice:

> "—man, bound
> By man's conditions neither less nor more,
> Obliged to estimate as fair or foul,
> Right, wrong, good, evil, what man's faculty

47. V, 627-631.

> Adjudges such,—how canst thou,—plainly bound
> To take man's truth for truth. . . .?"[48]

Jones admits that at times it appears as if Browning may compromise in order to hold both the religious and the moral positions, and he quotes from "Rabbi Ben Ezra" the line "Why time spins fast, why passive lies our clay" as apparent evidence that here at any rate Browning seems to advocate "a passive acquiescence in the divine benevolence; and he uses the dangerous metaphor of the clay and potter's wheel." Browning here is talking about the creation of man in terms of the formation of pots on a wheel, and it has nothing whatever to do with man's acquiescence or passivity as *man*, but man in embryo. Once the pots are formed, having taken shape from the hands of the Creator, they lead their own lives, and since Browning here is seeking to refute FitzGerald's figure in *The Rubáiyát* of ill-made pots which the unskillful Creator bungled through ineptitude or carelessness and which he smashed on the floor in a fit of pique, it becomes all the clearer that the life of man is not the brief moment of creation on the wheel, but the time thereafter. Jones contrasts this supposed doctrine of acquiescence—the moment on the wheel, which he equates with the doctrine of religion, *i.e.*, the doctrine that God could not have created evil—with the doctrine of morality, which is not acquiescent at all, but is indignant with the evils abounding in the creation.

Jones quotes Browning's "prayer" in support of his contention that, prompted by religion (which denies the existence of evil, according to Jones's definition), a perfect Creator must make a perfect creation:

> So, take and use Thy work:
> Amend what flaws may lurk,
> What strain o' the stuff, what warpings past the aim!
> My times be in Thy hand!

This evidence, even for Jones, seems to be singularly inadmissible. The lines include thrice the statement that man and his life are commonly ill made, with flaws, strains, and warpings, and such acquiescence as is clearly stated is in the hope that each man, with the help

48.  L1. 145-150.

of God's guidance, be allowed to perfect the defects that escaped the vigilance of God's quality control.

Jones explains Browning's solution to the contradiction between optimism (or religion) and ethics (or morality) in terms that are somewhat less than satisfactory:

> But, before trying to criticize the principle by means of which Browning sought to reconcile the moral and religious elements of human life, it may be well to give it a more explicit and careful statement.
>
> What, then, is that principle of unity between the divine and the human? How can we interpret the life of man as God's life in man, so that man, in attaining the moral ideal proper to his own nature, is at the same time fulfilling ends which may justly be called divine?
>
> The poet, in early life and in late life alike, has one answer to this question—an answer given with the confidence of complete conviction. The meeting point of God and man is love. Love, in other words, is, for the poet, the supreme principle both of morality and religion. Love, once for all, solves that contradiction between them which, both in theory and in practice, has embarrassed the world for so many ages. Love is the sublimest conception attainable by man; a life inspired by it is the most perfect form of goodness he can conceive; therefore, love is, at the same moment, man's moral ideal, and the very essence of Godhood.[49]

Jones's explanation of the role of love in Browning's philosophy is accurate, but it hardly explains away the dilemma he so carefully presents as not susceptible of solution, but perhaps it is just as well, for there was no dilemma and no conflict between optimism and ethics in the first place. It would have horrified Browning to find a professor of moral philosophy entangling his essentially simple philosophy in a net of casuistical definitions and discovering that he could not have held them on the ground that they were antagonistic.

49. Pp. 159-160.

W. Boyd Carpenter understands the simple vitality of Browning's poetry:

> Browning, perhaps more than other poets, demands that he shall be kept out of the hands of the theological anatomist; for Browning is the poet of life, of its anguish, its search, its doubt, its despair, its triumph. He does not find life through theology; he finds theology, so far as he finds it at all, through life.[50]

Browning was the least theoretical, the least abstruse and the most vital, the most practical poet who ever wrote philosophically. To Browning the least disturbing moral or theological problem was the problem of evil in a world created by a loving God. It is because Jones and others fail to see that the poet was not on the horns of a dilemma that menaced his faith that they suppose he *must* have been staggered by the problem and *must* have suffered agonies of spirit in a vain attempt to reconcile religion and ethics, and as a result he *must* have ended by denying the reality of evil. Browning loved life as few men have, and one of his earliest intuitive discoveries was the function of the pains of life. To postulate that he must have found a shattering contradiction between optimism and ethics is to misunderstand the fundamentals of his whole nature. He would have sensed a truly insoluble dilemma if he had found the world another planet worshipping the god Rephan and experiencing no growth or possibility of growth. One wonders why Jones believed that the ultimate solution to the assumed dilemma lay in the concept of love, when the supposed denial of the reality of evil appears to be a sufficient solution. If optimism and religion must fall in the presence of one single evil, a plain denial of evil does seem handy.

Henry C. Duffin, in his discussion of Browning's optimism, avoids the task of trying to solve the dilemma that Jones and Pigou fabricated. He affirms that Browning really "is by no means a complete optimist," and I applaud his wisdom. Half the decline in Browning's popularity in our day is a reaction to his alleged optimistic denial of the existence of evil, and his presumed contemptuous dis-

50. *The Religious Spirit of the Poets* (London, 1900), pp. 204-205.

missal of pain and sorrow—especially someone else's—as illusory. In a century which has sunk into depths of barbarism undreamed of by Genghis Khan and Atilla the Hun, men of good will resent a man reputed to report that "All's right with the world." The promise of immortality to the chosen few seems inadequate to account for the transcendent evil and suffering that lie about us. Of all the optimists who ever lived, Browning saw most steadily all the evils that inform the darkest pessimism. He was not an easy, shallow optimist, in spite of his fortunate upbringing and his providentially happy life; but the word *optimist* in our time has assumed a pejorative connotation of insensitivity, naïvete, and unwillingness to face unpleasant facts. Tell a man whose small son has perished under the wheels of a passing car that Browning denied the existence of evil, and he will loathe Browning the rest of his days. This fate has alienated many who have never read a line of Browning, and many who have; and it has all come about through misunderstanding.

What is an optimist? What is optimism? The *Merriam Webster Dictionary* says that in a philosophical sense it is (a) "the doctrine that the world is the best of possible worlds; (b) the doctrine that reality is essentially good; (c) the doctrine that the good of life overbalances the pain and evil of it." These three definitions should concern us here. I believe it is an untenable absurdity to try to maintain that Browning's optimism comes under definition *a*, unless one clearly stipulates that it holds true only in the sense that the plan of life is the best possible plan, because the world itself is so imperfect as to shake the stoutest heart and challenge the strongest faith. It is doubtful that his optimism fits comfortably under definition *b* either, for Browning held that life is three-fourths pain, and, as we have seen in *La Saisiaz,* he spoke *in propria persona* to the effect that in life the sorrows so far outweigh the joys that only the certainty of a second life of illimitable reward can make life tolerable. Only if "reality" is understood to include the next life does Browning's optimism fit definition *b*. Surely definition *c* is the one which fits Browning's optimism most perfectly, with the fewest qualifications necessary; but again one must insist on the proviso that the good of life overbalances the evil only if the balance is trimmed in the next world. In man's time on earth there are many joys, ranging from the simple joys of the earth and the flesh to the ineffable bliss afforded by "soul wine," the life of the spirit.

In "Saul" David sings to Saul, who is in a catatonic state, successively of the simple joys of earth—the shepherd's song, the reaper's song, the drinking songs, and the marriage chant; and then he sings of "manhood's prime vigor" and "the wild joys of living." All of these things are good, for "the wine of this life" is excellent, but Saul is not brought forth from his depression by them. It is sometimes forgotten that Browning originally published only the first nine sections of "Saul," in *Dramatic Romances* (1845). In the original form the poem ends with David's singing to Saul only of the "wine of this life" and ends with the words "King Saul." It seems likely that David's songs are destined to prove therapeutic in the cure of the ailing monarch, but in the expanded version it becomes clear that something more than physical joy must prevail upon Saul to effect a cure. David, the teacher or musical psychiatrist, learns far more and is changed even more fundamentally than is Saul, for it is upon him that the great light of revelation bursts and he sees the meaning of life and love and the relationship of love between God and man, and in a great epiphany he sees the Christ stand. David, who in the original version had only the songs of this life to sing to Saul, now discovers how paltry and inadequate—though still good—are these earthly joys. His true wisdom comes when he sees that "all's love, yet all's law" and thus knows by what means to "bid him awake/ From the dream." As DeVane observes, Browning's labors on *Christmas-Eve and Easter-Day* (1850) surely showed him the true course of the development of *Saul*, through his new and vital perception of the role of love, the "intensified bliss," in man's life.

The poem is one of the great optimistic poems of the world, and yet if one insists that optimism conform to one of the three definitions, it may fairly be argued that it is darkly pessimistic, if the affairs of this life end in oblivion. Good as are the wild joys of living, the lesson of "Saul" is that mankind's prime vigor faces sure decay and death, and the powerful mind is subject to devastating diseases, for which the delights of this life supply no anodyne. But, having said this, it is simply impossible to deny that the whole poem is as dynamic with the keen delights of life and its simple joys as can be found in English letters. It is true that "soul wine" is an element incomparably beyond the wine of this life, but, for all that, they are both wine. No writer could be more joyous in his "gust"—a favorite word of Browning's to convey his involuntary shout of joy in feeling the sun and breathing the air. It is impossible to imagine Browning, faced with the certainty that death closes all, seriously considering suicide, as Tennyson said he would do. Rather, like Arnold, it seems clear that he probably would have said that if there is no afterlife, "pitch this one high." This conviction is forced upon the reader, for Browning never thought of heaven in conventional Christian terms as a place of effortless delight. So great was his joy in the challenge and growth of life that in the lyric following "Two Camels" Ferishtah says that he cannot imagine heaven in other terms:

> What a heaven there may be? Let it but resemble
> Earth myself have known! No bliss that's finer, fuller,
> Only—bliss that lasts, they say, and fain would
>     I believe.[51]

Unique in Browning is his strangely dispirited and weary view of heaven in "Old Pictures in Florence":

*xxi*

> There's a fancy some lean to and others hate—
>     That, when this life is ended, begins
> New work for the soul in another state,
>     Where it strives and gets weary, loses and wins:
> Where the strong and the weak, this world's congeries,
>     Repeat in large what they practised in small,
> Through life after life in unlimited series;
>     Only the scale's to be changed, that's all.

*xxii*

> Yet I hardly know. When a soul has seen

51. Ll. 10-12.

> By the means of Evil that Good is best,
> And, through earth and its noise, what is heaven's serene,—
> When our faith in the same has stood the test—
> Why, the child grown man, you burn the rod,
> The uses of labor are surely done;
> There remaineth a rest for the people of God:
> And I have had troubles enough, for one.

Far more representative of Browning is the familiar passage from the "Parleying with Bernard de Mandeville":

> "Nay, after earth, comes peace
> Born out of life-long battle? Man's lip curves
> With scorn: there, also, what if justice swerves
> From dealing doom, sets free by no swift stroke
> Right fettered here by wrong, but leaves life's yoke—
> Death should loose man from—fresh laid, past
>         release?"[52]

If the gust of life, with its struggle and growth was so basic to Browning that heaven to him must be earth in large, it becomes apparent that he must have thought of life as a positive good, in and of itself without reference to a continuation in another world, and such a view constitutes optimism. To Browning the simple passage of time, with its inevitable growth, assures man that what *is* now surpasses what *was,* a belief that is the least tenable and the most destructive of his stature as a thinker; but in all fairness to Browning, he does not often insist upon it, and there is, fortunately, some room left for doubt about just how seriously he meant such a statement as "The first of the new in our race's story/ Beats the last of the old. . . ."[53] No pessimist could have written these lines or those from "The Guardian-Angel":

> O world, as God has made it! All is beauty:
> And knowing this, is love, and love is duty.
>     What further may be sought for or declared?

52. Ll. 56-61.        53. Ll. 155-156.

Here is the true note of Browning. It is undeniable and demonstrable that much of his exuberant delight in living was stirred by his unshakable faith that the plan of life is right and leads infallibly to eternal life, with a conspicuous resemblance to this one. But who can say that the bumptious *joie de vivre* in "At the Mermaid" is primarily informed by his expectation of heaven? In some of the most regrettable lines he ever wrote he unwisely said:

> I find earth not gray but rosy,
>     Heaven not grim but fair of hue.
> Do I stoop? I pluck a posy.
>     Do I stand and stare? All's blue.

Browning was not all of one piece. Happily, such a sentiment as this, especially one so embarrassingly expressed, is rare in Browning. One should be suspicious of generalizations based upon a few isolated quotations taken from context, especially when a dramatic character speaks the words. Browning was human, and human beings grow weary and tired and fretful. Thus, it is not surprising to find him, in the Epilogue to *Ferishtah's Fancies,* writing:

> Only, at heart's utmost joy and triumph, terror
>     Sudden turns the blood to ice: a chill wind
>         disencharms
> All the late enchantment! What if all be error—
>     If the halo irised round my head were, Love,
>         thine arms?

After writing twelve extended philosophical parables in defense of his optimistic faith, Browning wrote these lines and was honest enough to let them stand. They do not mean that he was faithless to his doctrine, nor do they mean that he was a pessimist. They mean that he was human—and honest and as admirable as any poet of his age.

G. K. Chesterton,[54] with his wonderful sixth sense which so often led him to see through the apparent to the real, compares Browning's

54. Pp. 175-176.

view of the infinitely relative and shifting nature of truth to the fable of the five blind men who encounter an elephant. One seizes its trunk and pronounces with confidence that an elephant is a kind of rough serpent of alarming size. A second finds its tail and affirms that an elephant is unquestionably a strange hairy rope. A third feels its side and pronounces that the animal is a wall, of dubious construction. A fourth encounters a leg and discovers the elephant to be a tree, peculiarly subject to the effects of undetectable breezes; and a fifth runs upon his tusk and makes the painful discovery that an elephant is a javelin. The fable, according to Chesterton, illustrates Browning's conception that man's perspective is sorely limited, error is a condition of life, and on earth truth can never be absolute. As long as men are men, truth will be colored by their experience and by their limited vision. But he can learn something, and it is supreme folly to deny the validity of knowledge solely because it is not total. Like the elephant, which has a most unusual shape, the whole creation has a most unusual shape indeed, and like the five blind men, each man gropes for knowledge of his universe with only partial success and often with outrageous error, but he has always the capacity to attain illimitable progress toward truth. Chesterton's view is so eloquent with truth that it illustrates perfectly Browning's whole attitude toward the mind:

> He held that it is necessary to listen to all sides of a question in order to discover the truth of it. But he held that there was a truth to discover. He held that justice was a mystery, but, not like the decadents, that justice was a delusion. He held, in other words, the true Browning doctrine, that in a dispute every one was to a certain extent right; not the decadent doctrine that in so mad a place as the world, every one must be by the very nature of things wrong. . . . But there is a vital distinction between the mystical view of Browning, that the blind men are misled because there is so much for them to learn, and the purely impressionist and agnostic view of the modern poet, that the blind men were misled because there was nothing for them to learn. To the impressionist artist of our time we are not

blind men groping after an elephant and naming it a tree or a serpent. We are maniacs, isolated in separate cells, and dreaming of trees and serpents without reason and without results.[55]

Chesterton denies that Browning's optimism was founded on conscious principles formulated by the poet. In other words, Browning did not reason his way to optimism, but rather analyzed his reason for being optimistic. His optimism was founded on joyous experience:

> Browning was, as most of his upholders and all his opponents say, an optimist. His theory, that man's sense of his own imperfection implies a design of perfection, is a very good argument for optimism. His theory that man's knowledge of and desire for self-sacrifice implies God's knowledge of and desire for self-sacrifice is another very good argument for optimism. But any one will make the deepest and blackest and most incurable mistake about Browning who imagines that his optimism was founded on any arguments for optimism. Because he had a strong intellect, because he had a strong power of conviction, he conceived and developed and asserted these doctrines of the incompleteness of Man and the sacrifice of Omnipotence. But these doctrines were the symptoms of his optimism, they were not its origin. It is surely obvious that no one can be argued into optimism since no one can be argued into happiness. Browning's optimism was not founded on opinions which were the work of Browning, but on life which was the work of God.[56]

The "Parleying with Gerard de Lairesse" is useful in forming an assessment of Browning's optimistic belief in the inevitability of progress in the quality of human life. In this parleying we see the fullest statement of Browning's evolutionary meliorism. Unlike Matthew Arnold, who looked back to the classical Greek age with such nostalgia that he normally discounted the modern in contrast, Browning felt that the passing scene of men and women and their

55. *Robert Browning,* pp. 175-176.     56. Pp. 179-180.

infinitely varied souls was of surpassing hope and interest. Gerard de Lairesse, the eighteenth-century painter of Dutch landscapes, and the author of *The Art of Painting,* which Browning read with delight in translation, preferred painting in the classical tradition, with its time-honored perfection of beauty and symmetry, to the romantic individualism of modern painting.

> Ah, but—because you were struck blind, could bless
> Your sense no longer with the actual view
> Of man and woman, those fair forms you drew
> In happier days so duteously and true,—
> Must I account my Gerard de Lairesse
> All sorrow-smitten? He was hindered too
> —Was this no hardship?—from producing, plain
> To us who still have eyes, the pageantry
> Which passed and passed before his busy brain
> And, captured on his canvas, showed our sky
> Traversed by flying shapes, earth stocked with brood
> Of monsters,—centaurs bestial, satyrs lewd,—
> Not without much Olympian glory, shapes
> Of god and goddess in their gay escapes
> From the severe serene: or haply paced
> The antique ways, god-counselled, nymph-embraced,
> Some early human kingly personage.[57]

Browning can hardly find it in his heart to wish the painter's blindness cured, so great was his objection to the dull, static paintings of the Dutch master, which he saw in the Dulwich Gallery, not far from his father's home in Camberwell. The classical antique may be all very well, but it is dead perfection, without possibility of improvement. Gerard de Lairesse loved the ideal and despised the "ugly actual"; whereas Browning found the actual of consuming interest, whether ugly or not, and despised the ideal, except as a goal for man in the real world to strive for. On earth an ideal attained is no longer an ideal—or woe betide! Lairesse, with his idealized myth-

57. **Ll.** 1-17.

ology, turned Holland into a land of faery, its eyes turned to the past. Browning prefers the world as God made it, vital, vibrant, full of the yeast of life:

> I who myself contentedly abide
> Awake, nor want the wings of dream,—who tramp
> Earth's common surface, rough, smooth, dry or damp,
> —I understand alternatives, no less
> —Conceive your soul's leap, Gerard de Lairesse!
> How were it could I mingle false with true,
> Boast, with the sights I see, your vision too?
> Advantage would it prove or detriment
> If I saw double? Could I gaze intent
> On Dryope plucking the blossoms red,
> As you, whereat her lote-tree writhed and bled,
> Yet lose no gain, no hard fast wide-awake
> Having and holding nature for the sake
> Of nature only—nymph and lote-tree thus
> Gained by the loss of fruit not fabulous,
> Apple of English homesteads. . . ?[58]

To Browning the answer is clear: to retreat to the past, to people the world with the fabulous is "Plain retrogression, this!" It is defeatism, a shrinking "from great to small/Sinking assuredly," the essence of stagnant pessimism: "If we no longer see as you of old,/ 'T is we see deeper. Progress for the bold!/You saw the body, 't is the soul we see."[59] His unbounded faith in the superiority of the present over the past, the actual over the fabulous, is unimpeachable evidence of his sturdy optimism; but one wonders whether *Oedipus Rex,* the *Iliad,* and *Electra* are markedly inferior to *Bleak House, In Memoriam,* "Empedocles on Etna," or even—and I include what I believe to be the supreme poetical fruits of the age— *Men and Women* and *The Ring and the Book.* Indeed, according to Browning's formula—"The first of the new . . . / Beats the last of the old . . ."—it may be argued that to Browning *Antigone* must be

58. Ll. 111-126.      59. Ll. 165-172.

inferior to "The Idiot Boy," but such a conclusion does unfair violence to the judgment and acumen of a great man and an idealistic principle.

Browning challenges Lairesse to take a walk through the countryside, such a walk as the painter described in his book, in which he went to great lengths to explain the right and the wrong in landscape painting. Browning's purpose is to demonstrate that his own poetic method—the modern psychological method—is superior to the classical method of the painter. In the four scenes depicted in the "walk," Browning's interest is in the impulses of the heart and soul. Even the satyr they meet in the forest is not merely a stock woodland inhabitant, but is a suffering, feeling human creature, abused and scorned by Lydia—a fine example of the soul under stress. At the end of the walk, Browning speaks directly to Lairesse perhaps the most optimistic lines extant in British poetry:

> Enough! Stop further fooling, De Lairesse!
> My fault, not yours! Some fitter way express
> Heart's satisfaction that the Past indeed
> Is past, gives way before Life's best and last,
> The all-including Future! What were life
> Did soul stand still therein, forego her strife
> Through the ambiguous Present to the goal
> Of some all-reconciling Future?[60]

Here is the voice of dynamic progress, a trumpet call to forging ahead in the strenuous pursuit of impossible ideals. Since man, Browning is sure, has responded heroically to his clarion call from the dawn of creation, modern man must be superior to the best of the ancient. It is somewhat dismaying that Browning did not detect the weakness of his logic here. The semantic problems that arise are nothing less than staggering. His lifelong insistence upon the relativity of knowledge and truth and values might, it seems, have suggested to him that civilizations and cultures may be labeled good, better, and best only by the very daring, the foolhardy, or the imperceptive.

60.  Ll. 363-370.

William C. DeVance ascribes Browning's almost blind faith in progress, as usual, to his rejection of intellect. His mind must have given the lie to his optimism, but since he clung to his dubious beliefs, he must have done so because he distrusted the testimony of his intellect. The truth of the matter is that he clung to his beliefs because his mind deduced from evidence what he believed to be valid, and his intuitive faculties supported his deductions eagerly—a perfect example of his lifelong insistence that the individual accepts as truth what his character, culture, history, bias, and desires present to him as truth.

# Chapter IV

# THE RING AND THE BOOK:
## BROWNING'S CONCEPT OF TRUTH

Well, now; there's nothing in or out o' the world
Good except truth. . . .

*—The Ring and the Book, I, 692-693*

Since the appearance of *The Ring and the Book* (1868-1869) a controversy has been waged over Browning's insistence that in writing his *opus* he remained faithful to the "Old Yellow Book" in point of fact. William C. DeVane put the problem succinctly: "How far did he give truth and truth only as he found it in his source? How far tenable is his own contention that he merely resuscitated, rather than created, the personages of the drama?"[1] It is not my purpose to review the long history of this debate in detail, which is summarized in DeVane's *Browning Handbook* for those who care to review it. I should like to examine the issue in the light of Browning's whole concept of truth, on which much light may be shed.

Browning himself initiated the debate by his repeated claims that he stayed with the spirit and the letter of his source, even when the evidence of his masterpiece seems to collide squarely with his contention. All parties to the debate have recognized that the "Old Yellow Book" is an uninspired and unimaginative court record, as court records commonly are. It could not have been anything else, if the ends of justice were to be served. *The Ring and the Book,* on the other hand, is the greatest poetic work of art in the Victorian Age, if not of the nineteenth century. It is patent to the least attentive observer that Browning did not remain literally faithful to his source

1. *A Browning Handbook* (New York, 1935), p. 299.

in detail, and it is preposterous to think that he believed he did so. Professor C. W. Hodell, in *The Making of a Great Poem, An Essay on the Relationship of "The Ring and the Book" to "The Old Yellow Book,"* establishes with careful scholarship what in a general way must be clear to all: the whole action, recorded in the source, is touched with the imagination of a great artist, and the characterization is dramatically altered by a poetic genius. One is dumbfounded to find Browning denying the fruits of his creative imagination. As DeVane notes, "The question indeed need never have risen save that Browning became more and more convinced as the years went on that he had merely read and reproduced the Old Yellow Book."[2] In *The Ring and the Book,* Guido is heightened in villainy and blackened with a dedicated malignity, Caponsacchi is altered from a rakish dandy to a Saint George—dashing and daring, to his own hurt, and moved by the loftiest selflessness; and Pompilia—in the source a pitiable but not particularly remarkable young, illiterate girl—is transfigured by the white radiance of perfect purity. J. E. Shaw's argument, in "The 'Donna Angelicata' in *The Ring and the Book,*"[3] that the character of Pompilia is rendered in terms of whiteness and purity because he cast her in the role of his dead wife, and that he saw the young, intrepid Canon as the young Browning, who on September 12, 1846, played Perseus to his Andromeda in a drama at 50 Wimpole Street, goes a long way to explain why he could not admit to any alteration of the characters as he found them.

Paul A. Cundiff, in the spring of 1959, reopened the whole matter in an essay entitled "Robert Browning: 'Our Human Speech,'"[4] which elicited a reply from Donald Smalley in the same journal in the fall of the same year.[5] Cundiff replied to Smalley in the spring of 1960, and Robert Langbaum, whose name appeared in the opposing essays, replied to them both in the same issue. The substance of the debate became less focused on whether Browning was in fact

2. *Handbook,* p. 299.
3. *Publications of the Modern Language Association,* XLI (March, 1926), 55-81.
4. *The Victorian Newsletter,* No. 15, pp. 1-8.
5. "Browning's View of Fact in *The Ring and the Book,*" No. 16, 1-8.

faithful to the fact in the "Old Yellow Book" and more on the nature of truth or fact as Browning uses the terms in his *opus*. The contest takes its origin very largely in the lamentable misinterpretation of Browning's view of the mind and man's relationship to the truth, which can be traced back to the grand source of error: Henry Jones. Among the most notable facts in Browning scholarship is the very long and exceedingly dark shadow cast by the Scottish professor of moral philosophy.

Cundiff's argument is of much interest and value, and I heartily accept much of it, but an equal portion I reluctantly reject. He holds that Browning did not intend to say that he "merely resuscitated . . . the personages of his drama," but was, in fact, fully aware of the invention and alteration he brought to the transformation of the "Old Yellow Book," and was conscious of the vast changes he made in mood, tone, character, and fact which everywhere abound. It seems to me that Cundiff is eminently correct in this belief. Indeed, one finds it difficult to conceive of serious dissent, which would be tantamount to concluding that Browning spoke to deceive or did not recognize the nature of the artistry he brought so successfully to the greatest poetic work of his life. What is fully apparent to all must have been equally apparent to Browning, who was the most conscious of artists. I disagree with J. E. Shaw's judgment, which Cundiff quotes, that *The Ring and the Book* is a "glorious misinterpretation of the *Old Yellow Book*," for surely *misinterpretation* carries the meaning of error and inadvertence, and it is strange to think that a great masterpiece would be informed throughout by such error and self-deception. Browning said that he read the "Old Yellow Book" eight times with care in the course of his composition, and his powers of observation and understanding were by no means small. His poetic account of his source is, rather, a glorious interpretation, and, it may be added, that Browning spent his artistic life in demonstrating and proving that everything in life comes down ultimately to interpretation and judgment by each individual, for this is the only "truth" man has. This is, indeed, what the work is about: the test of each man in interpreting and sifting truth from its matrix of lies and distortions, and rendering a decision, even though each man is peculiarly limited in judgment and subject to error and thus barred from attaining absolute truth. In life man must act even though, like the Pope, he may falsely condemn Guido through fradulent evidence, faulty judgment, or deficient faculties. But one must have the courage to act, knowing all the while the risk of error common to all men.

An emphasis I wish that Cundiff had included in his essay is that since Browning held knowledge to be relative and always imperfect, he surely would have recognized that his own interpretation of every detail in the "Old Yellow Book" must of necessity be relative and imperfect and individual. This is one of the bases of his whole philosophy; and to suppose that suddenly he would forget it when queried about his fidelity to the fact of his source is absurd. Just as the Pope read over the dreadful evidence of Guido's trial "through this sombre wintry day,/ With winter in my soul beyond the world's," so Browning read over the "Old Yellow Book," until the great plan occurred to him, a plan and an interpretation as unique as his fingerprint:

> "God who set me to judge thee, meted out
> So much of judging faculty, no more:
> Ask Him if I was slack in use thereof!"[6]

God does not demand uniformity of judgment from man "'i' the tricking lying world," for the world is made this way to test man's courage and virtue in bringing to bear the "judging faculty" God gave him, and no two faculties are alike. Browning brought this judging faculty to the reading of the "Old Yellow Book" and read it as we see it in his highly original and imaginative interpretation. In a fundamental sense Browning was right in affirming his fidelity to the original, for what one's judging faculty sees as true is indeed "truth." He saw it so because he was Browning, and, as all men must, he saw truth through the filter of his own life, with its hopes and disappointments and love. Pompilia was to him Elizabeth, "half angel and half bird," and Guido was to him all the impressions of villainy that had informed his spirit since his birth. In an ultimate

6.  X, 264-266.

sense he himself was Caponsacchi, rescuing a lady fair in distress. Through the poem runs a thread of chivalry and knighthood, influenced doubtless by the reproduction of Caravaggio's picture of Perseus rescuing Andromeda from the dragon, a picture which he kept before him as he sat at his desk. To the Pope temptations are seen as "reluctant dragons," to be met in bold encounter by Saint George. Browning knew he had profoundly altered the whole fabric of the original story, but he also knew that he had in the truest sense remained faithful to it, just as he perhaps knew that E. B. B., with the bulbous forehead, the somewhat infantile mouth, and the fragile body—as others might have seen her—might in truth by him alone be described as "lyric love," the bright angel-bird transfigured by love.

Cundiff finds in the ring metaphor evidence that Browning freely admits his sweeping departures from his source. Browning says that as the artificer mixes alloy with gold, so he mixes imagination (fancy) with truth (fact as recorded in the "Old Yellow Book"):

> . . . the artificer melts up wax
> With honey, so to speak; he mingles gold
> With gold's alloy, and, duly tempering both,
> Effects a manageable mass, then works:
> But his work ended, once the thing a ring,
> Oh, there's repristination! Just a spirt
> O' the proper fiery acid o'er its face,
> And forth the alloy unfastened flies in fume. . . .[7]

The repristination—the return to the original composition—as Cundiff points out, is only on the surface. After the strengthening alloy is fused with the soft gold and the ring has been formed, then the acid removes the surface alloy, leaving a film of pure gold on the surface. The sense seems clear that Browning intended by his metaphor to say that the work of art, whether ring or book, conveys the illusion of fidelity to facts through the alchemy of art, which shapes, sustains, and transfigures the inert mass of facts. What remains is in

7.  I, 17-24.

the highest sense *truth,* not in a figurative, but in the most actual
sense. That is what Browning means in the famous conclusion:

> So, British Public, who may like me yet,
> (Marry and amen!) learn one lesson hence
> Of many which whatever lives should teach:
> This lesson, that our human speech is naught,
> Our human testimony false, our fame
> And human estimation words and wind.
> Why take the artistic way to prove so much?
> Because, it is the glory and good of Art,
> That Art remains the one way possible
> Of speaking truth, to mouths like mine at least.[8]

Browning never intended to say that the fiery dash of acid removed
all the alloy of art, leaving just the gold (fact as reported during the
trial). It removed just enough to conceal his art, to rub away the
marks of the file's tooth. He was fully aware of how much alloy
remained. I suspect that the finished ring is somewhat short of ten
carats fine, and all lovers of Browning should rejoice. Had it been
otherwise, the affair Guido would long since have eroded to dust.

Browning gives a fine account of artistic fusion of alloy with fact
in the words of Dr. Bottinius, who is writing the speech he will read
to the court: the true artist does not merely reproduce cold, dead,
recognizable fact:

> Rather your artist turns abrupt from these,
> And preferably buries him and broods
> (Quite away from aught vulgar and extern)
> On the inner spectrum, filtered through the eye,
> His brain-deposit, bred of many a drop,
> *E pluribus unum:* and the wiser he!
> For in that brain,—their fancy sees at work,
> Could my lords peep indulged,—results alone,
> Not processes which nourish such results,

8. XII, 831-840.

Would they discover and appreciate,—life
Fed by digestion, not raw food itself,
No gobbets but smooth comfortable chyme
Secreted from each snapped-up crudity,—
Less distinct, part by part, but in the whole
Truer to the subject,—the main central truth
And soul o' the picture, would my Judges spy,—
Not those mere fragmentary studied facts
Which answer to the outward frame and flesh—
Not this nose, not that eyebrow, the other fact
Of man's staff, woman's stole or infant's clout,
But lo, a spirit-birth conceived of flesh,
Truth rare and real, not transcripts, fact and false.[9]

This is a perfect account of Browning's method and a spendid description of *The Ring and the Book*: a "spirit-birth," "Truth rare and real, not transcripts, fact and false." The difference between the source book and the work of art may be seen in the summary of the "Old Yellow Book" which occupies exactly ten lines (I, 119-129) of bald statement of the plot and the issue, and the twenty thousand lines of vital drama, quickened into life by the imagination of the artist—and all "true." Later in Book I, Browning shows his interest in the preservation of truth and the nature of truth:

Was this truth of force?
Able to take its own part as truth should,
Sufficient, self-sustaining? Why, if so—
Yonder's a fire, into it goes my book,
As who shall say me nay, and what the loss?
You know the tale already: I may ask,
Rather than think to tell you, more thereof,—
Ask you not merely who were he and she,
Husband and wife, what manner of mankind,
*But how you hold concerning this and that*
Other yet-unnamed actor in the piece.[10]

9.  IX, 87-107.      10.  I, 367-377. The italics are mine.

In ten lines he told the tale, but this sort of truth is nothing compared to one's own judgment on Caponsacchi's rescue of Pompilia (". . . was it right or wrong or both?"), the slaughter of Pompilia and the Comparini ("What say you to the right or wrong of that. . .?"), and even the question of Pompilia's relationship to the Comparini (". . . you know best"). This is the informing spirit of the work: "you know best." The Pope is tested through his judgment of things, Browning is equally tested in forming his own interpretation of right and wrong, and each reader is tested in like fashion. None of the views are exactly alike, being formed by individuals of diverse make and experience; but each view is judged by how it squares with the absolute vision, held only by God.

Cundiff notes:

> Browning has revealed that in *The Ring and the Book* his "business was to explain fact," but he would have been hard pressed indeed to find a uniformly acceptable interpretation of the contradictory facts of the *Old Yellow Book*. Even J. M. Gest's legal account of the story, through a historical, not a poetical version, provides matters of opinion which are subject to dispute.[11]

This is a singularly inept statement, for the point of *The Ring and the Book* is to demonstrate that there cannot be "a uniformly acceptable interpretation of the contradictory facts of the *Old Yellow Book*," and, indeed, Browning would not be "hard pressed," simply because it would not occur to him to try to find such an interpretation. *The Ring and the Book* was written to show that if a thousand men and women examine a given set of facts, there will be exactly one thousand differing views, at any given moment. They may agree substantially, but in detail no two will entirely coincide. This is why the hundred-year dispute concerning Browning's adherence to the fact of the "Old Yellow Book" is remarkably reminiscent of the dispute between the Big-endians and the Little-endians.

In the closing pages of his article, Cundiff comes to his disastrous

11. P. 5.

misinterpretation. He finds that in *The Ring and the Book* Browning "is in the process of scuttling knowledge":

> Browning's belief in his high calling is closely related to the reason for his intense agnosticism concerning knowledge. The belief that total or final truth is unattainable in this world was a stronghold of his faith. In *The Ring and the Book*, however, the entire distrust of intellectual knowledge and the complete reliance upon the heart evinced in Browning's later poems, had not reached an absolute division. Both Pompilia and the Pope are conscious of the value of knowledge as well as of its inadequacy to represent the finite. The difference between *The Ring and the Book* and later poems is that Browning was, in the former, in the process of scuttling knowledge, but had as yet insisted upon only the limits of knowledge. He felt that mankind's use of knowledge was narrowly limited and that only the artist, with his keener sensitivity and divine assistance, could make profitable use of knowledge.[12]

This statement, which bears the sign of Jones, is such a fusion of errors, mingled with half truths, that one approaches it as one does a game of jack-straws. To see the old sturdy fictions still hale and hearty after three quarters of a century is dismaying. I do not believe that repetition of the abundant and conclusive evidence of Browning's wholesome and boundless respect for the intellect—when properly used in wholeness with body and spirit—need occupy us long. I should like, however, to cite the Pope's clarion words on man's mind:

> Man's mind, what is it but a convex glass
> Wherein are gathered all the scattered points
> Picked out of the immensity of sky,
> To re-unite there, be our heaven for earth,
> Our known unknown, our God revealed to man?
> Existent somewhere, somehow, as a whole;
> Here, as a whole proportioned to our sense,—. . . .[13]

12. P. 5.        13. X, 1306-1312.

It is almost amusing to hear Browning charged with the supposedly anti-intellectual belief that "total or final truth is unattainable in this world," a belief held by every sane man, especially if he is trained in science and the pursuit of knowledge. I doubt not that Mr. Cundiff believes it too, and I strongly suspect he would be speechless with indignation to be charged, because of this rational belief, with "scuttling knowledge." Browning spent his artistic life preaching the doctrine that since man's conquest of truth is always partial, he is well advised to strive with renewed effort to climb toward the unattainable goal. To say that he scuttled knowledge because there is always room for growth of knowledge is to say that he advocated a state of pristine ignorance for man, in default of absolute knowledge —a belief which perfectly misunderstands Browning and his concept of life.

Cundiff quotes the lines, spoken by the Pope,

> No dose of purer truth than man digests,
> But truth with falsehood, milk that feeds him now,
> Not strong meat he may get to bear some day,

and he adds: "Consequently the heart or the soul is the only reliable source of truth for mankind. As the heart is schooled 'in things pertaining to God,' so will it be weaned gradually from the 'milk of truth.' "[14]

This is a non sequitur of unique purity. Because Browning says that in life man makes steady progress toward truth from birth to death, instead of being given absolute truth in the lump without effort, it seems to follow that the heart or soul is the only reliable source of truth! Because the arms are of limited use in flying like a bird, a sane man is advised to chop them off as imperfect instruments! How many scores of times did Browning gratefully pay homage to the wisdom of the Creator in denying man absolute knowledge, so that life would have its supreme function: to see whether man will resist precisely the weary dispirited renunciation of mind and of the pursuit of knowledge which Cundiff believes God recommends. He

14. P. 5.

also believes that the characters in *The Ring and the Book* who speak fail to attain truth because they *seek* for it: "Because they were still relying upon knowledge, *looking* for facts, they were unable to *feel* truth." In short, the theme of Browning's greatest poem is to scuttle knowledge, condemn the intellect, and to counsel man to rely solely on intuition and the heart. The Pope's judgment, he says, is the most satisfactory because "he makes it evident that this satisfaction was reached through an appeal, finally, to the heart." If he means that the Pope experienced an emotional surge of assurance that his judgment was as correct as he could make it, I agree; but if he means that the Pope made his decision by scuttling knowledge and relying wholly on the heart, I dissent completely. The old Pope makes it clear that he applied himself to the court records until he was as gray as the dismal wintry day—and he read them with all his faculties working together, and he reread the dreadful history of the popes to remind himself of the fact that as Pope he was as subject to error as any other man, and that in consequence he had to be doubly attentive to the evidence:

> Everywhere
> I see in the world the intellect of man,
> That sword, the energy his subtle spear,
> The knowledge which defends him like a shield—
> Everywhere; but they make not up, I think,
> The marvel of a soul like thine, earth's flower
> She holds up to the softened gaze of God![15]

Everywhere in Browning is the same sentiment: life's supreme ornament is the beautiful soul. But as Browning elevated the soul to a supreme position, he did not degrade the intellect correspondingly.

One is heartened to find Donald Smalley objecting to Cundiff's argument: "All in all, I see no very good reason for concluding that Browning in *The Ring and the Book* was in the process of 'scuttling knowledge' or evincing any new or growing belief that one should

15. X, 1008-1014.

allow heart rather than head to predominate in attempts to cope with the problems of life."[16] The only alteration I can make in Smalley's wise objection is that Browning devoted a vast amount of artistic energy from *Paracelsus* on to show that neither mind nor heart must predominate, but rather that they must work in harmony—always.

Cundiff proceeds to an examination of the second meaning of the word *truth* in the poem, and he finds that it is "based on his [Browning's] distrust of man's splintered and incomplete knowledge, that is, *fact*; on his idealistic attitude toward life; and on his acceptance of a calling as highly held as that of ancient priest or prophet. Wherever the particular and the general, the individual and the universal, are in conflict, Browning seems to reveal a consistent distrust of the particular and the individual."[17] One is almost convinced that this statement is the unhappy result of a transposition of words, for it is impossible to believe that anyone who has read Browning could believe that he—the greatest champion of individualism of his age, the tireless warrior against conformity and dogma—could be held to distrust the particular and the individual. He was the most consistent defender of the individual against conventional beliefs and stock patterns of behavior in Victorian literature. One's eager hope that the unfortunate statement is the fruit of inadvertence and not design is somewhat sustained by the next sentence: "Perhaps this is what Stopford Brooke meant when he wrote: '[Browning] hated the withering of the individual, nor did he believe that by that the world grew more and more.'" Brooke, of course, was very accurately speaking Browning's enduring love of individuals as opposed to masses, for the unit in the test of life is one man or one woman, alone before God. Cundiff's statement and Brooke's appear to be diametrically opposed: the one ascribing to Browning a consistent distrust in the individual and the other, a hatred of the withering away of the individual.

Cundiff supplies four quotations from the poem, which he calls "supporting passages" for his belief, but it is exceedingly difficult to see in what way they support his position:

16. Pp. 3-4.    17. P. 5.

      ... who trusts
To human testimony for a fact
Gets this sole fact—himself is proved a fool;
Man's speech being false, if but by consequence
That only strength is true: while man is weak,
And, since truth seems reserved for heaven not earth,
Plagued here by earth's prerogative of lies,
Should learn to love and long for what, one day,
Approved by life's probation, he may speak.[18]

What does the world, told truth, but lie the more?[19]

Truth rare and real, not transcripts, fact and false.[20]

     Expect nor question nor reply
At what we figure as God's judgment-bar!
None of this vile way by the barren words
Which, more than any deed, characterize
Man as made subject to a curse: no speech—
That still bursts o'er some lie which lurks inside,
As the split skin across the coppery snake,
And most denotes man! since, in all beside,
In hate or lust or guile or unbelief,
Out of some core of truth the excrescence comes,
And, in the last resort, the man may urge
"So was I made, a weak thing that gave way
To truth, to impulse only strong since true,
And hated, lusted, used guile, forewent faith."
But when man walks the garden of this world
For his own solace, and, unchecked by law,
Speaks or keeps silence as himself sees fit,
Without the least incumbency to lie.
—Why, can he tell you what a rose is like,
Or how the birds fly, and not slip to false
Though truth serve better? Man must tell his mate
Of you, me and himself, knowing he lies,

18. XII, 598-607.  19. X, 671.  20. IX, 107.

Knowing his fellow knows the same,—will think
"He lies, it is the method of a man!"
And yet will speak for answer "It is truth"
To him who shall rejoin "Again a lie!"
Therefore these filthy rags of speech, this coil
Of statement, comment, query and response,
Tatters all to contaminate for use,
Have no renewing: He, the Truth, is, too,
The Word. We men, in our degree, may know
There, simply, instantaneously....[21]

Cundiff alleges that in each one of these four significant passages Browning "scorns truth." "Truth [fact], on which Browning lavishes unnecessary derision in the above passages, seems subjected to belittlement wherever it appears in the poem." This position is among the most mistaken, the most pervasive, and the most unfortunate in the whole range of Browning criticism, and as long as it is believed, Browning will be fatally misunderstood—and at the very heart of his philosophy. Donald Smalley, who replies to Cundiff, assumes that the statements reflect Browning's contempt for the cold fact in the "Old Yellow Book," with the implication that his contempt served to justify his altering fact as he pleased. I cannot find any evidence in the work from beginning to end that reflects any contempt for fact or truth or the testimony of his source. Nothing could be clearer than that there is not the slightest basis for Cundiff's belief that Browning scorns truth.

I should like to examine these four quotations in some detail. In the first quotation, in which Browning is speaking, there is a fine statement of man's natural yearning for truth: since absolute truth is denied us in life, to spur us on toward truth, man should long for it all his days, as an earnest of his worthiness to receive the white light in the next life. There is no contempt for truth here. There is, rather, the central idea in Browning of the endless search for truth, the ultimate goal, along with love. When he says that "God is true/ And every man a liar," he is scorning neither man nor truth, for no

21. X, 347-377.

man can speak absolute truth in a world that prohibits absolutes. If scholars hold that Browning intends to convey the theme that since man has only partial truth he should scorn truth and give up the struggle, then Browning has signally failed to communicate, or scholarship has been bemused by Jones and later commentators following in his path. A man is a fool, Browning says, to accept any human testimony as wholly true, and in proof he supplies the biased and contradictory testimony of the Roman populace. Half-Rome sees Guido through the chagrin of his own cuckoldry as an example of virtue and manly action; whereas the Other Half-Rome holds the opposite opinion because he is eager for romance and feels chivalrous toward ladies in distress. Truth comes from within us, or rather we see truth as the product of all the forces and desires and frustrations that have made us what we are. This is what Paracelsus means when he says that truth is more a letting out of the light within us than letting it in. And when the Pope refers to "Man's speech being false," he reflects no scorn of man or truth, but rather acknowledges the infinite variations that bias makes truth assume to man. He knows that there can be no perfect agreement on any given body of fact, just as no two fingerprints are alike. If two men say "This is a beautiful day," they are not speaking the same thing, nor are they even talking of the same thing; but they both may open endless arguments with the nearest victim of hay fever.

The key passage that "truth seems reserved for heaven not earth" means simply what it says, that only in heaven will truth be separated from untruth. If Browning is revealing contempt for truth, as Cundiff believes, it seems most perverse to conceive heaven as a place where we shall finally have a fullness of what is contemptible. The lines—all of them quoted by Cundiff—are informed throughout with Browning's great reverence for truth and for man's gallant pursuit of it and his confident expectation of finding it pure and unalloyed in heaven.

The second quotation is much the same and proves nothing to convey hostility to truth. It might be recalled that Browning, speaking *in propria persona*, as a preface to his great work, said: "Well, now; there's nothing in nor out o' the world/ Good except truth. . . ."[22]

Dr. Bottinius's desire to find "Truth rare and real, not transcripts, fact and false" conveys no contempt for truth, but rather a desire to seize the essence of the truth through intuitive apperception. He yearns for "truth," but it is whatever will impress the court with his acumen and so win his case.

The final long quotation by the Pope, quoted by Cundiff, is such a clear refutation of Cundiff's argument that one is surprised to see it introduced as evidence. The Pope, again, is lamenting man's inability to grasp and hold truth, but he is not condemning man for being as he is nor God for making him so. Of all the speakers in Browning's gallery the Pope holds the steadiest vision of God's purpose in creating man imperfect in faculty and judgment. When he says that a man cannot really tell what a rose is, what it looks like, feels like, or smells like, he is saying nothing more than, this being true, how can one expect from him the living truth on matters of morality? If two men cannot agree about the texture of a rose petal, how shall they agree on Guido? We expect Guido to lie with all the skill that he can command, but should we be surprised to discover that even the radiant and saintly Pompilia lives only as a human being—*i.e.*, in partial error? She knows that mystery dominates man's life, and man is doomed to grope through error toward truth. Her final words express Browning's attitude toward truth—and life and death, with which it is one:

> Could we buy a wish
> Have what we will and get the future now,
> Would we wish ought done undone in the past?
> So, let him wait God's instant men call years;
> Meantime hold hard by truth and his great soul,
> Do out the duty! Through such souls alone
> God stooping shows sufficient of His light
> For us i' the dark to rise by. And I rise.

22. I, 692-693.

In Book I, Browning inquires into the reason for the wild divergence of opinion of the murders and discovers that plumb how deep soever a man will, he can never come to the end of such an enquiry:

> With this Half-Rome,—the source of swerving, call
> Over-belief in Guido's right and wrong
> Rather than in Pompilia's wrong and right:
> Who shall say how, who shall say why? 'T is there—
> The instinctive theorizing whence a fact
> Looks to the eye as the eye likes the look.
> Gossip in a public place, a sample-speech.
> Some worthy, with his previous hint to find
> A husband's side the safer. . . .[23]

There is little agreement to be expected from the principals in a barroom brawl, whether concerning the issue at stake, the proximate cause, guilt and innocence, or the heroism that marked their behavior, in contrast to the craven cowardice of the rest. But—and this is Browning's theme—the same disagreements, differing only in degree but not in kind, distinguish the gravest tribunals of the land, the most solemn ecumenical councils of the world, and every legislative body, from the Witenagemot to the House of Lords.

The Pope's words "He, the Truth, is, too,/ The Word," which Cundiff puts in block capitals for emphasis, mean only that absolute truth resides with God. It cannot in this context conceivably mean that man is doomed to total ignorance or that truth is a contemptible and illusory goal. If Browning has contempt for truth, it logically follows that he must have contempt for God, who *is* Truth, but in the welter of errors surrounding Browning criticism, I have not discovered this indictment. "Presumably an abiding distrust of truth [fact] caused Browning to accentuate so many times a word in conflict with his attitude toward life," Cundiff affirms, a statement that is somewhat clarified by his opinion that "Unequivocal conviction of the instability and fragmentary nature of man-conceived truth seems to have propelled Browning's loyalty beyond the external truth

23.  I, 851-859.

of fact to an essential truth." But it simply will not do to say that he rejected the facts of life—the life which he found of consuming interest—because they could not be complete and wholly true or that he found good only in the absolute truth which is God. This is the most sweeping misreading possible and on the most basic belief in Browning. The poet in "How It Strikes a Contemporary" is certainly not contemptuous of either mundane phenomena or partial truth, both of which fascinate him, for through them he is tested. Like Fra Lippo, to find the meaning—the "truth"—of life is his "meat and drink." Donald Smalley, in opposing Cundiff's notions, quotes from *Two Poets of Croisic* stanza CLII, which beautifully shows Browning's love of truth, mundane and absolute both:

> But truth, truth, that's the gold! and all the good
>     I find in fancy is, it serves to set
> Gold's inmost glint free, gold which comes up rude
>     And rayless from the mine. All fume and fret
> Of artistry beyond this point pursued
>     Brings out another sort of burnish: yet
> Always the ingot has its very own
> Value, a sparkle struck from truth alone.

Upon his discovery that Browning scorned truth and man's fragmented nature, Cundiff deduces a corollary that Browning believed in an artistic elect. He argues that Browning, like Wordsworth, defined a poet as a man "endowed with a more lively sensibility, more enthusiasm and tenderness, who has a greater knowledge of human nature, and a more comprehensive soul, than are supposed to be common among mankind." It is true that Browning believed that no two individuals are alike in any respect whatever, but it does not follow that he believed in an "artistic elect," even though the poet is gifted with heightened sensibilities. The most striking contrast may be seen in Tennyson's picture of the poet, dowered with the hate of hate and the love of love and with an absolute vision of God and his own soul, and Browning's picture of the poet as an unobtrusive lover of the world, scenting out the truths of life. Tennyson's poet is a prig; Browning's poet is a man among men, simple, unassuming, and above all vitally alive and in love with life. His concept of delight is to go to the Prado and "make the most of time." Tennyson's poet, being endowed with an unearthly and faultless view of God and life, is incapable of error; Browning's poet, like all other men, is wonderfully subject to all the errors which beset the mind and spirit of man, but he never retreats from life or his love of it. Browning asks in *The Ring and the Book*

> Let this old woe step on the stage again!
> Act itself o'er anew for men to judge,
> Not by the very sense and sight indeed—
> (Which take at best imperfect cognizance,
> Since, how heart moves brain, and how both move hand,
> What mortal ever in entirety saw?)
> —No dose of purer truth than man digests,
> But truth with falsehood, milk that feeds him now,
> Not strong meat he may get to bear some day—[24]

The conclusion to Book XII, cited earlier, is often held to reveal Browning's contempt of man's truth:

> So, British Public, who may like me yet,
> (Marry and amen!) learn one lesson hence
> Of many which whatever lives should teach:
> This lesson, that our human speech is naught,
> Our human testimony false, our fame
> And human estimation words and wind.
> Why take the artistic way to prove so much?
> Because, it is the glory and good of Art
> That Art remains the one way possible
> Of speaking truth, to mouths like mine at least.[25]

This passage, which seems perfectly clear, has proved inscrutable since its composition. In it has been discovered the sour, defeatist rejection of mind and of man's search for truth that Cundiff everywhere finds. Browning knew that communication is even less per-

24. I, 816-824.    25. XII, 831-840.

fect, of necessity, than man's concepts of truth, for nothing is transferred from man to man without the introduction of error, compounded upon error. But through art man can apprehend truth more nearly than through any other medium:

> How look a brother in the face and say
> "Thy right is wrong, eyes hast thou yet art blind,
> Thine ears are stuffed and stopped, despite
>    their length:
> And, oh, the foolishness thou countest faith!"[26]

In his article Cundiff introduces a most interesting concept, which is incidental to his thesis that Browning consciously departed from the facts in the "Old Yellow Book" and never intended to stick with them (a perfectly tenable thesis): that is, that Browning ascribes a dual meaning to the word *truth* or *fact*: "With the exception of God's truth, which is signalized in 'He, the Truth, is, too, the Word,' the word 'truth' in the poem seems always to refer either to 'fact-facts' or to a result accomplished by talents uncommon to man and attributable to the influx of divine guidance." Elsewhere in his article Cundiff adopts Browning's terms "Fanciless fact" and "Fanciful fact" to describe respectively objective truth of fact, and truth or fact altered by imagination.

The remarkable thing about this dualistic truth is that it represents only a poor fraction of the many subtle meanings Browning ascribes to truth in *The Ring and the Book*. Most frequently truth seems to mean what unquestionably *is*—a fact perceived by all men. Less often, as Cundiff notes, it means artistic truth, or fact colored by imagination. Browning first describes the "Old Yellow Book" as "pure crude fact," analogous to a pure gold nugget. (Half the ambiguity of the initial ring metaphor stems from Browning's use of gold as "crude fact," unshaped, untouched by imagination; for gold is traditionally used to signify the ultimate in quality or artistic worth.) When he found the book, his reaction was significant: he tossed it in the air, caught it, and twisted it by the crumpled vellum

26. XII, 841-844.

covers, in an ecstasy of delight, for he had gold worth the artistic shaping. When a lira made it his, he could not wait to read the pages, so great was his excitement, and he began its perusal while he walked from San Lorenzo, across the Santa Trinità bridge, and so on toward Casa Guidi by the Pitti Palace:

> Still read I on, from written title-page
> To written index, on, through street and street,
> At the Strozzi, at the Pillar, at the Bridge;
> Till, by the time I stood at home again
> In Casa Guidi by Felice Church,
> Under the doorway where the black begins
> With the first stone-slab of the staircase cold,
> I had mastered the contents, knew the whole truth. . . .[27]

This is a fine example of Browning's ambiguous use of *truth*. Even though the route home led through and around baskets and bedsteads and cast-off clothing, it seems clear that the walk required no more than an hour, or two at most. How then could he know the "whole truth"? Luckily the following lines make one reasonably sure that he intended to say only that he had mastered the outline, the "plot," of the murder story and the trial. The old Pope, in much the same vein, notes "I have mastered the whole matter: I nothing doubt," but every line of his great Book X illustrates Browning's theme that no one on earth can know the whole truth, for partial ignorance is man's distinguishing characteristic. The Pope means that he has done all that is humanly possible to serve the ends of justice. He has studied the evidence and been vigilant in his attention to fact and what to biased man passes for fact. Browning, after declaring that he learned the whole truth in his remarkable walk home, proceeds to state the "plot," as he read it, making it certain that this is the extent of the "whole truth" in his context:

> "A Roman murder-case:
> Position of the entire criminal cause
> Of Guido Franceschini, nobleman,

27. I, 109-115.

With certain Four the cutthroats in his pay,
Tried, all five, and found guilty and put to death
By heading or hanging as befitted ranks,
At Rome on February Twenty Two,
Since our salvation Sixteen Ninety Eight:
Wherein it is disputed if, and when,
Husbands may kill adulterous wives, yet 'scape
The customary forfeit."[28]

Before he reached the cool dark of Casa Guidi, he knew that within the crumpled covers of his book "lay absolutely truth,/Fanciless fact, the documents indeed. . . ."—*i.e.*, bald, unadorned fact, fact untouched by the alloy of art. Since the theme of the work is that man, from peon to Pope, is tested by his efforts, however unavailing, to discover absolute truth, the phrase cannot by any stretch of the sense mean that Browning saw, by the light of heaven, into the unsullied truth lying beyond the simple facts. He had a faithful transcript of the trial, the absolute truth on this level only, for it contained lies and bias and perjury along with the tainted truth.

When the old Pope is introduced, we see him sturdily defending the relativity of truth and even voicing an unpapal defense of heresy. Even the Molinists have a right to their version of truth and may have a light denied to others: " 'Leave them alone,' bade he, 'those Molinists!/ Who may have other light than we perceive,/ Or why is it the whole world hates them thus?' "[29] Here the "light" carries the connotation of revelation, truth gained through intuition—an emotional affirmation, a mystical conviction, the heavenly light. The Pope, infinitely wise and open-minded, respects revelation, along with all other avenues of truth, and has no fear of the dissent and doubts that may spring from its seeds. Each man is tested as an individual in the use of his talents, even the Molinists, even the Pope. He would be shocked to find Vida D. Scudder mistakenly say: "We have seen that the very theme of 'The Ring and the Book' is the

28. I, 119-129.    29. I, 311-313.

futility of human judgment. . . ."[30] The Pope has not the slightest twinge of futility in pronouncing his judgment. The only futility would arise from a defeatist refusal to judge at all because of fear of judging wrongly, or to withhold a verdict illimitably until absolute truth were held safe and sure.

In 1904 Arthur Temple Lyttelton found *The Ring and the Book* to mean that man must perceive the reality of absolute truth and seize it without pausing to debate the issue:

> Of all his poems, *The Ring and the Book* contains the finest and most complete presentation of Mr. Browning's theory of truth. For while the lesson he draws from the whole is
>
> > . . . That our human speech is nought,
> > Our human testimony false, our fame
> > And human estimation words and wind,
>
> the poem itself is a declaration of the reality of truth, of the utter blunder of the common conclusion in all such cases—"there is much to be said on both sides," or in other words there is no possibility of finding the truth, and therefore probably there is no truth; at least, we need not trouble about it. Unless the truth is seen purely and absolutely, without any mixture of error, the facts narrated are inexplicable, and all attempts to explain them plunge deeper and deeper into falsehood. Say there is some truth on Guido's side, some on Pompilia's and the whole becomes confusion worse confounded: defend Pompilia and Caponsacchi from any point of view but one, and the defense is a worse falsehood than the attack. . . . The conclusion would seem to be: There is truth, but it is almost impossible that men can discover it; this story is a labyrinth to which there is only one clue, any other will lead you utterly astray, and, apparently, only God can in such cases hold that one clue.[31]

30. *The Life of the Spirit in the Modern English Poets* (Boston, 1895), p. 234.
31. *Modern Poets of Faith, Doubt, and Paganism and Other Essays* (London, 1904), pp. 49-50.

In a vast work written to demonstrate that absolute truth is unobtainable in the mortal state, Lyttelton finds that Browning counsels the wisdom of catching absolute truth at a bound. In the elaborate symbol of the ring, on the edge of which men may sit and pronounce the relative truths that their bias and perspective demand, Lyttelton sees Browning scorning the confusion which must beset all those not blessed with tunnel vision, and he fancies that Browning urges man to plunge to the center of the ring, where lies absolute truth, and snatch it with resolution before the confusion of contradictory opinions and of his own human tendency to error paralyze his initiative. Browning's clear statement that man is not permitted entrance into the center of the ring, but must view truth from the vantage point of the circle, escapes Lyttelton. What he believes to be the poet's theme is precisely what Browning says cannot be done and must not be done. Here again appears the tedious charge that Browning, scorning the intellect, advised an intuitive seizure of absolute truth, without the pain and confusion that are the fruits of rational examination of evidence.

When the old Pope completes his wearisome examination of the court records and methodically arrives at his verdict, he briefly weighs the value of further delay in pronouncing sentence:

> Am I not Pope, and presently to die,
> And busied how to render my account,
> And shall I wait a day ere I decide
> On doing or not doing justice here?[32]

When Browning says that "Truth must prevail, the proverb vows," he is writing ironically, for he knows that, like most proverbs, this is one of the comfortable fictions that men live by. *Truth* here has the simple meaning of right and wrong, guilt and innocence, and it has nothing to do with a subtle probing for the nuances of truth that lie beneath the surface. Fortified by the proverb's easy assurance, Browning journeys to Rome to try "truth's power/ On likely people,"

32. I, 333-336.

but he finds that men have little regard for truth and less for the research that it demands. His pursuit of oral tradition and written records of the case elicits only snickers and disparagement. Why, he asks, should one seek the truth at all? Perhaps it were wise for him to rest content with the court records and seek no further:

> "Content you with your treasure of a book,
> And waive what's wanting! Take a friend's advice!
> It's not the custom of the country.
>
> . . . . . . . . . . . . . . . .
>
> Do you tell the story, now, in off-hand style,
> Straight from the book? Or simply here and there,
> (The while you vault it through the loose and large)
> Hang to a hint? Or is there book at all,
> And don't you deal in poetry, make-believe,
> And the white lies it sounds like?"[33]

Browning's point is that people by and large have a limited view of truth. Truth, they fancy, lies upon the surface for all to see who will. Poetry, which sees beyond the facts, is sheer make-believe, a tissue of white lies—to which, Browning says, "yes and no!" It depends on one's definition. To the "lingot truth" of the "Old Yellow Book" he adds fancy, which is as much fact as the gold ingot:

> Fancy with fact is just one fact the more;
> To-wit, that fancy has informed, transpierced,
> Thridded and so thrown fast the facts else free,
> As right through ring and ring runs the djereed
> And binds the loose, one bar without a break.
> I fused my live soul and that inert stuff,
> Before attempting smithcraft, on the night
> After the day when,—truth thus grasped and gained,—
> The book was shut and done with. . . .[34]

In this passage truth is fact fused with fancy, but, more important, it is truth rearranged ("the facts else free") and organized for artistic

33. I, 435-451.    34. I, 458-466.

purpose, as rings may be placed upon a spear, to give coherence and direction to them. The word *truth* ("truth thus grasped and gained") has a new dimension: it becomes the truth of revelation, the sudden apperception of meaning below the level of fact, the symbolism lying beneath the symbol. On first reading the "Old Yellow Book," he became engrossed in the story itself, and his art lay untouched by the strange account, until by an effort of the will, "to free myself and find the world," he tore himself from the book, and at length his artistic truth touched the bald fact and quickened it with life. This account is significant of Browning's thinking. Fancy and imagination must not be severed from the world of mundane fact, for life is always greater than art. When he was translated from the world on the wings of imagination, he felt obliged to return, for only by reference to the world can the worth of imagination be known. Unlike Keats, who yearned to remain in the land of faerie with the nightingale, Browning puts aside his book, steps out onto the terrace to note the lozenge-brickwork of the church opposite, to hear the chant rising from the cloister, and to watch the townsmen in their comings and goings, "A busy human sense beneath my feet." It is "the busy human sense" that is so characteristic of Browning. He never loses himself in an "O altitudo." In "Francis Furini" he expresses it perfectly:

> "Only by looking low, ere looking high,
> Comes penetration of the mystery."[35]

The poet who in Valladolid stops to watch the infinitely varied pageantry of life and who goes to the Prado to "make the most of time" is Browning, who knew that art divorced from life grows effete and precious. He is of all the poets of England the poet of life and the work-a-day world, a nineteenth-century Chaucer, indeed. He well knew that the remedy for death is life:

> The life in me abolished the death of things,
> Deep calling unto deep....[36]

35. I, 546-547.      36. I, 514-515.

That his art breathed life into the dead fact of the "Old Yellow Book" needs no proof other than the continued vitality of his masterpiece. The work is true to the spirit of the "Old Yellow Book," and to the fact as well, as seen beyond the fact by art:

> "How much of the tale was true?"
> I disappeared; the book grew all in all. . . .[37]

The squirt of the fiery acid removed the file marks of his work and took away the surface alloy, but deep within the ring the alloy lies beyond the power of the acid, and yet it appears to be the purest gold, as his book conveys the illusion of truth beyond the power of its source. In what sense is Browning using the word *true* in this query? Does he refer to the truth of correspondence? the truth of the spirit of the source? the truth of life and human nature? or the truth of his own imaginative interpretation of the gold? I think he may have all these senses in mind, but surely the primary sense is "how closely does my imaginative interpretation preserve the essential spirit of the original—adding, deepening, widening, but not falsifying?" When Browning insisted that he remained faithful to his source, this is what he meant:

> Lovers of dead truth, did ye fare the worse?
> Lovers of live truth, found ye false my tale?[38]

Browning, it has often been noted, was a poor historian. I should prefer to say that he classified himself as a lover of live truth, not dead. The "Old Yellow Book," he clearly says, should be thrown with all possible dispatch into the fire, unless one intends to breathe life into it. Untouched by imagination, it is indeed what Carlyle said it was: an Old Bailey story that wanted forgetting. Live truth to Browning is insight into human souls, their struggles through stress, their loves and hates and temptations and triumphs. The final utterance of Browning in Book XII, "That Art remains the one way possible/Of speaking truth, to mouths like mine at least," is clarified by his query in Book I:

37. I, 680-681.    38. I, 690-691.

Well, now; there's nothing in nor out o' the world
Good except truth: yet this, the something else,
What's this then, which proves good yet seems untrue?
This that I mixed with truth, motions of mine
That quickened, made the inertness malleolable
O' the gold was not mine,—what's your name for this?
Are means to the end, themselves in part the end?
Is fiction which makes fact alive, fact too?[39]

The answer to the last two questions is a ringing yes. The greatest
of life's truths is the truth of artistic purpose, provided it remain
solidly based on the truth of fact and life. The first of all facts—the
"very ABC of fact," he says, is "In the beginning God made heaven
and earth." In a basic sense this is the only fact that man cannot
alter or color, for man was not yet created, but since that primary fact
man has shared in the process of creation, for his imagination and
art have given meaning to life. Man is also a maker who "Repeats
God's process in man's due degree." The creation, without man,
would be meaningless, for all the eons of time and the formation
and leveling of whole ranges of mountains. Man

Creates, no, but resuscitates, perhaps.
Inalienable, the arch-prerogative
Which turns thought, act—conceives, expresses too!
No less, man, bounded, yearning to be free,
May so project his surplusage of soul
In search of body, so added self to self
By owning what lay ownerless before,—
So find, so fill full, so appropriate forms—
That, although nothing which had never life
Shall get life from him, be, not having been,
Yet, something dead may get to live again,
Something with too much life or not enough,
Which, either way imperfect, ended once:
An end whereat man's impulse intervenes,

39. I, 692-699.

> Makes new beginning, starts the dead alive,
> Completes the incomplete and saves the thing.[40]

Man is not granted the capacity to light a virgin wick, he says, but he may—and must—reillumine candles that once burned but now are dark. Original creation is for God, not for man, for he must relight the candles in darkness and sustain the life that is guttering to extinction. This is the function of art, and it is what Browning did in his shaping of the "Old Yellow Book."

The extended discussion of the function and method of the artist (I, 733-765) is both moving and enlightening. An artist, "by a special gift, an art of arts,/ More insight and more outsight and much more/ Will to use both of these than boasts my mates," can quicken the dead "Rag of flesh, scrap of bone," just as Elisha lay upon the corpse and breathed life again into his flesh.

Robert Langbaum, in *The Poetry of Experience; the Dramatic Monologue in Modern Literary Tradition,* holds that Browning's statement and practice were "that the facts themselves [in the "Old Yellow Book"], all of them, unselected and as they came to hand (their sordidness was all the better as a guarantee that they were unselected), were to yield the meaning."[41] In the light of Browning's clear statements upon the shaping power of the artist in fashioning something new and vital from something dead, this is an arresting statement. Browning's method was precisely that which he used in writing *Red Cotton Night-Cap Country,* a method he described in a letter to T. J. Nettleship:

> I believe it was as you say with the poem in question. I heard, first of all the merest sketch of the story on the spot. Milsand told me that the owner of the house had destroyed himself from remorse at having behaved unfilially to his mother. In a subsequent visit (I paid one every year while Milsand lived there) he told me some other particulars, and they at once struck me as likely to have been occasioned by religious considerations as well as

40. I, 712-727.    41. New York, 1957, p. 135.

passionate woman-love,—and I concluded that there was no intention of committing suicide; and I said at once that I would myself treat the subject *just so.*

Afterwards he procured me the legal documents. I collected the accounts current among the people of the neighbourhood, inspected the house and grounds, and convinced myself that I had guessed rightly enough in every respect. Indeed the facts are so exactly put down, that, in order to avoid the possibility of prosecution for Libel—that is, telling the exact truth—I changed all the names of persons and places, as they stood in the original "Proofs," and gave them as they are to be found in Mrs. Orr's Hand-book.[42]

In recasting the "Old Yellow Book" there was no need to change the names of the principals to avoid prosecution for libel, but Browning takes every artistic license that he believes will illumine the story as a work of art:

> ". . . prompt therein
> I enter, spark-like, put old powers to play,
> Push lines out to the limit, lead forth last
> (By a moonrise through a ruin of a crypt)
> What shall be mistily seen, murmuringly heard,
> Mistakenly felt: then write my name with Faust's!"
> Oh, Faust, why Faust? Was not Elisha once?—
> Who bade them lay his staff on a corpse-face.
> There was no voice, no hearing: he went in
> Therefore, and shut the door upon them twain,
> And prayed unto the Lord: and he went up
> And lay upon the corpse, dead on the couch,
> And put his mouth upon its mouth, his eyes
> Upon its eyes, his hands upon its hands,
> And stretched him on the flesh; the flesh waxed warm:
> And he returned, walked to and fro the house,

42. *Letters of Robert Browning Collected by Thomas J. Wise,* p. 309.

> And went up, stretched him on the flesh again,
> And the eyes opened. 'T is a credible feat
> With the right man and way.[43]

If one recalls the condition of Lazarus in the "Epistle of Karshish" after his return from the grave, one knows that the man who rose from the dead, with the truth of eternity burned into his brain, was the old Lazarus in name only. His mind, his heart, and his values were all profoundly altered by the dazzling vision; and when Browning breathed life in the old dead volume he found in Florence, the new book was altered in like degree. In London with the "Old Yellow Book," Browning feels the thrill of the new life that he will breathe into the yellow leaves:

> Enough of me!
> The Book! I turn its medicinable leaves
> In London now till, as in Florence erst,
> A spirit laughs and leaps through every limb,
> And lights my eye, and lifts me by the hair,
> Letting me have my will again with these
> —How title I the dead alive once more?[44]

His elation is not because he has such reverence for the fact of or in the ancient book that he will shape to his artistic needs, as Langbaum believes, and certainly it is not because he has contempt for the sordid and ugly truths that he finds in it, as Cundiff affirms. The words, "Letting me have my will again with these," explains his joy. He has magnificent raw gold to shape, and his joy is that of Michelangelo in beholding a splendid, unshaped block of marble awaiting his chisel. Neither artist creates the raw material, but each shapes and fashions what is there into a new life.

Browning's familiar discussion of the relativity of truth includes the analogy of men's attempts to reach into the depths of a pool to catch a "fact/ Fallen stonewise" into the deceptive depths. Man's senses are easily tricked, and the hand that gropes confidently for the submerged stone of truth falls wide of the mark. Man's capacity to

**43.** I, 747-765.     **44.** I, 765-771.

seize and hold truth is much diminished by his "prepossessions," Browning says. The "source of swerving" of Half-Rome and the Other Half-Rome is their "over-belief" in Guido's right, on the one hand, and in his wrong, on the other, beliefs which grow directly out of their respective cuckoldry or romantic aspirations. Half-Rome finds Guido a manful defender of home and virtue, for the plain reason that his wife is shamefully unfaithful; whereas the Other Half-Rome holds the contrary opinion, for the equally plain reason that he yearns for a wife. *Truth,* in fine, takes its appearance from

> The instinctive theorizing whence a fact
> Looks to the eye as the eye likes the look.[45]

Man fancies that he keeps his eyes round and open to the truth, whereas the universal malady is the "plague of squint." Truth is the daughter of bias and self-interest, masquerading in judicial robes.

When Browning announces that the first voice among the principals to be heard is that of Count Guido, summoned to the chamber

> Where Governor and Judges, summoned thence,
> Tommati, Venturini and the rest,
> Find the accused ripe for declaring truth,

Browning is using *truth* in a yet different sense: the sense of confession. To the judges a confession—ripped from a man by the rack or the screw—is the truth, whether it squares with fact or not. Guido has been broken by the *vigil* and torn with pincers and might well be considered ripe for confession, *i.e.,* the words that make for a clean, open-and-shut case. By means of torture, Browning says, the cord was "wont to tease the truth/ Out of loth witnesses . . . ," where *truth* again means simply confession, however false it may be. It is significant that at this point Browning launches the strongest attack he ever made upon organized religion. The attack seems equally directed against the raw brutality of condoning torture and in accepting false confessions wrung from tortured flesh:

45. I, 855-856.

Religion used to tell Humanity
She gave him warrant or denied him course.
And since the course was much to his own mind,
Of pinching flesh and pulling bone from bone
To unhusk truth a-hiding in its hulls,
Nor whisper of a warning stopped the way,
He, in their joint behalf, the burly slave,
Bestirred him, mauled and maimed all recusants,
While, prim in place, Religion overlooked;
And so had done till doomsday, never a sign
Nor sound of interference from her mouth,
But that at last the burly slave wiped brow,
Let eye give notice as if soul were there,
Muttered " 'T is a vile trick, foolish more than vile,
Should have been counted sin; I make it so:
At any rate no more of it for me—

Nay, for I break the torture-engine thus!"
Then did Religion start up, stare amain,
Look round for help and see none, smile and say
"What, broken is the rack? Well done of thee!
Did I forget to abrogate its use?
Be the mistake in common with us both!"[46]

In Browning's equally harsh attack in the poem upon the heartless, legalistic machinery of the law, we find yet another meaning of
*truth*.[47] In *The Ring and the Book* he reveals this contempt for

46. I, 977-998.
47. Browning's attitude toward the law is seen in his letter to Dr. Furnivall,
February 12, 1888, in which he comments upon the action for libel brought
against Furnivall by the actor Leonard Outram (*Letters of Robert Browning,
Collected by Thomas J. Wise,* p. 287):

I shall not comment on the disgraceful issue of the Trial, the grotesque
perversion of equity, whatever may be the ruling of the law—or rather,
the lawyers. I have always had a supreme contempt for the profession,
and the lawyers in my poems get the benefit thereof. I believe you have
the thorough sympathy of everybody worth caring for, and as for your
adversary—pity it is that you ever wasted a word on him. He was just
the fellow to make money out of a kick, the beggar!

> . . . the recognized machine,
> Elaborate display of pipe and wheel
> Framed to unchoke, pump up and pour apace
> Truth till a flowery foam shall wash the world?
> The patent truth-extracting process,—ha?
> Let us make that grave mystery turn one wheel,
> Give you a single grind of law at least![48]

Here truth is a legalistic travesty of fact. It is the mumbo-jumbo, the legal trick, the skillful showmanship and glib obfuscating language, which is designed to hide truth, while passing for it:

> Language that goes, goes, easy as a glove,
> O'er good and evil, smoothens both to one.[49]

Dominus Hyacinthus de Archangelis, the Pauperum Procurator, is a special object of Browning's detestation. Truth, to this pompous jurist, is what will further his ambitions. He regards the case as merely a splendid opportunity to outfox the Fisc and to parade his superior mastery of Latin and the law. To him it would be better to lose the case than to pass up the opportunity to gird at the Fisc's bad Latin and so miss the laughter of the Court.

The Pope's magnificent soliloquy is almost wholly devoted to the nature of truth, man's limited capacity to seize it, and the injunction placed upon him to judge in spite of the limited vision which mortality grants him. The scandalous schism among the popes of the early church, when pope damned pope and was in turn damned by his successor, he finds instructive. When forced to make momentous decisions, he turns to the sobering chronicle of papal error and duplicity as a reminder of the great truth that no man is infallible:

> Which of the judgments was infallible?
> Which of my predecessors spoke for God?
> And what availed Formosus that this cursed,
> That blessed, and then this other cursed again?[50]

48. I, 1102-1108.    49. I, 1172-1173.    50. X, 150-153.

No man—not king, not pope—has a special insight into truth, for every man is tested alike. The pursuit of truth, a concept which embraces virtue, integrity, and God, is man's destiny, and the way is always uphill and always uncertain. All a man can do is to bring to bear every talent he has in the pursuit:

> Truth, nowhere, lies yet everywhere in these—
> Not absolutely in a portion, yet
> Evolvible from the whole: evolved at last
> Painfully, held tenaciously by me.
> Therefore there is not any doubt to clear
> When I shall write the brief word presently
> And chink the hand-bell, which I pause to do.
> Irresolute? Not I, more than the mound
> With the pine-trees on it yonder! Some surmise,
> Perchance that man's wit is fallible,
> Mine may fail here? Suppose it so,—what then?[51]

The Pope's final question is in no sense a flippant disclaimer of responsibility. Rather it is the precise theme of the work: man is held guiltless if he does all in his power to make the right choice. Somewhere in "these filthy rags of speech, this coil/ Of statement, comment, query, and response,/ Tatters all too contaminate for use," lies truth, not as a gem lies hidden in clay, but as iron ore lies fused with its matrix. The metal of truth can never be absolutely freed from the dross of error, but man must never weary of trying.

The Pope finds Guido guilty because he was tested fairly and he elected failure; he did not even seek success. He was granted

> A solid intellect: the wit to seek,
> Wisdom to choose, and courage wherewithal
> To deal in whatsoever circumstance
> Should minister to man, make life succeed.
> Oh, and much drawback! what were earth without?[52]

51. X, 228-238.    52. X, 403-407.

In spite of these endowments, he preferred "just the vile of life" and called it truth. His life was a total fraud, for he skillfully cloaked evil in the robes of virtue. He was not deceived in his determination of truth, a pardonable fault if one has tried with all his mind and heart. He preferred evil. "The best he knew and feigned, the worst he took":

> Not one permissible impulse moves the man,
> From the mere liking of the eye and ear,
> To the true longing of the heart that loves,
> No trace of these: but all to instigate,
> Is what sinks man past level of the brute
> Whose appetite if brutish is a truth.[53]

*Truth* here means virtue, goodness, rectitude, all of which Guido has scorned in favor of his brutish appetites; and lies are the negation of all principle. It must be made quite clear that Guido's fault lies not in his exercising individual choice. His fault lies simply in his refusal in good faith to find the truth, to make the moral choice. The Pope finely expresses the issues of life when he wearily tells of his awesome decision:

> I find the truth, dispart the shine from shade,
> As a mere man may, with no special touch
> O' the lynx-gift in each ordinary orb. . . .[54]

As explained earlier, the Pope does not mean that he believes he has attained absolute truth or complete certitude— although he says, "I . . . profess no doubt/ While I pronounce. . . ." He professes no doubt that he has done all he can to assure a fair verdict, nothing more, for man can do no more. Each man must find out what to him is the truth, "Life's business being just the terrible choice." As he uses the word *truth* in this context, the Pope means merely that he too has fashioned a ring of the gold of truth and the alloy of man's vision of truth. Nothing in all of Browning so artistically conveys the great theme of courage in the face of terrible choice, in

53. X, 536-541.     54. X, 1238-1240.

which man is doomed to find imperfect truth, as seen in his comparison of the sparks of man's truth to the light of the sun.

> Yet my poor spark had for its source, the sun;
> Thither I sent the great looks which compel
> Light from its fount: all that I do and am
> Comes from the truth, or seen or else surmised,
> Remembered or divined, as mere man may:
> I know just so, nor otherwise. As I know,
> I speak,—what should I know, then, and how speak
> Were there a wild mistake of eye or brain
> As to recorded governance above?
> If my own breath, only, blew coal alight
> I styled celestial and the morning-star?
> I, who in this world act resolvedly,
> Dispose of men, their bodies and their souls,
> As they acknowledge or gainsay the light
> I show them,—shall I too lack courage?—leave
> I, too, the post of me, like those I blame?
> Refuse, with kindred inconsistency,
> To grapple danger whereby souls grow strong?
> I am near the end; but still not at the end;
> All to the very end is trial in life:
> At this stage is the trial of my soul
> Danger to face, or danger to refuse?
> Shall I dare try the doubt now, or not dare?[55]

No clearer utterance than this may be found to illustrate Browning's vision of truth. From birth to death man is denied the assurance every man seeks that his spark, which he thinks comes from the sun—the source of all light—is in reality not a product of his "wild mistake of eye or brain." Perhaps what one styles the purest light of the morning star is in reality but a spark from lowly coal, blown into light by man's breath, and not truth at all. The thought is chilling to the Pope, who deals in life and death, but he knows that

55. X, 1280-1302.

to allow fear or indecision to paralyze action is to be worse than the
men he must condemn. Thus, he acts with resolution, never refusing "To grapple danger whereby souls grow strong"—and, he might
have added, whereby they are judged. Whatever man does in life
is fraught with risk, whether man faces the danger or refuses to do
so, but the last course of action assures failure.

Even God is largely unknown, in any objective way. The Pope
understands Him only "as represented to me/ In such conception as
my soul allows. . . ," and such a conception often seems to man
woefully inadequate. "Under Thy measureless, my atom width!"
It is important to note that he does not deny man at least an atom
width of truth in this life. It may not be much in relation to the
Absolute, but it is sufficient for his needs. After the passage in which
he calls man's mind a convex glass, or lens, which gathers the light
from Infinity and focuses it in small so that it may be understood by
the mind of man, he says that no two minds will see the focused
rays the same, for no two eyes and minds are identical, and no two
will conceive alike

> . . . the absolute immensity, the whole
> *Appreciable solely by Thyself,*—
> Here, by the little mind of man, reduced
> To littleness that suits his faculty,
> In the degree appreciable too;
> Between Thee and ourselves—nay even, again,
> Below us, to the extreme of the minute,
> Appreciable by how many and what diverse
> Modes of the life Thou madest be![56]

The plan of life and the nature of God are beyond man's full comprehension, and far beyond the comprehension of all other living
things. Of only one thing can man be sure: it is a perfect plan,
made by a power perfect beyond the measure of man's mind. But
man's search for truth is also his search for God, wherein are evolved
the moral qualities of man. There is no injunction that all men

---

56. X, 1314-1322. The italics are mine.

agree on the nature of truth or God. Life is to "compel him strive,/ Which means, in man, as good as reach the goal. . . ." For the Aretine Archbishop, who refused redress to Pompilia, the Pope has boundless contempt, for a man's election of the moral choice should reflect his capacity, his talents, and his training. The unworthy cleric stands almost alone in his guilt, for of all men among the dramatis personae he is most endowed with the gifts that compel the moral choice, but he denied both his gifts and his office. Men of such peculiar gifts, the Pope says, should

<blockquote>
Outstrip!<br>
Or else stop race you boast runs neck and neck,<br>
You with the wings, they with the feet,—for shame![57]
</blockquote>

These lines interpret very well Pippa's song "All things rank the same with God." If there is anything that is certain in Browning it is that all things do not rank the same with God. Indeed, life is a vast scale of values against which man is judged. Pippa, like the Pope, means that each man is judged alike, the man of great talents as well as the man of few, but their choices are judged in relation to their capacities. The archbishop should outstrip other men, but he actually falls behind, and his sins are thrice compounded accordingly. Men with wings should outstrip men with feet, but they are both counted equal in God's sight if they use their talents fully in the race, regardless of who "wins."

Near the conclusion of his great soliloquy the Pope enunciates one of the most stirring (and unpapal) defenses of private judgment in all matters, religious and secular, to be found in English poetry. Everything in life is undergoing change, and what was true yesterday may not be true today. Thus, dogma is worse than useless, for it binds men's minds to the dead body of yesterday's truth. Each man must judge for himself. "How can I speak but as I know?" he asks.

<blockquote>
And as that limner not untruly limns<br>
Who draws an object round or square, which square<br>
Or round seems to the unassisted eye,
</blockquote>

57.  X, 1580-1582.

Though Galileo's tube display the same
Oval or oblong,—so, who controverts
I rendered rightly what proves wrongly wrought
Beside Paul's picture? Mine was true for me.[58]

Indeed, man's freedom of judgment is almost without limit, for even "what gods do, man may criticize,/ Applaud, condemn,—how should he fear the truth?—" And here truth is unmistakably man's private judgment.

At the conclusion, the Pope expresses little hope for Guido's salvation, abandoned in evil as he is, unless the truth comes upon him in a blinding revelation or vision, as by lightning: "And Guido see, one instant, and be saved."

The sermon of the Augustinian monk, delivered at San Lorenzo, on the case of Guido, is one of Browning's fullest statements on truth and its nature. The monk's sermon, which takes as its text "Let God be true, and every man/ A liar," makes the point, standard in Browning, that it is folly to conclude from the trial "that truth/ May look for vindication from the world. . . ." Truth is far too relative a concept on earth to solicit God's aegis and support, for if God's view of truth became unmistakable to man, then the trial of life would be destroyed, just as Lazarus's life was destroyed by his discovery of absolute truth. As the monk employs the term here, truth means not absolute truth but virtue, purity, innocence:

> Because Pompilia's purity prevails,
> Conclude you, all truth triumphs in the end?[59]

To conclude so, he says, would be the twin of Noah's pronouncing there was no further danger because of the safe return of the dove, an event that might afford no valid assurance for the lark, the thrush, and the culver. The world teems with evil, and everywhere truth is at bay:

> "'Though this one breast, by miracle, return,
> No wave rolls by, in all the waste, but bears
> Within it some dead dove-like thing as dear,

58. X, 1721-1727.    59. XII, 469-470.

> Beauty made blank and harmlessness destroyed!'
> How many chaste and noble sister-fames
> Wanted the extricating hand, so lie
> Strangled, for one Pompilia proud above
> The welter, plucked from the world's calumny,
> Stupidity, simplicity,—who cares?"[60]

The monk knows that in life one can be certain only of uncertainty. He is not absolutely certain of the wisdom of his renunciation of the world and its pleasures. He made a choice of a way of life and he will live by it, but he has moments of serious misgiving, reflecting, of course, Browning's vigorous anti-asceticism:

> "I have long since renounced your world, ye know:
> Yet what forbids I weigh the prize forgone,
> The worldly worth? I dare, as I were dead,
> Disinterestedly judge this and that
> Good ye account good: but God tries the heart.
> Still, if you question me of my content
> At having put each human pleasure by,
> I answer, at the urgency of truth:
> As this world seems, I dare not say I know
> —Apart from Christ's assurance which decides—
> Whether I have not failed to taste much joy."[61]

The monk concludes by affirming the wisdom of his choice, for earthly fame he denounces as a bubble of vanity, a sentiment to which Bottinius gives short shrift:

> Didst ever touch such ampollosity
> As the monk's own bubble, let alone its spite?
> What's his speech for, but just the fame he flouts?[62]

Bottinius condemns the monk's sermon root and branch and especially reprehends his attack on the law as proving that he cares not a fig

60.  XII, 480-488.      61.  XII, 611-621.      62.  XII, 644-646.

for truth. In one of Browning's most successful passages of sustained irony the lawyer proves the monk's charge while attempting to disprove it. He recounts how the Monastery of the Convertites, where the court consigned Pompilia after her capture at Castelnuovo, is now seeking to claim her estate, under the law granting a monastery rights to the property of sinners dying within its walls, and the court, while condemning Guido, neglected to pronounce Pompilia innocent. Bottinius has been retained to represent the claimants:

> It follows that Pompilia, unrelieved
> By formal sentence from imputed fault,
> Remains unfit to have and to dispose
> Of property which law provides shall lapse:
> Wherefore the Monastery claims its due:
> And whose, pray, whose the office, but the Fisc's?
> Who but I institute procedure next
> Against the person of dishonest life,
> Pompilia, whom last week I sainted so?[63]

To this unprincipled lawyer, truth means only fame and profit. He represents one of the lowest views of truth in all of Browning.

Although *The Ring and the Book* is a study of equal boldness and subtlety in the relativity of truth, it is neither a cynical condemnation of truth as unobtainable or illusory nor a weary invitation to each man to embrace as truth whatever lie his bias and self-interest find congenial. The confused, contradictory testimony of the trial is life in little, wherein not Guido alone is on trial. Each principal in the case, together with the judges, the Pope, and the Roman populace who find for or against Guido in accordance with their nature, is likewise on trial. Every man is judged by his courage and resolution in confronting life and finding light in darkness. In the final lines of the last book, Browning acknowledges that his own soul is on trial as he labors to shape the gold of fact into a ring of art, an act in which he is as fully judged as was Guido:

63. XII, 699-707.

And save the soul! If this intent save mine,—
If the rough ore be rounded to a ring,
Render all duty which good ring should do,
And, failing grace, succeed in guardianship,—
Might mine but lie outside thine, Lyric Love,
Thy rare gold ring of verse (the poet praised)
Linking our England to his Italy!

# Chapter V

# THE CHRISTIAN EXISTENTIALIST:
# THE KINETICS OF DEVELOPMENT
# OF THE SOUL

I GET TO SING OF LOVE, WHEN GROWN TOO GRAY
FOR BEING BELOVED: SHE TURNS TO THAT YOUNG MAN,
THE MUSCLES ALL A-RIPPLE ON HIS BACK.

—"Cleon"

Browning's dedication of *Sordello* to J. Milsand of Dijon in 1863 includes the most quoted prose statement that the poet left concerning his literary credo:

> The historical decoration was purposely of no more importance than a background requires; and my stress lay on the incidents in the development of a soul: little else is worth study. I, at least, always thought so; you, with many known and unknown to me, think so; others may one day think so. . . .

Familiar though this striking statement of literary faith is, it has proved not entirely clear. Indeed, it has upon occasion proved to be entirely confusing, if one may judge from the conclusions not infrequently drawn by his critics, who have, strangely enough, inferred that the development need not have direction or purpose. It has been commonly recognized that by development Browning always implied struggle against evil, frustration, failure, and doubt; but the precise nature of the struggle and its dynamics have remained moot. Furthermore, the religious and philosophical bases of this development, though much discussed, leave a few things to be noted. It is strange that Browning has not been recognized as perhaps the most important

225

and dynamic spokesman of Christian existentialism in Victorian poetry. The dedication of *Sordello* to Milsand is a statement of existentialism, as are most of his important works, directly or indirectly.

One hesitates to apply the terms *existential* or *existentialism* to Browning, for they are not only anachronistic but also as beclouded as any philosophical or literary terms in the language. No one reacts with ennui to them, for they are semantically ambiguous and provocative. Nearly everyone has his own private definition or association or emotion that he attaches with greater or lesser accuracy to them. Nearly everyone has a particular literary figure with whom the word is associated. Perhaps in our time the name Jean Paul Sartre or Albert Camus is most commonly linked with existentialism, or perhaps Sören Kierkegaard, Paul Tillich, Karl Jaspers, or Gabriel Marcel. The immeasurable gulf separating Sartre, say, and Browning in both their lives and philosophies in no way precludes their equal right to be called existentialists. The terms is capacious and protean, and it affords room for the militant atheist, the reflective agnostic, the epicurean materialist, the carpe diem philosopher, on the one hand, and the pious believer, the joyous mystic who has attained the peace that passeth all understanding, on the other hand.

Miguel de Unamuno, the great existentialist sage of Salamanca, was a student and profound admirer of Robert Browning. He read him to good purpose and found in his poetry the spirit and the vision which helped to shape the philosophy of one of Spain's greatest spirits: the concept of life as dynamic struggle; the concept of growth through moral exercise; the vision of life as a becoming, not simply a being—growth, not attainment; the intense individualism which everywhere marks Browning's theory of life; the view of truth as something kinetic and growing with the needs and development of the individual; the insistence on free and open inquiry on all matters vital to life: scientific, esthetic, or moral. It is not my purpose to assess the nature of the influence Browning exercised over the younger man, or its degree. Such an assessment would be a prodigious job and endless, for Unamuno was a tireless and retentive student of the world's great literature—in fifteen languages. Nevertheless, although a thousand influences operated on Unamuno's agile mind, one is struck by the many parallel ideas held by the two men (along with inevitable differences), which suggest, if not borrowing, at least the Spaniard's awareness of the kinship of ideas he shared with Browning. One is tempted to say that Unamuno might well have formulated the two basic ideas in his reading of life from studying *Pauline, Paracelsus,* and *Sordello* alone, not to mention almost all the later works: (1) the concept of vocation, the committed life, which a man attains only when, through struggle and dedication, he finds himself and his purpose in life; and (2) the concept of existence as struggle and growth. In *The Tragic Sense of Life* Unamuno affirms that a man attains selfhood through these two avenues, and Browning everywhere does likewise. Even the "transcendental pessimism" which marks the Spaniard might be traced to Browning. In *The Tragic Sense of Life* he states his categorical imperative, which is very close to Browning: "Let life be lived in such a way, with such dedication to goodness and the highest, that if, after all, it is annihilation which finally awaits us, that will be an injustice." This is what Browning meant when he wrote the Epilogue to *Ferishtah's Fancies,* with the astonishing and soul-searching doubt marking the concluding lines:

"Was it for mere fool's-play, make-believe and mumming
    So we battled it like men, not boylike sulked
        or whined?
Each of us heard clang God's 'Come!' and each was coming:
    Soldiers all, to forward-face, not sneaks to lag
        behind!

"How of the field's fortune? That concerned our Leader!
    Led, we struck our stroke nor cared for doings left
        and right:
Each on his sole head, failer or succeeder,
    Lay the blame or lit the praise: no care for
        cowards: fight!"

.    .    .    .    .    .    .    .    .    .    .    .    .    .    .

> Only, at heart's utmost joy and triumph, terror
>    Sudden turns the blood to ice: a chill wind
>       disencharms
> All the late enchantment! What if all be error—
>    If the halo irised round my head were,
>       Love, thine arms?

One of the peculiarities of literary criticism is that even today Browning is almost universally regarded as an incurable optimist, blind to the grim reality of life, and insensitive to the suffering that he could not see—a critical error of the most ruinous character. Unquestionably his reputation would profit substantially by minimizing his optimism—or at least seeing it for what it really was—and emphasizing his humanity and consistent vision of human frailty, sin, and suffering. Of what value is optimism in a world under the dominion of evil and malignant forces, unless it has been tried by the worst the world has to offer and perhaps has tasted the bitterness of defeat?

Perhaps the most striking difference between the philosophies of Browning and Unamuno is seen in the contrast offered in the two quotations which follow, the first of which Browning wrote in his final volume of poetry, and the second of which Unamuno wrote for inscription on his tombstone:

> No, at noonday in the bustle of man's work-time
>    Greet the unseen with a cheer!
> Bid him forward, breast and back as either should be,
>    "Strive and thrive!" cry "Speed,—fight on, fare ever
>       There as here!"

> Lay me, Eternal Father, in thy bosom,
> That mysterious home:
> I will sleep here, far from life's fierce struggle
> I come all undone.

Browning sees the hereafter as a continuation of the struggle, a place of unending trial and heroic effort and growth. Unamuno sees it in more traditional Christian terms as a place of peace, rest, and reward.

Both men concur in their fundamental faith in the vital function of action in meeting the test of life. Thought is to both men important, but existence transcends essence, doing is greater than being, and growth is superior to attainment. Both share the existential view that man exists dynamically as an individual and as a part of the divine order of creation, which challenges him and his faith by its mystery. Both men recognize that the uncommitted life is the life of the failure who refuses to follow the "tourney-regulations"[1] or—what is much the same thing—who refuses to take the test of life at all.

J. Hillis Miller, writing in *The Disappearance of God,* finds in Browning evidence of his thesis that many readers of the last century, as well as of our own, felt that "the impossibility of a face-to-face confrontation with God" diminished man's life and impoverished his spirit. He believes Browning felt that man's inability to meet God and to seize absolute truth, which is God, results in incompleteness. In one sense Miller is right: man *is* doomed to incompleteness, for completeness means stagnation and death. Man's incompleteness—man's inability to confront God—is the foundation stone in the whole structure of God's plan, not, as Miller supposes, a cause of diminution of man. Man's "nothing perfect" is to spur man on the endless road toward perfection. Lazarus, as has been shown, is a conspicuously tragic victim of the blight of soul that accrues to the man who, while yet on earth, has confronted God and has thus seen the White Radiance. Miller says:

> Though Browning's poetry is so different in atmosphere from, say, Matthew Arnold's, though his world is a universe of plenitude rather than poverty, he is like Arnold and like many other English writers of the nineteenth century in experiencing in his own way the withdrawal of God and the consequent impoverishment of man and his surroundings. Browning does not disbelieve in God, but he finds it impossible to approach him directly. He begins with the feeling that he contains everything in his vast potentiality. The attempt to actualize that possibility leads him

1. "The Two Poets of Croisic," 1. 498.

to discover his inner nothingness, and his exclusion from the substance of being.[2]

Far from affirming that man and his surroundings are impoverished by God's plan, Browning never wearied of preaching the gospel of existential and dynamic growth toward God, toward truth, and toward the larger and nobler life—always through doubt and imperfection and trial. Not once did Browning, in life or in verse, discover his inward nothingness, precisely because he could make illimitable progress toward God, for indeed "the prize is in the process," not in the attainment. Life is glorious because it challenges man to go onward, not because it confers upon him completion and ease of spirit —a principle enunciated by George Santayana, in a colossal misreading of Browning, whom he failed to understand—but because it does not.

Perhaps it would be helpful at this point to attempt a somewhat fuller definition of what existentialism is, in order to see more clearly which meanings apply to Browning. The atheistical existentialism which variously marks Albert Camus, Simone de Beauvoir, and Jean Paul Sartre is fundamentally alien to Browning. The concept of life as absurd, associated with Camus's *The Stranger*, for example, is almost precisely the opposite of Browning's belief, although his life, letters, and works all attest to the fact that he knew despair, but his philosophy was not rooted in it; it did not begin in it. Rather, it was dedicated to eternal struggle against it. The existential belief that life is a meaningless set of fortuitous experiences, leading from nothing to nowhere, is not Browning's, nor is its corollary that since life is a pointless, unplanned practical joke, man should face this dreary cosmic truth by frenetically existing, hungrily seeking sensual experience in lieu of meaning. To Browning, life always has point and meaning, so long as man accepts its challenge.

Carl Michalson, in his essay "What Is Existentialism?"[3] attempts to cut through the semantic thicket which has grown up around *existentialism*. The term, he admits, is almost impossible to define,

2. P. 99.
3. *Christianity and the Existentialists* (New York, 1956), pp. 1-22.

for it is not so much a system of thought as it is action. It is what a man does, more than what a man thinks, although it is both, for the two are inseparable. Michalson includes in his attempts at definition several perceptive statements that apply in varying degrees to Browning:

1. "To exist is what a man is." This statement at first seems either meaningless or platitudinous. In fact, it is neither. It implies an awareness that man has only one state: being. When the state of non-being obtains, he is no longer man. He has ceased to exist. In short, it implies the individual's awareness of oblivion as a state which erases being and the be-er simultaneously; and each man, upon becoming aware of this most basic of all facts must counter it with what assuredly must be the foundation of his view of life. Browning met the fact by a simple denial that death robs man of being, but rather confers upon him life illimitably heightened in every capacity. Perhaps the existential idea that would have repelled Browning most is Hemingway's strange answer to the riddle of death: to conquer death, man must become death's agent. He must kill, for in the act of killing, man for a moment is God or is Death, a belief which led to the death of many magnificent beasts which died unaware, not of their bloody agony, but of their role in conquering death as they died.

2. "The existential man immerses himself in his moods to find within them a trustworthy index to reality. . . . To exist is to take seriously these messages from deep within oneself." Michalson finds that the strong reliance upon subjectivity and personal moods is the existentialist's guide to truth, the touchstone of his belief. "Some truths are not really true until they are related to an existing individual," he affirms, a statement that summarizes much of Browning's subjective view of truth. A strong sense of identity, of separateness—of inscape, as Hopkins called it—marks this form of existentialism. When Kierkegaard made the famous statement, "My category is the individual," he perfectly expressed this heightened sense of identity, which is also Browning's.

3. "To exist is to be unique." It might well be argued that Browning, second only to Hopkins, was the Victorian poet of the uniqueness of the individual.

4. ". . . to exist is to be with and for another." Browning expressed it more succinctly: "Love is best." There is no contradiction between statements 3 and 4. Man is a social animal, needing love and human communion. Only through love and dedication to others can man fully develop his own potential, his own uniqueness.

5. "To exist is to be human." No poet of the age more consistently grounded his art in humanity and life than did Browning. He was in love with life and with humanity to the extraordinary degree that he could not conceive of heaven in other than earthly terms. Browning is the poet of humanity.

6. "To exist is to value personal authority more highly than scientific exactitude." This is not an antirational attitude. It does not imply rejection of the mind. Rather it places the responsibility for human life and conduct squarely upon the individual, who, of course, does not necessarily reject the intellect, science, or convention. But in the end, the individual is supreme. Each man lives alone, each man *is* an island (in spite of John Donne, as Matthew Arnold well knew) estranged from all other men by the bitter, salt, and unplumbed sea. Although man is a social being, no man can live another man's life for him, or fully comprehend the mind and heart of any other man. Browning's concept of the test of each man individually and man's right and duty to seek out the truth and his own values is a corollary to this principle.

7. "Existentialism is a method of interpreting life which is based upon an attitude of seriousness in living." Although Browning advocated greeting the unseen with a shout, no frivolity is implied. The shout is to be one of heroic joy and courage. Under this heading Michalson observes that the existential interest in the individual life, or biography, is far more than the usual concern with the "life" of man. Rather the existential interest in biography imparts an illuminating insight into the uniqueness not only of the man, but of the reader. He should become alive in his own life and direction and uniqueness and should discern unsuspected labyrinths in his own soul. It is in the truest sense an exercise in the wisest of dicta: "Know thyself."

H. Richard Niebuhr, in his essay on Sören Kierkegaard, remarks that "True Christianity as it exists in living subjects, or as living selves become themselves by becoming true Christians, is a becoming, not being. It is becoming eternal."[4] This dynamic becoming, rather than static being, is central in his definition of Christian existentialism. This becoming is not by any means a simple matter of development without struggle and pain, nor is it a simple change regardless of direction:

> This becoming a Christian is not a painless process of growth, or, for that matter, even a growth accompanied by certain growing pains. It is a becoming by the self of what it is not. It is becoming what it is not possible for the self to become. If we say that it is becoming what it is possible for God to make us become, we must not forget that it is a becoming of free men who must make themselves. . . .

> As the individual becomes a Christian he believes. But faith is not something that he possesses; it is a constant struggle, a faith renewed and in the face of repeated doubt. It is a faith that has been tried, is being tried, and that will be tried. To believe is not to *be* a believer, but to become a believer in every moment, without confidence in the soul's power to believe, but only with confidence now that tomorrow God will give it faith as a wholly new and wonderful act of grace.[5]

Here is a splendid statement of Browning's central philosophical and religious position, which informs everything he wrote. Evolutionary growth and development are so striking in Browning that few have failed to note them from the beginning of his career, but just how existential and central they are in his poetry invites further examination. Paul Tillich believes that "most creative art, literature and philosophy in the twentieth century is in its very essence existentialist," and he adds, "Existentialism as a universal element in all thinking is the attempt of man to describe his existence and its conflicts, the origin of these conflicts, and the anticipation of overcoming them."[6] He believes that wherever man's predicament is described

4. Michalson, p. 40.    5. *Idem.*    6. Michalson, p. 129.

poetically or artistically existential elements are present. Wherever the dignity of man as an individual is affirmed in the face of the dehumanizing forces of a mechanical society, we have existentialism. Existentialism is a cry in defiance of the forces that seek to reduce the individual to a statistic.

John F. Hayward's definition of existentialism serves to place Browning squarely among the ranks of the existentialists: "'Existentialism,' in contrast to 'Essentialism,' affirms that being transcends thought, that existence transcends essence, that the immediate and experiential transcends the conceptual and universal. It is a reversal of Plato for whom 'Essence' or 'Idea' is richer in quality, in duration, and in the power of being than physical phenomena."[7]

On December 19, 1863, two and a half years after the death of his wife, Browning wrote to Isa Blagden:

> Yes—the years go—we are in the *third* [i.e., the third year after the death of E.B.B.]: at first, when you were here, the business was of the hardest, for nothing seemed *doing,* nothing *growing,* —only the emptiness and weariness of it all: now, there seems really *use* in the process, & fruit. Pen is evidently the better for my being here, so it is all easier to go on with: if I live, I suppose I shall get done in five or six years more: but enough of me.[8]

The dark night of the soul through which Browning agonized after June, 1861, is glimpsed in this rare, highly personal revelation, which he could write only to his dearest Isa. The emphasis on the fact that nothing was *doing* is the most remarkable part of the passage. This was the vilest form of death: nothing growing, no progress, not even a meaningful struggle against the phantoms of inanition, loneliness, and stagnation. It must not be thought, of course, that Browning really had given in to such phantoms, for the evidence of his productivity and life abundantly proves otherwise. The letters he wrote in the years after the death of his wife are testimonials to his

---

7. *Existentialism and Religious Liberalism* (Boston, 1962), p. 17.
8. *Dearest Isa: Robert Browning's Letters to Isabella Blagden,* ed. McAleer, p. 182. The italics are mine.

activity and courage in the face of the greatest trial he ever met in life. Perhaps the sense of *nothing doing,* which seemed to be a dragon in his path, owed something to the fact that the "Old Yellow Book," which Browning knew he had to turn to practical account, lay before him like an insoluble puzzle. Not until the following year while on vacation in Spain would the absolutely brilliant plan and theme occur to him—not unsuitably in the *Pas de Roland,* where the gallant French hero, who was also ever a fighter, kicked a hole in the mountain to form a pass. The splendid plan must have enlivened his spirit. On August 19, 1865, he again wrote to Isa Blagden: "So good luck to my great venture, the murder-poem, which I do hope will strike you and all good lovers of mine."[9] The whole tone of the letter is more bouyant and happy than the earlier one. He had found his great task, and at last something was *doing.*

It has long been noted that the wellsprings of existentialism may be traced to Kierkegaard's reaction to Hegelian rationalism, which affirmed "that existence itself was rational and therefore could be put inside logic." As William Barrett says, Hegel "demanded not only that the universe be intelligible in its totality, for which he needed to point an Absolute, but also that it be intelligible to him, Hegel— at which point he leaped into the Absolute's mind and declared himself privy to its secrets."[10] If Kierkegaard in Denmark opposed this position, Browning opposed it equally in England. *Pauline, Paracelsus,* and *Sordello* parallel Kierkegaard's opposition to Hegelien rationalism, as they oppose the kind of hubris seen in Hegel's declaration that he was privy to the secrets of the Absolute. Browning spent his poetic life dramatically illuminating the folly of demanding full intellectual understanding of life and most especially of attempting to leap into the mind of God, the essence of hubris. When Rossetti discovered the anonymous manuscript of *Pauline* in the British Museum and shrewdly surmised from the style and matter that only one man could be the author, Browning was forced to acknowledge the authorship of a poem he hoped was dead and forgotten. In his

9.  *Dearest Isa,* p. 220.
10.  William Barrett, *What Is Existentialism?* (New York, 1964), pp. 43-44.

collected works, he confessed that he acknowledged and retained the work "with extreme repugnance" and only to forestall pirated editions of dubious accuracy.

*Pauline* is Browning's first study of the progress of a soul—his own. In it he traces his development and failure on his journey to self-realization as a poet. At the root of this highly subjective poem lie Browning's latent guilt feelings that stemmed from his self-indulgence and sloth. He is suffering from the pangs of self-recrimination growing out of his uncommitted, egocentric life:

> Still I can lay my soul bare in its fall,
> Since all the wandering and all the weakness
> Will be a saddest comment on the song. . . .[11]

He professes the greatest admiration for Shelley, the Sun-Treader, who is "as a star" to men—to give them direction and purpose. He recognizes in Shelley the committed life, the life that had what Browning felt his lacked: purpose and courageous dedication. Shelley was wholly committed to the cause of human rights and bettering the quality of human life, through literature and through direct action, as in Ireland. Browning contrasts himself with his mentor, likening himself to "a girl one has silently loved long/ In her first loneliness in some retreat. . . ."—perhaps his father's library within the protective home, where the young Browning read to excess:

> I am to sing whilst ebbing day dies soft,
> As a lean scholar dies worn o'er his book. . . .[12]

Here is a picture of stasis, "essence" rather than "existence," futile shadows playing on a wall, not life and dynamic action. He has a strong feeling of personal identity, he says, and a deep consciousness of self, a thirst to know and do all; but he has yet no focus, no goal:

> I am made up of an intensest life,
> Of a most clear idea of consciousness
> Of self, distinct from all its qualities,
> From all affections, passions, feelings, powers;

11.  Ll. 124-126.    12.  Ll. 252-253.

theme appears in "The Statue and the Bust," where Browning, after affirming that life is *doing,* is action, not stagnation, concludes:

> Stake your counter as boldly every whit,
> Venture as warily, use the same skill,
> Do your best, whether winning or losing it,
>
> If you choose to play!—is my principle.
> Let a man contend to the uttermost
> For his life's set prize, be it what it will!

The sense of this disputed passage is not that it is of no consequence what man does so long as he does it with gusto. Rather it means that once a man has made a choice—and in Browning the choice is always to be a moral choice—he then must live by his decision with confidence. No theme in Browning is more fully supported than the injunction that dynamism must have moral direction, but few critical assumptions have passed more fully into dogma than the opposite belief. Hoxie Neale Fairchild is perhaps the most confident purveyor of this significant fallacy. None of his several expressions of it serves to show more clearly than this how really disastrous to Browning's reputation the charge is, which reduces Browning to the level of an amoral cynic:

> This endless chase which "takes up one's life" must be shown as good in itself: not a chase for the sake of catching, but a chase for the sake of chasing. . . .
> It is therefore our duty, according to Browning's philosophy, to lash ourselves into such a state of admiration for the world that everything in it will appear beautiful whether it happens to be beautiful or not. . . .
> In other words, heaven keys life to a higher pitch, and perpetuates our most intense moments of irrational activity. The same old race must continue, but faster, faster. Browning holds, with Rupert Brooke's pious fish,

> > That somewhere, beyond space and time
> > Is wetter water, slimier slime.

The affirmation that failure is a great blessing, that it matters little what we do so long as we do it hard enough, and that this bad life is a good life if we are men enough to close our eyes and swallow it whole—these are crystallized in Pippa's doctrine "All service ranks the same with God." The less we accomplish, the more ardently we hope that God lacks discrimination.[19]

Taken in order of their appearance, this asserts that to Browning 1) Life is a purposeless and childish exercise in calisthenics; 2) Man should seek out failure on the principle that the worse he is the better he is; 3) Man must sing equal praises for the evil and the good, the beautiful and the ugly; 4) Heaven will augment illimitably the irrationality, purposelessness, and evil of life; and 5) God is the prince of brutish bounders who can see through neither the stupidity and immorality of his plan of life nor man's egocentric exploitation of it. Since these views have met very wide critical acceptance, one is forcibly struck with the vitality and worth that Browning's poetry must have to survive at all. No poet of major stature that I can recall has in our day been so misread and so uncritically maligned as Browning.

Edward Berdoe, who is commonly discredited as being a Browning idolator, took quite an opposite position in 1899, when one could without undue danger to his scholarly standing find things to admire in the poet: "No failure discourages Browning; if the aim be right, the effort properly directed, he cares nothing about success."[20] And he quotes as evidence the following:

> Better have failed in the high aim, as I
> Than vulgarly in the low aim succeed.
> —*The Inn Album*

> 'T is not what man Does which exalts him, but
> What man Would do.
> —"Saul"

19. "The Classic Poets of English Literature," *The Literary Digest International Book Review*, August, 1925, p. 608.
20. *Browning and the Christian Faith* (2nd ed.; London, 1899), p. 104.

That low man seeks a little thing to do. . . .
—"A Grammarian's Funeral"

Not on the vulgar mass
Called "work" must sentence pass,
Things done, that took the eye and had the price. . . .
—"Rabbi Ben Ezra"

How the world is made for each of us!
How all we perceive and know in it
Tends to some moment's product thus,
When a soul declares itself—to wit,
By its fruit—the thing it does!
—"By the Fire-side"

Berdoe's interpretation, not Fairchild's is supported by all the evidence, and especially by the moral crisis in the life of the poet confessing his sins to Pauline. He is aware of the fact that life must have purpose and meaning. Torture racks him as he vainly searches for his true original course, as Arnold later called it.

Steeped in Romanticism, Pauline's lover tries to find purpose and fulfillment in Keatsian adoration of nature:

I can live all the life of plants, and gaze
Drowsily on the bees that flit and play,
Or bare my breast for sunbeams which will kill,
Or open in the night of sounds, to look
For the dim stars. . . .[21]

His heart informs him that such communion with nature is not his true goal. It may be a means to an end, but it is not the definite object to which he must dedicate his life. Man's most challenging test is to find his goal, often after much frustration and blind wandering. Although he perceives that communion with nature is a misdirection of his energies, he fancies that nature with Pauline in a wild retreat, far away from the frustrations of the world, may be his true destiny. The imagery he uses to describe his desire to escape the world and

21.  Ll. 716-720.

retire to the innermost sanctuary of the forest (which is strikingly similar to the later description of Goito in *Sordello*) is most revealing of the struggle in the young Browning between a romantic yearning for escape to lotus-blossom land and the growing conviction that life is to be lived in the world of men:

> Shall we stay here
> With the wild hawks? No, ere the hot noon come,
> Dive we down—safe! See this our new retreat
> Walled in with a sloped mound of matted shrubs,
> Dark, tangled, old and green, still sloping down
> To a small pool whose waters lie asleep
> Amid the trailing boughs turned water-plants:
> And tall trees overarch to keep us in,
>
> . . . . . . . . . . . . . . . . . . . . . . . . . . . . . . . . . . . . . . . . . . . . . .
>
> Deeper in!
> Shut thy soft eyes—now look—still deeper in!
> This is the very heart of the woods all round
> Mountain-like heaped above us. . . .[22]

As he asks Pauline to follow him into this strangely Freudian nest, he knows that he is being deceived by idleness, sloth, and stagnation; and he cries: "O God, where do they tend—these struggling aims?" It is not too difficult to hear another and earlier cry: "O God, my God, why hast thou forsaken me?"

Betty Miller discovers, very properly, I think, that in the poem "Browning has recognised in the spiritual independence of Shelley a principle of conduct whereby to measure, in the years to come, not only the sum of his poetic achievement, but the very nature of human integrity itself."[23] In short, Shelley symbolized the committed life.

The poet vows to give over his morbid introspection:

> No more of the past! I'll look within no more.
> I have too trusted my own lawless wants,

22. L1. 747-767.
23. *Robert Browning: A Portrait* (New York, 1952), p. 9.

Too trusted my vain self, vague intuition—
Draining soul's wine alone in the still night. . . .[24]

Inexplicably, he still seeks redemption in romantic flight with Pauline. He seeks to escape from the cage of his own ego and flee to the prison of a make-believe world of faerie, where Pauline will sing her native songs to him or recount old stories of dead knights—strange behavior in a man who has just renounced all forms of retreat, especially from the past. When this palls, he will read to her great lays, by way of diversion. Meanwhile they are to be "like twin Gods," unemployed except in their entertainments and communion with nature. It is all rather hastily bundled up, as if Browning were not sure how to finish the poem, or had not known from the beginning precisely what he was trying to say. I believe that *Pauline* is unique in this respect among his works. All the rest, whatever their faults, reveal the sure hand of the artist and a steady planned development. But *Pauline,* beautiful as it is in isolated passages, stumbles and sputters to a puzzlingly unsure end. In this fact one can see the real perplexity of the young Browning. He was seeking something to commit his life to, and he could not find it. No poem so clearly shows the morbid questing that marked his life at this time.

*Paracelsus* continues the quest for direction to the dynamic, existential life, and the answer he propounds informs all his later poetry. Paracelsus represents the committed life, but he is committed unwisely: he chooses to dedicate his life solely to amassing knowledge, by whatever means lies before him, including necromancy and conjuring. He scorns love and emotion as useless obstacles to his monomaniacal pursuit of knowledge. The poem has been often misread as a warning against the evils of intellect and as a dramatic parable illustrating the wisdom of pursuing intuition and love instead. It is, rather, a plea for wholeness, balance, and full development of personality.

Paracelsus suffers from one other serious disability: he clings to the past, detesting change; and to Browning this is a form of death. In

24. L1. 937-940.

speaking to Aprile, the poet, of his early joy in hearing Michal sing, in days before his emotional life dried up, he expresses hope that things have remained static:

> Ah, those children quite
> Unsettle the pure picture in my mind:
> A girl, she was so perfect, so distinct:
> No change, no change! Not but this added grace
> May blend and harmonize with its compeers,
> And Michal may become her motherhood;
> But 't is a change, and I detest all change,
> And most a change in aught I loved long since.[25]

I should like at this point to comment on certain aspects of Betty Miller's strictures on *Paracelsus* in her *Robert Browning: A Portrait*, a book dedicated to debunking the character of the poet. Miss Miller discovers in the poem the clearest evidence that Browning was, and realized that he was, a sickly, sheltered, emotionally stunted mamma's boy, who grew up in a household that was a militant matriarchy. Browning is presented throughout the book, and with much "evidence" from *Paracelsus,* as an invertebrate, a sponge. In the stage directions to Scene I—"Würzburg; a garden in the environs. 1512"— she discovers with a clairvoyant insight that commands immediate admiration, incontrovertible evidence of autobiography: "The scene takes shape; it is an autumn evening in the year 1507 [sic]. . . . it is plain enough that 'Wurzeburg, with its church and spire, and garden-walls and all that they contain' is in fact pre-Victorian Camberwell; the garden in the environs, 'limited Alone by one old populous green wall', none other than the suburban garden of Browning's early home in Hanover Cottage."[26]

Of course! How could one have been blind to what is so obvious when called boldly to our attention? The facts are indisputable, in much the same fashion that Shakespeare's seacoast of Bohemia is in reality Brighton and Birnham Wood is Eden. No evidence of her

25. III, 38-45.    26. P. 4.

contention is apparently needed, and she supplies none. This is the method used throughout the book: confident assertion is considered both indictment and evidence. Browning's error—or Miss Miller's—in dating the action of the drama perhaps we should pass over in silence.

Miss Miller discovers that Festus and Michal, the harmoniously married couple, represent quite clearly Father and Mother, by reason of the initial letters F and M of their names, a fact that passed unnoticed for a hundred and twenty years or so, in much the same fashion that heretofore critical narcolepsy has concealed Milton's aversion to brothers and sisters, clearly seen in his hatred of Belial and Satan. Festus and Michal, it should be noted, are unrelated in the drama to Paracelsus, a strange mischance if Browning were busily engaged in adumbrating the family's maternal domination. The purpose of these two characters, far from revealing their struggle for dominance, is precisely to show the love and harmony that inform their lives. They are the wholeness of love and knowledge that neither Paracelsus nor Aprile can attain. No poorer example in the whole range of British literature could be found to illustrate domestic infelicity than this admirable couple. Miss Miller makes the case that Robert Browning, Senior, like Festus allegedly, remained a child under the tight rein of his wife. Furnivall, she reports, had heard Browning "speak of his father, but never of his mother, probably because he saw little of her," an ominous bit of evidence to establish the fact that the young poet was an exceedingly pathetic victim of momism.

Some boys, it is true, who are neurotically attached to their mothers' apron strings are rather inclined to speak of them often and indeed to see a great deal of them, domineering people rarely keeping in the background unobtrusively. But Browning's momism, apparently, was of the silent and distant sort.

Miss Miller remarks:

Meeting, five years after her marriage, an elderly gentleman who submitted to having his face washed and his hair brushed for

him by a briskly impatient daughter, Elizabeth Barrett Browning
was moved to remark that "the relations of life seem reversed in
their case, and the father appears the child of the child."[27]

Although there is no evidence that this elderly gentleman, whose
daughter washed his face, was in any way related to the Brownings,
or that Elizabeth Barrett Browning implied a connection with life in
the Browning household, Miss Miller finds in the story weighty
evidence that the poet's father was in a similar condition, a dismay-
ingly distorted use of evidence.

*Pauline,* as everyone knows, is markedly autobiographical, but
there is little evidence that *Paracelsus* is so in like degree. Browning
had recently read John Stuart Mill's harsh comments in the back of
his review copy of the earlier poem, and he had repudiated both
Shelley and any further morbid self-consciousness. His selection of a
historical character to illustrate the sin of hubris is significant. I have
no doubt that the poem reflects certain problems that were very real
to Browning, and it seems clear that the respective choices of life
made by Paracelsus and Aprile represent alternate choices attractive
to the young Browning, but the weight of evidence is conclusive that

27. P. 7. In contrast to Betty Miller's view of Browning, one might recall
that of William Wetmore Story, written to Pen Browning the day after the
death of the poet, December 12, 1889. Story and Browning were intimates
for many years and spent literally thousands of hours together in the greatest
of accord and amity. This is his appraisal of the character of Robert Browning (*Browning to His American Friends,* ed. Gertrude Reese Hudson [New
York, 1965], p. 197): "He was one of my oldest and dearest and most valued
friends—and the world seems poor now that he has gone—Yes! for it is not
only a loss to us who were his personal friends, it is a terrible loss to the
world—that nothing can ever make up—The last words he said to us when we
said good-bye to him at Asolo were 'We have been friends for forty years—
aye—more than forty years—and with never a break'—How true it was—There
was never a break—never a cloud on our friendship for a moment—and the
more I knew him the more I loved him—and the more I admired him—He
was one of the best and noblest of men—Alas! that I should have to say, he
was—I do not think that a small or mean thought ever knocked at the door
of his spirit—much less even—was allowed to enter—Ever large hearted as large
minded, grand in all his impulses—generous in all his feelings—vivid in his
enthusiasms and the most living man I ever knew—I cannot believe it possible
that he has gone from us forever—"

Browning never thought of identifying himself with the sixteenth-century doctor. Paracelsus is no more Browning than is the Great Duke Ferdinand or Sludge. It is true that the quest of Paracelsus illustrates Browning's own search for a viable set of values and in this sense alone it is autobiographical.

In *Pauline, Paracelsus,* and *Sordello,* Browning is trying to come to grips with the most pressing problem of his young life: what is the duty of an aspiring poet to himself, to man, and to God? All three poems reject pride or hubris as the most fatal of sins and reject self-indulgent sloth, and the last two espouse with especial vigor the need for wholeness and dynamic aspiration toward a worthy goal. Paracelsus discovers too late that he has pursued knowledge at the expense of love and his emotional life and that he has attained only hubris and fatal imbalance. His existential drive to *become* has been misdirected. He can no longer enjoy nature or poetry or music; and his soul withers with the dry and static knowledge that he so yearned for: ". . . the few truths/ Got at a life's cost. . . ." The poet Aprile, his counterpart in hubris, has sought only love at the expense of knowledge, and he too fails for want of wholeness. On his deathbed Paracelsus confesses his sin of pride and imbalance, and Festus, mistaking his intent, says:

> But all comes
> To the same thing. 'T is fruitless for mankind
> To fret themselves with what concerns them not;
> They are no use that way: they should lie down
> Content as God has made them, nor go mad
> In thriveless cares to better what is ill.[28]

Paracelsus in horror rebukes him for this disastrous misinterpretation, shouting: "no, no; mistake me not; let me not work/ More harm than I have worked!" The great lesson he has learned is not anti-intellectualism, as many critics have inferred, but rather wholeness and dynamic dedication to improving the life of man. Paracelsus was granted "a searching and impetuous soul" with which to attain "New strifes, new triumphs:—doubtless a strong soul. . . ." "Progress is/

28.  V, 575-580.

The law of life, man is not Man as yet," an excellent statement of existentialism. Paracelsus sees that each man has an obligation of dynamically evolving toward perfection. Inaction, unwholeness, and pride are the cardinal sins of man, Paracelsus discovers. Paracelsus knows that he has failed, but not absolutely, for he has aspired and yearned and struggled, albeit for one thing only. There are hope and a certain nobility in man's

> . . . faint aspirings, dim
> Struggles for truth, their poorest fallacies,
> Their prejudice and fears and cares and doubts;
> All with a touch of nobleness, despite
> Their error, upward tending all though weak,
> Like plants in mines which never saw the sun,
> But dream of him, and guess where he may be,
> And do their best to climb and get to him.
> All this I knew not, and I failed. Let men
> Regard me, and the poet dead long ago
> Who loved too rashly; and shape forth a third
> And better-tempered spirit, warned by both. . . .[29]

*Sordello* is a study of the craft of the poet and how he best may attain the heights in his craft. It is throughout a repudiation of preciousness, sloth, inaction, isolation, and Wordsworthian retreat to nature, and it is a plea for dynamic growth and social responsibility. The story of Sordello, the medieval troubador, is the chronicle of his trial-and-error groping toward poet-craft, his failure, and his death. The young poet by nature tends to be a recluse, living in an ivory tower, communing with nature and himself and letting the world pass by unheeded. Stewart Walker Holmes[30] is correct in seeing a partial identity between Sordello and Browning, as I have attempted to show in my *Triple Soul*, but the work is not truly autobiographical. Sordello lives in Goito, "a drowsy paradise" of self-indulgent quiet, a lotus-blossom land of irresponsible faerie:

29. V, 876-887.
30. "Browning's *Sordello* and Jung: Browning's *Sordello* in the Light of Jung's Theory of Types," *Publications of the Modern Language Association,* LVI (September, 1941), 758-796.

> Ah, but to find
> A certain mood enervate such a mind,
> Counsel it slumber in the solitude
> Thus reached nor, stooping, task for mankind's good
> Its nature just as life and time accord
> "—Too narrow an arena to reward
> Emprise—the world's occasion worthless since
> Not absolutely fitted to evince
> Its mastery!"[31]

In Goito, luxuriating in his "fancies infantine," stagnates Sordello, playing at life and rejecting its test. He wants to mix with men, drive dynamically toward a goal, like young Ecelin, but, he knows that in *doing* there is always the risk of failure. Activity, he fears, may be retrograde, and Sordello is terrified of failure. Thus he

> . . . left each abortive boy's-attempt,
> For feats, from failure happily excempt,
> In fancy at his beck.[32]

He vows that someday he will enter into life and meet its demands like a man, "though I must abide/ With dreams now," until such time as he may "acquire an instrument/ For acting what these people act. . . ." Here is one of Browning's enduring themes: man must never evade life because he fears he is not ready for it, is not equipped to meet its demands, or feels that greater apprenticeship is required to assure success. Success is not of first importance, or, to put it more accurately, success *is* the process, the action, the existential commitment, the courageous joining in battle—provided always that the goal is what one believes to be worthy. Man is tested by his will, by what he "would do," and by what he does with the talents and circumstances that direct his life. But Sordello chooses "Song, not deeds." When he does break away and flees to Mantua, he is quite unprepared for life and its struggles, and as a result he is split, the "Poet's half" at war with the "man portion":

31. I, 554-561.     32. I, 827-829.

> Weeks, months, years went by,
> And lo, Sordello vanished utterly,
> Sundered in twain; each spectral part at strife
> With each; one jarred against another life;
> The Poet thwarting hopelessly the Man—
> Who, fooled no longer, free in fancy ran
> Here, there. . . .[33]

Perhaps the most destructive, pernicious, and useless strife is this psychic split whereby man wars against himself and is impotent to fight the warrior's fight against evil. In this sort of internecine war man's dynamism turns inward and chaos ensues. Browning never speaks of the necessity of fighting the evils of life without implying the necessity of wholeness as a condition of the struggle. "The complete Sordello, Man and Bard," is gone and he is left impotent by the "internal struggle to be one/ Which frittered him incessantly piecemeal. . . ." There is no doubt about Browning's judgment of such an internal struggle: the Man must triumph over the Bard, if they cannot fight as equals side by side. Life is greater than art. For Sordello "The obvious if not the only shelter lay/ In deeds. . . ." No theme is more pervasive in Browning than this insistence that life must be lived, not theorized upon. As a poet Sordello is crippled, for to be a poet, one must first be a man, and as a man he is a failure, his conversation being that of an unworldly child, and in consequence his verse coming "only not to a stand-still."

His moment of truth arrives when he learns the great lesson:

> "Would you have your songs endure?
> Build on the human heart!—why, to be sure
> Yours is one sort of heart—but I mean theirs,
> Ours, every one's, the healthy heart one cares
> To build on!"[34]

From this point on Browning over and over again illustrated this great principle of existential living. But the implementation of the

33. II, 655-661.    34. II, 797-801.

principle, far from being simple, is fraught with challenge and danger. It is life's principal business, and life *is* danger. Sordello, the recluse, discovers that the body and the passions are vital to life, "To balance the ethereality." Browning calls the body "the Machine for Acting Will"—and the Acting Will is the soul. Nothing could more typify Browning's growing awareness of the need for vitalism, dynamism, existentialism than this definition of soul: Acting Will. Now Sordello learns that life is a process of growth, a becoming, not a being only, an eternal striving with body, mind, and soul upward— the triple soul of man which must work in harmony if man is to achieve his potential. Every man, however "bounded," strives to become:

> The common sort, the crowd,
> Exist, perceive; with Being are endowed,
> However slight, distinct from what they See,
> However bounded; Happiness must be,
> To feed the first by gleanings from the last,
> Attain its qualities, and slow or fast
> Become what they behold; such peace-in-strife,
> By transmutation, is the Use of Life,
> The Alien turning Native to the soul
> Or body—which instructs me; I am whole
> There and demand a Palma; had the world
> Been from my soul to a like distance hurled,
> 'T were Happiness to make it one with me:
> Whereas I must, ere I begin to Be,
> Include a world, in flesh, I comprehend
> In spirit now. . . .[35]

A similar theme is presented more dramatically in "Cleon," where the greatest of Greek artists, who has written his country's deathless love odes, is painfully aware that he has grown too old for loving and that the young slave girl turns instinctively to the young rower. Cleon has written of love, but he has not loved, and life is greater than the greatest love ode:

35.  III, 159-174.

I can write love-odes; thy fair slave's an ode.
I get to sing of love, when grown too gray
For being beloved: she turns to that young man,
The muscles all a-ripple on his back.[36]

Fra Lippo Lippi, commenting on the beauty and the power and the wonder of the creation, asks a perfectly existential question:

What's it all about?
To be passed over, despised? or dwelt upon,
Wondered at? oh, this last of course!—you say.
But why not do as well as say,—paint these
Just as they are, careless what comes of it?
God's works—paint any one, and count it crime
To let a truth slip.[37]

Life is for living first, for art second. In the middle of a painting, ironically of St. Jerome pounding his chest with a rock to subdue the flesh, Lippo hears the titter of girlish laughter outside and in a trice rips up curtain, counterpane, and coverlet to make a ladder to further his flight to life. One of the lessons that Sordello learns is that men of action are rightly preferred by the world to theoreticians and effete artists, however famous, who know not the shock of battle in life's lists:

Alack,
Not so unwisely does the crowd dispense
On Salinguerras praise in preference
To the Sordellos: men of action, these!
Who, seeing just as little as you please,
Yet turn that little to account,—engage
With, do not gaze at,—carry on, a stage,
The work o' the world, not merely make report
The work existed ere their day![38]

In life one must act, not passively contemplate. One must not *think* his life away. Thought should lead to action. Sordello says of the

36. Ll. 296-299.     37. Ll. 290-296.     38. III, 915-924.

general Taurello Saliguerra that he is "one/ Of happier fate, and all I should have done/ He does; the people's good being paramount/ With him. . . ." It is unthinkable that Sordello would have professed such envy had Saliguerra been a vicious tyrant, opposed to the people's welfare. Activism is no excuse for tyranny, and individualism is never divorced from responsibility. Man's acts are of supreme importance, but more important than the fact of the act is the intent of the act—its direction, its fruits. Browning says that Goito, the drowsy paradise, palled on Sordello because it was perfection, which on earth is death to man. Man must seek the whole by its parts, knowing all the while that if the whole were ever attained, "naught were gained/ But leave to look—not leave to do." Like Carlyle, Browning said, "Whatsoever thy hand findeth to do, do it with all thy whole might. Work while it is called Today; for the Night cometh, wherein no man can work." Browning expressed it somewhat differently in *Sordello*:

> Oh life, life-breath,
> Life-blood,—ere sleep, come travail, life ere death!
> This life stream on my soul, direct, oblique,
> But always streaming! Hindrances? They pique:
> Helps? Such . . . but why repeat, my soul o'ertops
> Each height, then every depth profoundlier drops?
> Enough that I can live, and would live! Wait
> For some transcendent life reserved by Fate
> To follow this? Oh, never![39]

The Mantuan troubador, facing death and failure, realizes that man must live within the limitations of life and ask only for "firmer arm and fleeter foot" in the arena of life, not "mad wings" to carry him above the fray. Man must learn to walk and run before he can be trusted with wings.

In the conclusion to "Gerard de Lairesse," Browning speaks of the dynamic, existential nature of life. He repudiates the belief that the Greek culture was man's highest achievement, for if progress is the law of life, modern civilization must be better than the old:

39. VI, 355-363.

> Let things be—not seem,
> I counsel rather,—do, and nowise dream!
> Earth's young significance is all to learn:
> The dead Greek lore lies buried in the urn
> Where who seeks fire finds ashes.[40]

"The Eagle," the first in the series of *Ferishtah's Fancies,* illustrates life's principle of dynamic action. As Ferishtah, who is not yet a dervish, walks through the wood, he sees a raven's nest of starving younglings, the mother lying dead at the foot of the tree. As he watches, musing upon their certain fate, an eagle sweeps down and feeds the open beaks with meat clutched in its talons. In admiration, Ferishtah concludes that the moral to be drawn from this extraordinary instance is clear: take no thought for the morrow, for God will provide. Sustained by this comforting reflection, Ferishtah goes home and ponders in a rapture upon the beneficence of providence, scorning meat and drink the while, as well as labor. Only the eventual pangs of hunger and lightness of head instruct him that the moral he so missed is quite otherwise than that which his folly drew. In a dream God reproaches him:

> "Hast thou marked my deed?
> Which part assigned by providence dost judge
> Was meant for man's example? Should he play
> The helpless weakling, or the helpful strength
> That captures prey and saves the perishing?
> Sluggard, arise: work, eat, then feed who lack!"

Repentant, Ferishtah rises and goes to Ispahan to minister to the needy.

Browning's "Parleying with Daniel Bartoli" gives an account of an aspect of existentialism which interested him all his life: the subjecting of a man's statement of principle to the test of action. Browning, like John Stuart Mill, knew that most men live by their principles just up to the point where they must be tested through action. In the poem Browning is contrasting his view of a saintly woman with the

40.  Ll. 389-393.

view expressed by the seventeenth-century Jesuit Daniel Bartoli. Bartoli's vast book, *De' Simboli Trasportati al Morale,* was devoted to discovering moral lessons to be drawn from the wonders of nature and from fabulous and stock tales of heroism, commonly involving lions. Browning again reveals his opposition to dreaming of ancient myth and fable and the marvelous, when all about one lies the real world of transcendent wonder and interest and life. Browning alleges that Bartoli presents idealized accounts of saintly women, whom he, the poet, will contrast with his ideas of truly saintly women. DeVane, in his *Browning's Parleyings,* points out that in point of fact Bartoli says nothing about the saintliness of women, and suggests that Browning may have confused Daniello Bartoli with Adolfo Bartoli, a historian of Italian literature, who has much to say about saintly lives.[41] In any event, Browning objects to the stock portraits of pallid, static, bloodless women. The mood is the same as that in "Pictor Ignotus," in which the painter, confessing his craven fear of the vulgar world of haggling and hawking of wares, resolves to continue painting

> "These endless cloisters and eternal aisles
>     With the same series, Virgin, Babe and Saint,
>  With the same cold, calm, beautiful regard,—
>     At least no merchant traffics in my heart."

Browning begins the parleying with one of his favorite ideas: the real or the historic is of greater interest and value to man than the purely fabulous or legendary:

> Don, the divinest women that have walked
> Our world were scarce those saints of whom we talked.
> My saint, for instance—worship if you will!
> 'T is pity poets need historians' skill:
> What legendary's worth a chronicle?[42]

He recounts the story of a certain duke who is forced to sign away two of his dukedoms to the king as an inheritance after the duke's death. At his sister's house, where the instrument is being drawn up

41. P. 60.　　42. Ll. 1-5.

but is yet unsigned, he meets a lovely and gentle girl, daughter of a humble druggist. In spite of the disparity in their positions and the advice of his sister, he resolves to marry her:

> "Sure as fate,
> I wed that woman—what a woman is
> Now that I know, who never knew till this!"
> So swore the duke. "I wed her: once again—
> Rave, rate, and reason—spend your breath in vain!"

The banns are read, and the Duke commands a simple ceremony, stripped of all pomp, as is appropriate to their simple human passion. He even renounces his courtly privilege of supplementing his domestic bliss with the embraces of mistresses, so true is his devotion. In the meanwhile, back at the palace, the king, after an interview with the Duke's hostile sister, sends a wily minister to break off the marriage unless the bride-to-be will persuade the duke to sign the ruinous instrument. As an additional reward, the minister promises that she will become a favorite of the court. The penalty for noncompliance is imprisonment. She returns to the duke, who is at the table, and before the assembled guests, demands that he tear up the tyrannous document as evidence of his manhood and honor. She knows that she can never marry him. If he fails to sign the agreement, she will go to prison; if he signs it, he betrays his honor and she will scorn him. She pleads with him to choose the path of honor:

> "Never dare alienate God's gift you hold
> Simply in trust for him! Choose muck for gold?
> Could you so stumble in your choice, cajoled
> By what I count my least of worthiness
> —The youth, the beauty,—you renounce them—yes,
> With all that's most too: love as well you lose,
> Slain by what slays in you the honor! Choose!
> Dear—yet my husband—dare I love you yet?"[43]

43.  L1. 194-201.

The duke sputters and fumes, but in the end he signs the agreement. She is taken to prison for her noncompliance, and they never meet again. The gifts he gave her she returns, among them a necklace which, Browning says, "I know not round what neck/ They took to sparkling, in good time—weeks thence." The duke's honor was found wanting in the test, and he proved that he and she were "not of one sort at all, one size/ As souls go. . . ." She represents the true saint, a person who rises to lofty heights of selflessness and who regards deeds, not words, as the measure of a man.

As DeVane surmises, the after-history is a thinly disguised account of Browning's elopement with E.B.B., for the noble girl marries a man much her junior, but her equal in steadfast love:

> They were wed.
> Whereon from camp and court alike he fled,
> Renounced the sun-king, dropped off into night,
> Evermore lost, a ruined satellite:
> And, oh, the exquisite deliciousness
> That lapped him in obscurity! You guess
> Such joy is fugitive: she died full soon.
> He did his best to die—as sun, so moon
> Left him, turned dusk to darkness absolute.
> Failing of death—why, saintship seemed to suit:
> Yes, your sort, Don! He trembled on the verge
> Of monkhood: trick of cowl and taste of scourge
> He tried: then, kicked not at the pricks perverse,
> But took again, for better or for worse,
> The old way in the world, and, much the same
> Man o' the outside, fairly played life's game.[44]

If DeVane is right in reading autobiography into these lines—and I think he is right—they are unique in their illumination of the dark days that succeeded the death of Browning's beloved wife. What is principally notable about this passage is the implicit picture of the true male saint: he is not the man who in grief will shun the world

44. L1. 229-244.

and put on the cowl and apply the scourge, as the crushed spirit often prompts. The true saint is the man who conquers his grief as best he can and plays the game of life to the end. Unlike the duke, Browning was a man whose word and action were one. He returned to London after his wife's death and entered into a life as full and dynamic as literary history affords, and he wrote many of his greatest works.

G. K. Chesterton, who loved a paradox beyond all other men, remarked that after the death of his wife, when he left the room where she died, Browning "closing the door of that room behind him, closed a door in himself, and none ever saw Browning upon earth again but only a splendid surface."[45] Like most paradoxes, this one is difficult to assess. It is not immediately clear whether it is the most incisive judgment passed on the poet or whether it is the most blind. I believe it is the latter, and Browning's whole dynamic life and literary output support my judgment. Browning spent his life counseling men to greet the blows of fate with manly courage, never to take the veil or don the cowl, and never to retire from life behind any mask. The trial by test is precisely to determine whether one will refuse to take refuge behind any form of make-believe or painted front. We know that Browning never believed that one should allow the public to look within his private life, as he so forcefully states in "House" and "Shop" and elsewhere; but this is not what Chesterton means. He means that Browning put on a false face to the world, hid behind a mask, and played a role before the world, keeping it at bay. This I refuse to believe. The last poem in the Browning canon, "Epilogue" to *Asolando,* published on the day of his death, is the most direct evidence that he slammed shut no doors in his breast and that he refused to don the mask of the mummer before life:

> Oh to love so, be so loved, yet so mistaken!
>     What had I on earth to do
> With the slothful, with the mawkish, the unmanly?
>     Like the aimless, helpless, hopeless, did I drivel
>         —Being—who?

45. *Robert Browning,* p. 104.

No psychic wound drove him underground. To believe that he put a facade before him to deceive the world is to deny a large part of what he wrote and believed in most. In "The Two Poets of Croisic" he clearly proclaims his principle of facing up to life with something more than stoical fortitude. Life, especially in crisis, demands verve and action:

> No, we must play the pageant out, observe
>   The tourney-regulations, and regard
> Success—to meet the blunted spear nor swerve,
>   Failure—to break no bones yet fall on sward;
> Must prove we have—not courage? well, then—nerve![46]

The actual application of the tourney rules to an individual situation is, predictably, a matter demanding the greatest delicacy in moral matters. No formula fits. In "Ivàn Ivànovitch" we have a moral problem that provokes diverse moral judgments, in spite of the fact that the Russian who tells the story to Browning confidently affirms that the old folktale has been told to children, time out of mind,

> . . . for a moral that's behind,
> Which children quickly seize.

The story is a terrible tale of a Russian mother's midnight flight from a pack of wolves. The sleigh, drawn by a single horse, is unable to outdistance the slavering wolves, and she, to gain time, flings her children one by one into the gaping jaws. Even the baby is torn from under her body, but her dreadful stratagem succeeds, in that she is drawn by the dying horse safely into the village, where she gasps out her horrible story to the carpenter, Ivàn Ivànovitch, who listens, axe in hand. At the end of the tale, as she sinks to the ground, he, without a moment's hesitation, decapitates her with one careful blow, and pronounces with measured finality:

> "It had to be:
> I could no other: God it was bade 'act for Me!'"

46. Ll. 497-501.

The case is immediately brought before the Lord of the Land, who pronounces Ivàn guilty of murder. But the ancient "Pope" of the village, to whom the case is appealed, sees the issue otherwise. De-Vane finds the Pope "somewhat like the Pope in *The Ring and the Book*," and with "a comparable philosophy."[47] In point of fact, the gulf that separates the two popes is as wide as can be imagined. The Pope who judges Guido spends much of his long monologue explaining that in life he, along with all other men, must act on imperfect evidence and with fallible judgment, even in matters of life and death. The one thing denied to man is absolute certainty, it will be recalled. The Pope who judges Ivàn is of quite another persuasion:

> "Ay, children, I am old—
> How old, myself have got to know no longer. Rolled
> Quite round, my orb of life, from infancy to age,
> Seems passing back again to youth. A certain stage
> At least I reach, or dream I reach, where I discern
> Truer truths, laws behold more lawlike than we learn
> When first we set our foot to tread the course I trod
> With man to guide my steps: who leads me now is God.
> 'Your young men shall see visions:' and in my youth I saw
> And paid obedience to man's visionary law:
> 'Your old men shall dream dreams:' and, in my age, a hand
> Conducts me through the cloud round law to where I stand
> Firm on its base,—know cause, who, before, knew effect."[48]

The Pope now believes that he is infallible because God leads him through the night of doubt into the white radiance of absolute truth. He has unshakable assurance and is confident, not that he has merely done the best he could in judgment making, but that he has been divinely guided to perfect truth. In short, according to Browning's lifelong pronouncements on the subject, this Pope is a madman, for only the mad fancy themselves the emissaries of God. Ivàn also is a madman, for he blandly affirms that he acted under the direct injunction of God. It is significant that most people who disavow responsi-

47. *A Browning Handbook*, p. 393.        48. L1. 309-321.

bility for an act and who ascribe the act to the special command of God have committed an act of singular brutality. When Ivàn is apprised of the Pope's favorable verdict, he is entirely unmoved, as madmen are who think themselves under the special guidance of God. He merely remarks, "How otherwise?"

The moral issues in the poem have provoked such partisan sentiment and debate that the poem might well be considered one of the casuistical pieces, except for its brevity and sketchy development. Tennyson is reported to have defended the frantic mother's actions, saying, "I think the woman was right. The wolves would have eaten them all. She might have saved part by what she did."

Browning does not reveal in the poem the rationale for the Pope's "decision," if it may be called so. The mother, in telling her story, reveals that she is primarily concerned with two things: 1) desire to extenuate, if not exculpate, her guilt, by insisting that she did all in her power to shield the children and that they were torn from her arms or from under her sheltering body, and 2) joy in her survival from the jaws of the wolves. Grief over the loss of her children, though powerful, is a poor third in her heart. The leader of the pack of wolves, Satan-face, she insists tore the flesh from her shoulder as she tried to shield her children, and she felt his great fangs grate upon her bones; and yet, when the horrified townspeople pick up her headless body, they discover that "the body shows no trace/ Of harm done. . . ." Throughout her account she lies to preserve her own position in the village and to enable her to live with herself after her crime. She is like a captain of a ship explaining why he was the first off a ship that went down with all hands. The Pope pronounces that the measure of her betrayal of the most sacred gift— the miracle of life—must be some extraordinary retribution. If Ivàn had not been handy, the sky would surely have opened and some dire punishment would have been delivered; thus, he believes, Ivàn may properly be considered God's instrument of justice:

"I hold that, failing human sense,
The very earth had oped, sky fallen, to efface
Humanity's new wrong, motherhood's first disgrace.

> Earth oped not, neither fell the sky, for prompt was found
> A man and man enough, head-sober and heart-sound,
> Ready to hear God's voice, resolute to obey.
> Ivàn Ivànovitch, I hold, has done, this day,
> No otherwise than did, in ages long ago,
> Moses when he made known the purport of that flow
> Of fire athwart the law's twain-tables! I proclaim
> Ivàn Ivànovitch God's servant!"[49]

It is strange that this poem has not been recognized as one of Browning's poems dealing with psychosis, ranking with "Johannes Agricola in Meditation" and "Porphyria's Lover." It is a poem of special importance in countering the absurd notion so widely held that to Browning dynamic action is always good, regardless of its direction or purpose. In this poem we have three acts of shocking impetuosity: the murder of the children, the murder of the mother, and the mad and reckless verdict of the senile Pope. It is clear that to Browning all three of these dynamic acts are evil and all three principals are mad. I think that Browning would have disagreed with Tennyson's judgment on the woman's act, which forcibly reminds me of the most shattering of stories to issue from the savagery of World War II, a story that almost certainly would have intrigued Browning with its moral questions. The story concerns the brutal S.S. man who was implored by the frantic Jewish mother to spare her three small children, who were being loaded into a truck destined for the crematorium. After a moment's hellish reflection, he told her, "You may keep one." The stricken mother, after a long moment, turned and fled, leaving the three children to perish. I doubt not that Tennyson would have condemned her action, for she could have saved one—but only for a short while, we know. There is no doubt that Browning would have applauded her act. Could she select one child, a favorite, and let the other two go to their deaths knowing that they had been rejected? Could a mother select one child *first* to be thrown into the jaws of wolves, and later a *second,* and finally a *third?*

49. L1. 372-382.

Her unmotherly guilt, of course, in no way gave Iván any right to behead her on the spot, and the old Pope's senile dementia conferred no wisdom or truth upon his verdict. To Browning action is desirable, but, again, it must be considered, moral action, and those who attempt to picture Browning as an amoral barbarian besmirch a Christian existentialist who spent a substantial part of his poetic life deploring barbarism in its several forms.

# SELECTED BIBLIOGRAPHY

Anon. Review of *Fifine at the Fair, Old and New,* November, 1872, 609.

Baker, Joseph E. "Religious Implications in Browning's Poetry," *Philological Quarterly,* October, 1957, XXXVI, No. 4, 436-452.

————, *"Pippa Passes" and Shorter Poems,* New York, 1947.

Barrett, William, *What Is Existentialism?,* New York, 1964.

Berdoe, Edward, *Browning and the Christian Faith,* 2nd ed., London, 1897.

Boyeson, Hjalmar Hjorth, *Literary and Social Silhouettes,* New York, 1904.

Bury, John, "Browning's Philosophy," *Browning Studies,* London, 1895.

Carpenter, W. Boyd, *The Religious Spirit of the Poets,* London, 1900.

Chesterton, G. K., *Robert Browning,* New York, 1908.

Cohen, J. M., *Robert Browning,* London, 1952.

Crawford, A. W., "Browning's Ideal of Life, an Interpretation of 'An Epistle of Karshish,'" *Methodist Review,* March, 1909, XCI, No. 2, 264-269.

Crowell, Norton B., *The Triple Soul: Browning's Theory of Knowledge,* Albuquerque, New Mexico, 1963.

Cundiff, Paul A., "Robert Browning: 'Our Human Speech,'" *The Victorian Newsletter,* 1959, No. 15, 1-9.

Curle, Richard, *Robert Browning and Julia Wedgewood, a Broken Friendship, at Revealed in Their Letters,* London, 1937.

DeVane, William C., *A Browning Handbook,* New York, 1935; 2nd ed., 1955.

————, *Browning's Parleyings, the Autobiography of a Mind,* New Haven, 1927.

Drew, Phillip, "Henry Jones on Browning's Optimism," *Victorian Poetry,* II (1964), 29-41.

Duffin, Henry C., *Amphibian, A Reconsideration of Browning,* London, 1956.

Dunsany, Lord, "Browning Is Blougram," *Nineteenth Century and After,* April, 1946, CXXXIX, 175-177.

Fairchild, Hoxie N., "The Classical Poets of English Literature," *The Literary Digest International Book Review,* August, 1925, iii, 608-609.

————, "Browning's 'Whatever Is, Is Right,'" *College English,* April, 1951, XII, 377-382.

Gladstone, Mary, *Her Diaries and Letters,* ed. Lucy Masterman, New York, 1930.

Haywood, John F., *Existentialism and Religious Liberalism,* Boston, 1962.

Hitner, John M., *Browning's Pessimism in "Fifine at the Fair,"* Colchester, England, 1962.

Holmes, Stewart Walker, "Browning: Semantic Stutterer," *Publications of the Modern Language Association,* 1945, LX, 231-255.

――――, "Browning's *Sordello* and Jung: Browning's *Sordello* in the Light of Jung's Theory of Types," *Publications of the Modern Language Association,* 1941, LVI, 758-796.

Honan, Park, *Browning's Characters: A Study in Poetic Technique,* New Haven, 1961.

Hood, Thurman L., *Letters of Robert Browning Collected by Thomas J. Wise,* New Haven, 1933.

Hutton, Richard Holt, *Brief Literary Criticisms,* London, 1906.

Jones, Henry, *Browning as a Philosophical and Religious Teacher,* Glasgow, 1902.

Kenmare, Dallas, *An End To Darkness, A Modern Approach to Robert Browning and His Work,* London, 1962.

King, Roma A., Jr., *The Bow and the Lyre, The Art of Robert Browning,* Ann Arbor, 1964.

Lake, Mrs. Percy, *The Ethics of Browning's Poems,* London, 1897.

Langbaum, Robert, "The Importance of Fact in *The Ring and the Book,"* *The Victorian Newsletter,* No. 17, 1960.

Litzinger, Boyd, *Time's Revenges: Browning's Reputation as a Thinker, 1887-1962,* Knoxville, Kentucky, 1964.

Lyttelton, Arthur Temple, *Modern Poets of Faith, Doubt, and Paganism and Other Essays,* London, 1904.

McAleer, Edward C., *Dearest Isa: Robert Browning's Letters to Isabella Blagden,* Austin, Texas, 1951.

――――, *Learned Lady: Letters from Robert Browning to Mrs. Thomas FitzGerald, 1876-1889,* Cambridge, Massachusetts, 1966.

Mellone, Sydney H., *Leaders of Religious Thought in the Nineteenth Century,* Edinburgh, 1902.

Michalson, Carl, *Christianity and the Existentialists,* New York, 1956.

Miller, Betty, *Robert Browning: A Portrait,* 1952.

Miller, J. Hillis, *The Disappearance of God,* Cambridge, Massachusetts, 1963.

Noyes, Alfred, "In White Cotton Night-Cap Country," *The Speaker,* June 13, 1903, 252-253.

Orr, Mrs. Sutherland, *Life and Letters of Robert Browning,* Boston, 1908.

Phelps, William Lyon, "Browning, Schopenhauer, and Music," *North American Review,* October, 1917, CCVI, 623.

Pigou, Arthur C., *Browning as a Philosophical Teacher,* London, 1901.

Priestley, F. E. L., "Browning's Apologetics," *University of Toronto Quarterly,* January, 1946, XV, No. 2, 1939-1947.

Raymond, William O., *The Infinite Moment and Other Essays in Robert Browning,* 2nd ed., Toronto, 1965.

Revell, William F., *Browning's Criticism of Life,* London, 1892.

Ridenour, George M., "Browning's Music Poems: Fancy and Fact," *Publications of the Modern Language Association,* LXXVIII (1963), 369-377.

Robertson, W., "La Saisiaz," *London Browning Society Papers,* XI, No. 51, London, 1889, ii, 312-332.

Russell, Frances T., *One Word More on Robert Browning,* Palo Alto, 1927.

Santayana, George, *Interpretations of Poetry and Religion,* New York, 1900.

Scudder, Vida D., *The Life of the Spirit in the Modern English Poets,* Boston, 1895.

Shaw, J. E., "The 'Donna Angelicata' in *The Ring and the Book,*" *Publications of the Modern Language Association,* March, 1926, XLI, 55-81.

Smalley, Donald, "Browning's View of Fact in *The Ring and the Book,*" *The Victorian Newsletter,* 1959, No. 16, 1-9.

Strong, Augustus H., *The Great Poets and Their Theology,* Philadelphia, 1897.

Symons, Arthur, *An Introduction to the Study of Browning,* London, 1886.

————, "Robert Browning as a Religious Poet," *The Wesleyan-Methodist Magazine,* December, 1882, VI, 943-947.

Whitla, William, *The Central Truth: The Incarnation in Browning's Poetry,* Toronto, 1963.

Wickstead, Philip H., "Robert Browning," *Contemporary Review,* January, 1903, LXXXIII, 86-99.

Wormhoudt, Arthur, *The Demon-Lover: A Psychoanalytical Approach to Literature,* New York, 1949.

# INDEX